Childhood
South Africans recall their past

Childhood

South Africans recall their past

ADRIAN HADLAND

PENGUIN BOOKS

PENGUIN BOOKS

Published by the Penguin Group
Penguin Books Ltd, 80 Strand, London WC2R 0RL, England
Penguin Group (USA) Inc, 375 Hudson Street, New York, New York 10014, USA
Penguin Group (Canada), 90 Eglinton Avenue East, Suite 700, Toronto, Ontario,
Canada M4P 2Y3 (a division of Pearson Penguin Canada Inc)
Penguin Ireland, 25 St Stephen's Green, Dublin 2, Ireland (a division of Penguin
Books Ltd)
Penguin Group (Australia), 250 Camberwell Road, Camberwell, Victoria 3124,
Australia (a division of Pearson Australia Group Pty Ltd)
Penguin Books India Pvt Ltd, 11 Community Centre, Panchsheel Park,
New Delhi – 110 017, India
Penguin Group (NZ), Cnr Rosedale and Airborne Roads, Albany, Auckland 1310,
New Zealand (a division of Pearson New Zealand Ltd)
Penguin Books (South Africa) (Pty) Ltd, 24 Sturdee Avenue, Rosebank,
Johannesburg 2196, South Africa

Penguin Books (South Africa) (Pty) Ltd, Registered Offices:
24 Sturdee Avenue, Rosebank, Johannesburg 2196, South Africa

www.penguinbooks.co.za

First published by Penguin Books (South Africa) (Pty) Ltd 2005

Selection Copyright © Adrian Hadland 2005
Introduction © Adrian Hadland 2005
Individual contributions © The authors

All rights reserved
The moral right of the author has been asserted

ISBN 0 143 02471 X

Typeset by CJH Design in 10.5/13pt Palatino
Cover design: Flame Design, Cape Town
Printed and bound by Interpak Books, Pietermaritzburg

Except in the United States of America, this book is sold subject to the condition
that it shall not, by way of trade or otherwise, be lent, resold, hired out or
otherwise circulated without the publisher's prior consent in any form of binding
or cover other than that in which it is published and without a similar condition
including this condition being imposed on the subsequent purchaser.

I would like to dedicate this book to the memory of my father, Brian.
I hope his gift of gentleness, love and laughter will be mine too.

'Life is not what one lived, but what one remembers and how one remembers it in order to recount it'

– Gabriel Garcia Marquez
(Living to Tell the Tale, Penguin, London, 2004)

Contents

Acknowledgements	viii
Introduction	1
Peter Abrahams	10
Raymond Ackerman	16
Dugmore Boetie	20
Breyten Breytenbach	29
Rrekgetsi Chimeloane	35
JM Coetzee	42
Denis Hirson	44
Ronnie Kasrils	47
Ahmed Kathrada	53
Zazah Khuzwayo	59
Ellen Kuzwayo	69
Sindiwe Magona	78
Katie Makanya	88
Miriam Makeba	98
Rian Malan	103
Nelson Mandela	109
Winnie Mandela	118
Cecil Margo	122
Don Mattera	131
William Bloke Modisane	135
Stephen Mokone	145
Es'kia Mphahlele	154
Patrick Mynhardt	165
Mbulelo Vizikhungo Mzamane	172
Alan Paton	184
William Plomer	191
Mamphela Ramphele	198
Antony Sher	208
Gillian Slovo	213
Thomas Stubbs	220
Chris van Wyk	229
Albert Wessels	240
Donald Woods	245
References	254
Copyright Acknowledgements	254

Acknowledgements

I would like to thank the staff at the University of Cape Town's African Studies library who were sent scampering, patiently, speedily and repeatedly into the darkest vaults in search of often obscure texts – only to be told all too often that they were not necessary after all. Also my gratitude goes to my colleagues at the Human Sciences Research Council, in particular Linda Richter, Andy Dawes and Leslie Swartz from the Child, Youth and Family Development research programme, whose interest, expertise and advice were most helpful. Thanks to my publisher and friend, Jeremy Boraine and his team at Penguin. Thanks to my cousin, Richard, for drawing my attention to the vicissitudes of family history and memory. And, finally, thanks to my wife, muse and soulmate, Jackie and our beautiful baby boy, Nicholas, for being such an important part of everything I do.

Introduction
Adrian Hadland

There is something magical about childhood. It defines so much of who we are and what matters to us. Childhood places an irrevocable stamp on our identity, on our dreams and on our expectations. But childhood is elusive and recalling it is a complex process. Memory is unreliable. Images grow dim. We remember things which we think were important at the time, but were they? We mix up clips of old family movies and the recollections of others with what actually happened. We pass on family stories from generation to generation with all the conviction of truth, only to find someone else has a different version. Trauma, too, is a notorious shaper of memory. So how do we know what is true?

Take one of your earliest memories and dust it off. Ask a brother or sister, or anyone who was actually there, what they remember about that particular moment on that particular day. The chances are, they will have a very different perspective of what happened. Childhood, in other words, is mediated. The act of putting it down on paper, of constructing a narrative around our earliest memories, is even more complex and even more mediated. When you throw into the mix a country as splintered and as fraught as South Africa, the narratives of childhood that emerge present a very different picture. These narratives have to wrestle not only with the unreliability of memory but also with a context of social and political upheaval. Race, class, politics, privilege and poverty all have a different shade when viewed through the lenses of childhood. Children cope with the consequences of these processes more often than they try to understand the reasons why they exist. The result is a poignant, uncluttered look at what it really means to have lived in South Africa at various stages in its difficult history.

This book, *Childhood: South Africans remember their past*, presents a unique and diverse perspective of South African history and literature. It showcases the writing of some of the country's finest authors and personalities, all peering back through time, in an attempt to recall their own youthful responses and feelings. You will find in this book recollections of profound, historical moments as well as memories of ordinary, mundane ones. Here, side by side, brilliant literary genius is highlighted with the memoirs of political leaders and with the recollections of fellow South Africans from a range of backgrounds, regions and periods. Here you will find industrialists and poets, vagabonds and farmers, refugees and entertainers. You will even find the remembered childhoods of an 1820 settler and a high court judge. Together, they represent the rich patina of life in South Africa seen from every angle.

This is a book about family, about siblings and about communities. It highlights human warmth and bemoans its cruelty. It brings together a collection of texts that begin to define who we are as individuals but also who we are as a nation. In spite of the diverse background, interests and contexts of each of those who have contributed to this collection, common themes can be discerned. Each writer, whether president or villain, was able to step back and ask profound questions about their childhood lives and environments. Each sensed injustice just as they nurtured a powerful strength of spirit. Each weighed up inequity just as they nourished the determined hope that things can, and must, get better. Seldom do any of the writers collapse in a heap of individual desperation. They look instead to family, to friends and to their community to help them build a path to a better life. Scholars might argue whether these are universal rather than South African traits. Perhaps we all share the building blocks of the human condition but find ourselves accentuating different elements depending on our cultural and temporal contexts.

There is no question these voices emanate from the same family. Their concerns are too familiar, their strategies for coping too common and their routes out too similar for it to be otherwise. The question then becomes, to which family can these almost three dozen people from three different centuries belong?

Children played an extraordinarily important role in South Africa's transition from apartheid pariah state to a new, model democracy. All too often, it was children who occupied the frontline of resistance. It was children who suffered most keenly the terrible consequences of decades of racial segregation. It was they whose development was stifled by poor education, whose growth was stunted by poverty and whose futures were curtailed by the mad vision of apartheid's political champions. But if one looks back over almost a century of South African history, children appear again and again not just as the most vulnerable victims but also as one of the country's most potent political and social forces.

Yet, like many countries, South Africa has largely failed to record the opinions, experiences and hopes of its children. As renowned psycholgist and historian Lloyd de Mause once observed: 'Historians have concentrated so much on the noisy sandbox of history, with its fantastic castles and magnificent battles, that they have generally ignored what is going on in the homes around the playground'. (De Mause, 1974:1) Even here, in South Africa, with our history, it is still the children who are the silent ones.

This anthology seeks to take a small step to rectify the imbalance. In it will be heard the remembered voices of a variety of South African children going back close to 200 years. Of course in many cases, the adults they became are far better known than the ordinary children they once were. Many are indeed household names in the new South Africa, like former president Nelson Mandela or Nobel laureate for literature JM Coetzee. Others are less well known, or are not known at all. Only their testimonies remain.

Considerable limitations had to be imposed to find the components of a manageable, quality anthology. Decisions had to be made about important and controversial debates. In all, some 2000 published texts were considered. All were principally autobiographical, published in English and all were South African. This immediately excluded non-published work, a particular pity given this country's rich if unrecorded oral tradition. The very fact of publication introduces its own matrix of bias – gender, racial and class – which implicitly distorts what is available and why. The objective, however, was to mine what was at hand in the hope of finding a rich collage of childhood experience that would inform, intrigue and inspire. I believe that, at least, has been successfully achieved.

Many of the 2000 preliminary texts did not consider childhood important and brushed past in the briefest fashion possible. Many more omitted it altogether. William Plomer, one of the contributors to this book, voiced the following warning: 'Autobiographers who enlarge at length upon their trivial recollections of infancy are to be shunned like lakes bewitched'.

A fair number of authors coped with the awkwardness of remembering their childhoods by leaning on ill-considered or even clichéd passages that contribute little of interest. In fact, by the time the skimpers and the dodgers had been excised, only 60 or 70 works of any substance remained. Some searching questions were asked of those that remained: Had a writer presented a unique or original view of childhood? Was the work interesting? Was it well written? Did it help piece together our history in a way that was helpful, revealing, honest or funny? And, one of the most important questions: was it surprising?

Narrowing down this shortlist into the final collection of 33 then became a question of opinion. There will inevitably be texts, or portions of texts, that have cried out for inclusion or are a reader's favourite and offence may have been courted. In several cases the hard question was not so much whether to include the work, but deciding on which bit to include. One of the toughest was Denis Hirson's *I Remember King Kong*, cascading as it is with such a rich flow of images that may or may not have personal resonance. In the end, the final decision on extracts and on authors came down to personal choice. This was premised on the belief that in the banquet that was offered to the reader, there would be more than sufficient to sate the palate and inspire the spirit. If a chord is struck, the reader is encouraged to seek out the full and original text. To this end, full bibliographical details of each extract are provided at the end of this book.

You will find in this collection many surprising essays. Several are even shocking. Few contain a more powerful image than Cecil Margo's in which the former judge writes about the terrifying sight of his mother, hair and clothes aflame, running towards him screaming. Writers you might expect to portray childhoods of poverty or squalor, such as Nelson Mandela, find happiness, laughter and great pleasure in simple things. Others you might anticipate will reflect lavishly on a life of wealth and advantage, instead invoke sadness and loss. Take the extract from celebrity businessman Raymond Ackerman's work, *Hearing Grasshoppers Jump*. Few will envy Ackerman's experience of testifying as a key witness in his parents' ugly custody battle. The sounds he remembers most, as you will read in his extract, are those of slamming doors and the shouting of his parents. Perhaps a reader might have expected a more sedate, carefree childhood in the Ackerman household.

In fact, few childhoods in this collection are easy or carefree. This is due in large measure to the terrible adversity suffered not only by this collection of writers but by the overwhelming majority of South African children for the last 300 years and more. One particular noticeable commonality is the fact that virtually every author included in this anthology was subjected to corporal punishment as a child. Just about the only one who wasn't, JM Coetzee, was so terrified of the prospect of corporal punishment that avoiding it overwhelmed his childlike perspective on life. It might be tempting to draw a connection between beaten children and autobiography writers, but in truth corporal punishment has been ubiquitous in South African households for a very long time. It has only recently been outlawed in schools.

In spite of the tough conditions of many of the childhoods represented in this volume, this collection is a very long way from being an assortment of grim extracts recalling bitter or pointless lives. This is in part because children play with the hand they are dealt. They are rarely given any choices over parental care or home environment. The world is as the world does. It is often only later, as children grow older and become more aware of the world around them, that they start to locate their own experiences within a wider context. It is perhaps to this that contributor Peter Abrahams refers when he writes that when we were children we just didn't ask the right questions.

It would be remiss, at this point, not to mention in passing that there are many controversies underpinning a collection of this kind. For instance, the very nature and definition of childhood is hotly disputed, and has been for decades. Some, such as French social scientist Philippe Aries, argue that childhood as we know it didn't exist until the 15th century. To give this debate a local dimension, consider the different points at which South African children go through rites of passage symbolising their entrance into adulthood. South Africa has a population with a richly varied assortment of values, traditions, religions and ways of life and young people migrate from childhood into adulthood at different times and in different ways. Sociologist Sandra Burman has shown in her recent work that Jewish families don't consider children who have gone through their bat/barmitzvahs to be fully fledged adults whereas this is very much the case in many rural areas of South Africa following the initiation of young men. (Burman, 1990: 11)

A second debate worth mentioning concerns the question: what is an autobiography? A translator's footnote to Breyten Breytenbach's *A Season in Paradise* (an extract of which is also found in this collection) reads as follows: 'Fact and fantasy are often indistinguishable in this book, and nowhere more so than in these reminiscences of early childhood'. How is it, one might ask, that fact and fantasy can be blurred in a work of autobiography? At root is the unreliability and mutability of memory together with the elusive nature of truth itself. The consequence is many different forms of autobiographical writing and many theories about what autobiographical writing is. One can see even from this collection how stories about onself are treated differently. Margaret McCord, for example, writes an autobiography on behalf of someone else (Katie Makanya). This is not a biography, as one might suppose, as it is written in the first person with the assistance of the subject. JM Coetzee, on the other hand, takes the unusual narrative stance of writing about himself in the third person. Coetzee even questions out aloud the veracity of his early recollections: 'It is a magnificent first memory ... but is it true?' The contemporary literature lists at least eight different forms of autobiographical writing, each with distinct, if at times overlapping, characteristics. These are: life writing, life narrative, autobiography, confessional writing, memoir, creative non-fiction, ego document and diary.

But even this range of forms fails to capture the full, nuanced landscape of contemporary autobiographical writing, particularly in South Africa. Take for instance the combination of forms demonstrated in *Walter and Albertina Sisulu: In our Lifetime,* in which a writer presents the lives of both her in-laws and includes narrative about herself. Alternatively, take Luli Callinicos's biography of Oliver Tambo that is part (posthumous) autobiography and part biography.

One element that all the works in this collection include and that is implicit in all forms of autobiography, is the role of memory. Memory is undeniably an important tool in the production of a narrative about oneself. For unless a comprehensive personal diary is available of the period one wishes to recall, what other means are there short of the opinions of others? But memory is a fickle muse. It is also an extremely unreliable process that seldom does the truth any favours.

The discipline that has focused most attention on the subject of individual memory is psychology. The vulnerability of memory to suggestion and embellishment lies in the manner in which memories are coded, stored and then recalled. Each stage seems fraught with the potential for error. An experience is remembered when the brain parcels out its various parts. In the business of re-assembling, all sorts of distortions, part memories and mood-specific details may be added in or subtracted from the mix. (Begley, 1994: 2) Wallis Wilde-Menozzi has written a wonderfully powerful essay on memoir and memory which includes the beautiful lines: 'Memory waits quite often, like a train in a tunnel, until it senses a green light. Memory is alive, hunkering, sometimes submerged, but often not. It is just kept in the dark. When it re-emerges ... reality is re-evaluated'. (Wilde-Menozzi, 2001: 44)

What psychology has long argued, developments in neurobiology now back up. Says researcher Bob Holmes: 'The latest findings in neurobiology about how the brain stores memory strengthen the notion that the human mind has a remarkable ability to spin a web of fantasy about a few scraps of remembered fact, or to seriously distort an almost complete memory by inventing a few crucial details'. (Holmes, 1994: 32) While the frailty of human memory is demonstrable enough in 'normal' circumstances, this is particularly exaggerated in situations of trauma or stress or where severe depression is involved. It has been repeatedly noted, for instance, that for individuals with some forms of mood disturbance (such as stress, trauma or depression), retrieval of specific autobiographical memories are particularly difficult. (Swales et al, 2001: 321)

In a landmark study undertaken by sociologist Linda Williams, an extraordinary level of memory suppression was evident among women who had suffered sexual abuse as children. The study traced 100 women who had been hospitalised as children due to sexual abuse. A third of the women reported no memory whatever of the abuse. (Holmes, 1994: 34) It may seem rather extreme to use child sexual abuse to illustrate memory frailty, but it is worth noting that a recent survey of 200 contemporary memoirs found the largest category 'by far' concerned depictions of childhood and, in particular, narratives concerning incest, abuse, alcoholism and impoverishment. (Adams, 2002) There are certainly many of the above themes evident in this anthology.

Since the advent of democracy, a large number of autobiographies have been produced by South African political figures, literary ones as well as many others. Indeed, if one counts the life story narratives told by 20 000 people to the Truth and Reconciliation Commission from 1996 to 2001, autobiographies have become something of a national obsession. Perhaps this is a natural consequence of a country and its people attempting to reconcile the trauma of a conflict-ridden past to a future of reconciliation and hope.

There is certainly no question that a growing interest has arisen concerning what it is that distinguishes South Africa's 'new' national identity. Studies have already shown that South Africans are increasingly identifying with a broader South African identity. (Roefs, 2002: 12) As deputy arts, culture, science and technology minister Brigitte Mabandla pointed out in 1998: 'We have embarked upon an exciting new voyage of discovery as we begin to explore and define who we are as a people.' (Mabandla, 1998)

The underlying premise of current debates is that there is a need to understand the national character and identity in order to promote what is positive and beneficial and in order to suppress what is divisive and destructive. This becomes more urgent given the fractured past and the diverse cultural and linguistic composition of the national character. The delineation of the national identity becomes an imperative, a tool for democratic consolidation. But where does one look for the features of a national identity? I would suggest that the texts and life stories which constitute the national narrative, as exclusive and limited as they are, are a good starting place. It is my contention that some of the features of this national identity will become evident from a study of these texts.

The debates, however, do not negate the need for, or the interest in, how South Africa's past has been experienced by its children. It may even provoke a more dedicated attempt to record the experiences of children in the present and even in the future. In closing, may I offer one last caveat. As illustrative as texts can be, there will always be a space between a life and its record, no matter the craft or art of the author. As Anne Chisholm has written in the *New Statesman*: 'As for the readers, they know, or they should know, that the full truth about any human life is hard to find, hard to tell and certainly not to be found between the covers of a book.' (Chisholm, 2001: 43)

References

Adams, L. 2002. Almost Famous: The rise of the 'nobody' memoir, *The Washington Monthly*, Vol 34, no 4 (April 2002), pp42-47.

Begley, S & Brant, M. 1994. You must remember this: How the brain forms 'false memories', *Newsweek*, Vol 124, issue 13.

Burman, S. 1990. *Growing up in a divided society*. Chicago: Northwestern University Press.

Chisholm, A. 2001. Secrets and Lies, *New Statesman*, Vol 130, May 14, 2001, pp41-43.

De Mause, L (ed). 1974. *The History of Childhood*. New York: Harper & Row.

Holmes, Bob. 1994. When memory plays us false. *New Scientist*, Issue 1935, 23 July 1994 pp32-35.

Mabandla, B. 1998. Preface to *Arts and Heritage 1998: Guide to South African Arts, Culture and Heritage*. Pretoria: Department of Arts, Culture, Science and Technology.

Roefs, M. 2002. Public Participation and perceived (in)justice in South Africa, 1995-2000, unpublished Doctoral Thesis, Social Psychology, Free University, Amsterdam.

Swales, MA & Williams, MG. 2001. Specificity of autobiographical memory and mood disturbance in adolescents, *Cognition and Emotion*, Vol 15(3), pp321-331.

Wilde-Menozzi, W. 2001. Cross-cultural stories in *Southwest Review*, Vol 86 (1), (winter), pp34-46.

The Coyaba Chronicles: Reflections on The Black Experience in the 20th Century

Peter Abrahams

We are fast coming to the close of the twentieth century. By the time these chronicles are made public we will, I suspect, be into the twenty-first century. I did not expect to live this long. As far as I know, no other member of my family has lived to the ripe old age of eighty. My mother made it to her early sixties. My brother, Lolly, my sister, Tibby (Margaret or Maggie), and my cousin, Catherine, did not. Catherine died young, perhaps in her early forties. She suffered from 'St Vitus' Dance' and a wife-beating husband. My Aunt Mattie, Catherine's mother, she who accused me of stealing a half-crown all of seventy years ago, was an old person in her late fifties, with swollen legs and feet, when she died.

Why does that accusation linger? I knew it was false; she found that out later without telling me how.

Almost sixty years ago, when I last saw Aunt Mattie, just before I left South Africa for good, she apologised painfully, awkwardly. She was a shadow of the tough old Skokiaan Queen of my childhood days. We embraced. The intensely passionate hurt of youth had long since gone. All I remembered at that last meeting was how hard she had struggled to keep our family together.

Aunt Mattie, formally Margaret DuPlessis; her younger sister, Angelina, (Limmie to everybody) my mother; Lolly and Tibby, my elder brother and sister and Catherine, Aunt Mattie's only child; and me, the youngest: that was my circle of love, the people who made up my world, the first humans whose faces and sounds and smells and movements illuminated my consciousness. The two DuPlessis sisters, with four children between them, and no men to support them. There had been a fifth child, my sister Natalie, nearest in age to me, a year older, who died in early childhood, before she became part of my memory bank. There is the memory of my father; a tall, thin dark presence, a mineworker who died early. The most lingering image is of being lifted up to look my last on the dead face that I associated with my mother's laughter and the tranquil sounds of haunting music. As long as he was with us Aunt Mattie was not a dominant presence. When he died, she became the cornerstone of our lives.

My mother went to work in the homes of white folk, usually living in and looking after their children. The money was small. Aunt Mattie stayed home and managed the family. In the Vrededorp of my childhood that was difficult. Finding our daily bread was a struggle. Aunt Mattie tried all sorts of things. We sold vegetables, then firewood, from a pushcart. As long as Lolly was prepared to lead us through the streets of Vrededorp and Fordsburg, and Braamfontein, pushing the loaded handcart, it worked. When he found a girlfriend and a job for himself, and when he spent more time at his girlfriend's than at our place, the firewood enterprise collapsed.

So Aunt Mattie brewed the illicit Skokiaan, the 'kaffir beer', and sold it to the mine boys – a shilling for a small tin-full, one-and-six-pence for a slightly larger one – at weekends when they were allowed out of the mine compounds. I remember Aunt Mattie went to jail many times when she was caught in the Saturday night police raids. The usual Monday morning magistrates' court sittings were packed with prisoners' relatives, come to pay the fines or to swear, nearly always in vain, that the accused was not the guilty person. The sentence, a monotonous routine, was fourteen days or twenty-one shillings; or, for the bigger fish, one month or forty to forty-five shillings. Those who could, paid up and went back to their trade. Those who could not, served their time then went back to their illicit brewing. The State collected quite a bit of money from these 'Skokiaan fines'. Once, I recall, we could not raise the twenty-one shillings and Aunt Mattie spent a fortnight in jail. It was a miserable fortnight for all of us. But we had a party the day she came home, and all the neighbours came to celebrate, bringing food and drink which lasted us for three days.

Aunt Mattie always stood out among the prisoners. She was one of those almost white Coloureds; all the others had the subtle variation of pigmentation – from a Mongolian light-yellow through to a rich reddish-brown or near-black – which the world of white folk sweepingly lumped together as black. So except for such rare cases as near-white Aunt Mattie, and the occasional other Coloured Skokiaan Queen, the Monday morning prisoner line-ups were all comprised of black women. But for all that, this near-white woman, dressed as voluminously as all the other black women prisoners, down to the elaborately tied kerchief or *Doekie* on her head, seemed not out of place.

Every now and then we had seen some other Coloured woman lined up in the dock among the Skokiaan Queens; not as fair as Aunt Mattie, not with grey-green eyes and 'European' hair, but seemingly much more awkward, embarrassed and out of place. I have a vivid memory of Aunt Mattie in animated conversation with her fellow prisoners before the white magistrate entered and the world became silent. There she was, wedged between a row of black women, all taller than she was. She was short, just over five feet, heavy-bodied, squarish and squat, as are Boer women after generations of walking the vast African veld and eating the heavy Dutch-style Afrikaner food. She could have been one of them – if she were not my Aunt Mattie. She and a very tall statuesque and austere-faced woman were talking 'nineteen to the dozen', as Tibby and her friends used to say. Those around them listened eagerly. It seemed normal at the time, but now I wonder what language they were speaking. Most of the black women who lived in the lower end of Vrededorp came from the countryside and were there to be near their menfolk who worked in the mines. They spoke neither English nor Afrikaans. I knew Aunt Mattie had a nodding acquaintance with English, but Afrikaans was her language; she thought and cursed in Afrikaans. She made it sound beautiful when she spoke softly to my mother when the two of them were alone and thought no one was listening. There was a hint of sadness when that gentleness was between them. Years later, and in strange and distant lands, I slowly grew to recognise that shared quiet gentleness. It was a thing of shared memories, of remembrances of other times and other lives. What were these memories? Where had these two sisters come from? Why was one near-white and the other as near-black as makes no difference? It is one of the great regrets of my life that I did not have the sense to ask these questions of Aunt Mattie and my mother. We do not ask the right questions when we are young, so we miss the important answers. Now it is too late to ask, too late for the illuminating answers, and the unanswered questions haunt us for a lifetime. In what language was she talking to that big and beautiful black Skokiaan Queen in the Marshall Square prisoners' dock that Monday morning? Why was she so at ease among those women? Questions without answers. That big woman became the prototype for Leah in *Mine Boy*.

Of all my immediate family Aunt Mattie was, looking back over more than sixty years, the least concerned with the colour and shade consciousness which defined every aspect of South African life. Perhaps, without my realising it, she helped to shape for me a way of looking at my world. I should have given her the credit for this in *Tell Freedom*. I did not because I did not recognise it at that time, or its influence in the shaping of my views on my world.

One day, in the cold Vrededorp winter, I returned to our yard. We were either living at 21st or 22nd Street, the lower and blacker end of Vrededorp, when I saw this little man, black as only one from Nyasaland could be. He did not look like a mine boy. I was between ten and twelve at the time but he was no taller than I was and not much heavier. He had small hands, tapering fingers, and there was a beakiness to his face: pointy nose, pointy lips, pointy ears. And then he smiled at something

Aunt Mattie had said in a language I did not understand. And the whole world seemed to glow. Then, as suddenly as it came, the smile was gone and we were back in drab, shanty Vrededorp.

When the rest of the family came home in ones and twos they all looked surprised at the presence of the little black man. Aunt Mattie said nothing and behaved as though everything was normal; we all knew her so nobody said anything – within her hearing. Tibby and Catherine had much to say out in the yard, so that Aunt Mattie couldn't hear. She called him Pickanin – a variation on piccaninny – little one – so we called him that behind their backs. When my mother came from work that night Aunt Mattie silenced her with one of her 'looks'.

Pickanin stayed the night – with Aunt Mattie. When we got up next morning he was gone. We did not see him all day nor that night, nor the next night. But on the third morning, before sunrise, Pickanin was back. With him he brought a donkey cart piled high with firewood drawn by a big handsome strong Jenny. Aunt Mattie glowed as she welcomed him with a hot mug of coffee and a plate of cornmeal porridge. She warned us off with her eyes, and the two of them sat quietly talking and sipping coffee for the best part of an hour. Then Pickanin put on his battered trilby, adjusted his jacket, cracked his small whip and drove the cart in the direction of white Fordsburg.

For many days and weeks this new routine dominated our lives. Pickanin was the man of the house now and we all accepted it because Aunt Mattie would brook nothing else. Tibby was as irreverent as ever, she and Catherine were forever snickering about the strange little new black man in Aunt Mattie's life.

One day I was ordered to go with him on his selling trip. It was my first time close to him. We walked up one street and down another called out; 'Firewood! Firewood!' until we had sold more than half the wood. I noticed his gentleness with the donkey, how he caressed her neck when nobody was looking; how she nuzzled against his shoulder when he adjusted her harness or gave her a snack of fodder or a drink of water when we paused. At one point when there were no people about, no customers, and we had paused from calling 'Firewood! Firewood! Shilling a bundle!', the donkey was directly behind him and he could not see her face. She raised her head, pushed it forward and stretched out her lips as far as they would go, and bared her teeth at his back. I burst out laughing. I couldn't help myself. I had never seen anything like that.

Without turning, Pickanin said: 'She mock me', the words filled with laughter. And suddenly they were both my friends, the big beautiful grey donkey and the blackest little man I had ever seen up to then. I could see why Aunt Mattie liked him. In the days that followed, going out selling firewood with Pickanin and his donkey became an adventure I looked forward to.

It ended all too suddenly. One morning he did not load the little cart with firewood from the stockpile in the far corner of our yard. He and Aunt Mattie talked quietly for a while. Then he looked at me with a twinkle in his eyes.

'Bye, Lee. I leaving.'

'Why?' I cried.

'Family die me shamba. Must go take care.'

'Will you come back?'

A rare smile lit up the little face. He looked at me as he looked at his donkey when no one was looking.

'Don't know.' It was a whisper. 'Remember me ...'

I nuzzled against the donkey's neck. And then Aunt Mattie and I watched him leading his donkey and cart out of our lives. This little incident had been out of my mind for all these years until just now, as I reflect on Aunt Mattie. So much I would have liked to ask, but I did not know how at the time. Who were they really, these two women who shaped me? Where did they come from? Where were they born? Where did they go to school? Who were their parents? Did they have any other relatives beside each other? Why were they the kind of women they were, who could turn poky little backyard rooms in Vrededorp, Johannesburg, racist South Africa, into homes filled with love and sanctuaries where strangers sometimes paused for rest before moving on? So much I would have liked to know about my Aunt Mattie and her sister, my mother. In a coldly hostile and cruel place they somehow taught us how to be gentle, how to laugh, how to love, how to survive.

One of the things about the Vrededorp of my childhood was the coming and going of strangers. All manner of people came, staying for a day or many days, or weeks, or even years. And then they left. I do not remember anyone in the family ever asking where they came from or where they went. We depended on Aunt Mattie's judgement. She decided who to give shelter and who to turn away. We did not always agree with her choices, but her decisions were final. We either liked it or lumped it. And, looking back, I think my Aunt Mattie was quite a judge of character, despite that mistake of accusing me of stealing her – or rather, the family's – half-crown. Wherever you are, dear stern and beloved old lady, thank you. I wish I got to know you and your background better. All the years of my life I have remembered how you cared for my mother, your little sister, after she was nearly burnt to death; how you and Tibby and Catherine brought her back to life by your sheer will for her to stay alive. Above all, I remember the deep passion for 'family' you instilled in all of us. I was hugely blessed in the strong women who raised and shaped my way of looking at the world during those key early years.

Peter Abrahams was born in Vrededorp, Johannesburg in 1919. After college he settled in Britain to fulfil has ambition of becoming a writer. A writing assignment in Jamaica resulted in a permanent move for him and his family to Kingston in 1959, where he continued his career as a novelist, editor, and political commentator. His early books look, optimistically, at a world without racial boundaries, while his later works are more political, venturing into topics such as emancipation and colonialism. Abrahams was one of the first black writers of the 1940s and 50s, and was a tremendous influence for authors such as Chinua Achebe and Ngugi wa Thiong'o.
Book Extracted: *The Coyaba Chronicles: Reflections on The Black Experience in the 20th Century* (Indiana University Press, Indianapolis, 2001)

Hearing Grasshoppers Jump
Raymond Ackerman

… When I think back to my early childhood, the noises I remember most are shouting – and the sound of slamming doors. There were some happy times – I think on the whole I *was* a happy child – but the warfare within my parents' marriage ultimately overwhelmed everything.

Although my parents' relationship soured soon after their marriage, my sister Moyra was born in 1922, my brother Kenneth in 1928, and I myself on 10 March 1931 in Claremont, Cape Town. I gather that my parents had me in an attempt to shore up their crumbling relationship but, if so, it did not work. When I was quite small, and as my father's business prospered, our family moved to Bishopscourt to a lovely house named Le Rêve – 'The Dream' – for the majestic outlook from the grounds of the property.

In retrospect, our childhood was very strange: sometimes happy, but often very, very sad. I don't remember anything of a real home life, mainly because my father and mother were always fighting. We had a nurse and a governess looking after us. Sometimes we wouldn't see my mother for a month at a time; she would stay locked in her room. I am sure that today she would be diagnosed and treated as a depressive, but things were different then.

I know that the austerity which characterised my father had been fashioned by the hardships of his own upbringing, but in his determination not to spoil his children he sometimes overdid it. When Ken and I were on holiday from school – prep school and high school – he would tell us, 'Right boys, you can't be lazy now.' He would put the housekeeper in charge of us and we had to do three hours' work in the garden every day. I resented that, wanting to go off and have some leisure time but, under the scrutiny of our overseer, this was not possible.

Most of the happy times which I remember revolved around sharing sport with my father. Sport always formed a strong bond between us. He used to be a soccer goalie and was a very keen player in his youth until a bad accident to his arm ended his footballing activities. Later, we played a lot of golf together. Conversely, as sport bonded my father and me, so it complicated the difficult relationship between my father and Ken who, as an asthmatic, was not able to play sport competitively.

During my early childhood my father was away for long periods on buying trips overseas. When he came back he would put me on his shoulders and walk with me around the house and garden. I valued those times very much. One day, I remember, he bathed my brother and me. As we were brushing our teeth he told us we must always push the tube from the bottom upwards so as not to waste toothpaste. Whenever I squeeze a tube of toothpaste today, I push it from the bottom. I remember that bath so clearly because we had so little contact with my mother and father.

On his travels overseas, buying goods for Ackermans, my father picked up marketing ideas which he recognised, to his great credit, as winning strategies with the potential to work in South Africa. So it was that local consumers were introduced to house brands with catchy names such as Ackra, Ackersley and Ackersown, some of which are still in use fifty years on. As well as the trademark 1/11 Ackermans price tag, my father introduced the concept of in-store sales held on a basis so regular that stores were on sale more often than not. The purpose of this – then a daringly different device – was to create a sense of excitement, a carnival atmosphere to heighten customer expectations and draw them in.

Mass marketing techniques introduced into South African retailing by my father were soon widely copied by other chain-store traders. Many of his innovations remain an important part of modern retail marketing to this day. Without doubt, my father – the most adventurous and dynamic member of the original Ackermans trio – was South Africa's first mass marketer. He certainly taught me the importance of keeping retail trading exciting for consumers.

The Great Depression of the 1930s created a chill trading climate for South African business. Even though Ackermans succeeded in attracting new cash customers into the stores during that testing time, the Depression was actually only one of their problems. My father's avowed intent never to borrow money placed his business under enormous constraint. Without borrowing, Ackermans could not compete with new enterprises playing on the retail stage, among them OK Bazaars and Woolworths. These lively new chains traded unfettered by the crippling commission on sales that still hobbled Ackermans. They also borrowed freely to buy stock ahead.

The Great Depression, the commission paid to Mauerberger, competition and outdated financial constraints conspired among them to put Ackermans under severe stress. Around this time my father did persuade Mauerberger to reduce the vexed 10 percent commission to 7, 5 percent, and it ultimately went as low as 5 percent. Even so, it remained an enormous impediment. To see it in context, in my company today we are lucky to make 3 percent on sales, pre-tax. Imagine what giving away

10, 7 or even 5 percent to someone else would do to our prices.

In 1938, the year before the outbreak of the Second World War – the event which finally drove Ackermans to the wall – tensions within my parents' marriage built up beyond any chance of reconciliation and my father started divorce proceedings. He left the family home in Bishopscourt and moved into a little rented house in Claremont.

I was seven years old when I suddenly found myself in the centre of a bitter child custody battle between my parents. Unusually for the time, my father had decided to sue for custody because, so he told me, he thought that he was the right person to bring us up; that we would have very unhappy lives in the custody of Rachel, our mother. The divorce attracted plenty of unwelcome publicity and was extensively written up in law books because it was so unusual for a father to seek custody of children at that time.

But my father was convinced that my mother was the wrong person to bring us up. Over the years she had become very isolated and the divorce merely deepened an already thoroughly depressed state. The custody fight became a very vicious one. One day, I remember, we were told to attend a meeting with my father's lawyer in Kirstenbosch Gardens. We had to ensure that this meeting was kept secret from my mother. In the serene setting of the beautiful botanical gardens beneath Table Mountain's Skeleton Gorge, my brother, sister and I were coached by the lawyer to say in court that we didn't like our mother and didn't want to live with her.

Coaching was also carried on by our governess with whom we'd grown up. She had no time for my mother and had, besides, been told that if she looked after us children during the divorce she could come and live with us afterwards and keep her position as family governess.

Just before the divorce proceedings started, as part of the process of building up a case for my father, my sister Moyra was told to plan for us children to run away from the Bishopscourt house where we still lived with my mother. We ran away at about 6.30 p.m. one evening, just before supper. Our governess made sandwiches for us and we rode off on our bicycles, each carrying a little school bag.

When we reached our father's house we refused to go back to Bishopscourt, just as we'd been told. My father's lawyers were then able to say that we had run away from our mother to our father on our own initiative, had left our mother and gone to our father of our own free will. It was all part of the legal game played in my father's bid to win custody, but it was very, very cruel to my mother.

Rachel did try to fight the legal onslaught against her but she lacked resources and was anyway in a terrible state. As the 'baby' of the family I had been specially coached to cry and scream in the courtroom. When I was called before the court during the divorce proceedings I did as I was told and screamed, 'I don't want to stay with my mother.' I was the key witness and was told afterwards that my performance secured custody for my father.

It was a terrible burden for a seven-year-old to bear and it had a huge effect on my life. I still wake up in the middle of the night with that scene in the court echoing in my head. My mother was so angry and embittered, she was never really able to forgive me for the role I was taught to play in the custody battle. She never remarried and remained all her life a very unhappy woman. It took the warmth, wisdom and kindness of my future wife, Wendy, to bring some sort of peace and reconciliation between Rachel and me – but in 1938, the year of the divorce, bitter reproach predictably reigned supreme ...

Raymond Ackerman was born in Cape Town in 1931, and is most famous for having turned a small Cape Town retail group known as Pick 'n Pay, which he bought in 1966, into a major retailer within the South African market. Now, Pick 'n Pay consists of over 300 supermarkets and hypermarkets and about 160 franchised outlets, and employs over 30 000 people. Ackerman has received numerous awards, including an Honorary Doctorate in Commerce from the University of Cape Town (2001), and was named as one of the first 'Four Outstanding Young South Africans' in 1965.
Book Extracted: *Hearing Grasshoppers Jump* (David Philip, Cape Town, 2001)

Familiarity is the Kingdom of the Lost
Dugmore Boetie

'Say "*mother*"! Go on, say "*mother*", you son of a bitch!'

Wham! Wham! went the leather strap.

'Say "*mother*", damn you! Louder, you little bastard, louder!' she shrieked.

The strap went wild all over my face, head, and neck. It was as if she was suffering more than me.

My mouth opened, and instead of the word 'mother' a clot of blood rolled out. It was followed by a distinct '*Futsek!*' She shrieked and swung a frying pan, cracking four of my ribs. I pushed and her skinny body fell to the greedy flames of a healthy fire-galley.

Maybe I had broken her back, or maybe she was just too exhausted to lift herself. Anyway, my mother just fried and fried and fried...

'Where is he?'

'We've got him in bed thirteen.'

'How is he?'

'Oh, his ribs are coming on fine and we took the stitches out of his right thigh this morning. It's the cut above his eye that seems to worry him. He'll soon be out of here.'

'You're a social worker, aren't you?'

'Yes, Nurse.'

'I wonder how old he is?'

'Between seven and eight, I'd say.'

'God,' said the nurse.

'What's going to happen to him when he gets out of here?'

They were many now, all ringed around my bed discussing me as if I had fallen from heaven and had broken a wing. The one not in uniform shrugged her shoulders and said:

'These cases are many; they might be different, but the pattern is the same. Take this one – he's too young to be sent to a reformatory and too old to be placed in a crèche. Children of the gods above and the gutters below. One day, with God's help, the Government will build a home for them.'

My ribs were not fully healed when I ran away from hospital. I walked back to Sophiatown where I got myself a job at the Good Street bus depot. It was more voluntary than fixed.

I worked without asking permission from anybody. I busied myself sweeping stationary buses with an improvised rag broom.

At night, I would wait for the last bus to come in. It had to be the last bus because you never knew which one might pull out first. The last bus would come in between eleven thirty and twelve midnight and then I'd coil myself on the back seat and sleep.

When the first bus pulled out at four a.m. I would get up and stand at the corner of Good Street and Main Road to wait for the baker's horse-cart. Right on time I would hear the clop-clop echoes of the horses' hoofs on the tar road as they galloped towards Newlands. This was a daily routine. They were delivering fresh-baked bread to the white inhabitants of Newlands.

I would stand hidden behind one of the shop pillars and watch the driver till I was sure that all his attention was centred on the road before him, then I would dart swiftly out of my hiding place and without hesitation jump lightly on the back step of the van. Sometimes I would just sit there with my bare feet dangling while I enjoyed the ride.

One morning I was too hungry to brag. I pulled at the thick wire loop to swing the door open, but nothing happened. Then I noticed that the van was freshly painted. The paint made it difficult for me to lift the loop; it needed stronger hands. Hands that materialised right out of the tar road. Or so it seemed. One minute I was struggling with the wire loop and the next I knew, a different pair of hands appeared mysteriously and lifted the loop without effort.

'Jump!' was all he said.

I did. We retreated up Main Road with four loaves of fresh-baked bread under our armpits. When we came to the spot where he had so mysteriously appeared, he stopped and eyed me speculatively.

'Where's your home, boy?'

I shook my head. 'No home.'

'Where d'you sleep?'

'At the bus depot in Good Street, on the back seat of the last bus.'

He had a big dent in his forehead and it was throbbing violently as if it was inhaling and exhaling. He was very much undecided about something. What made him come to a quick decision was the shouting we heard from the still-receding baker's cart.

We had forgotten to close the back door of the van. The door was flapping wildly in the wind and someone was hailing the driver, hoping to draw his attention.

'In here,' said my new-found father. He threw himself on to his stomach and, sliding crabwise, vanished into the gutter.

I was still undecided when I felt his fingers closing around my ankle in a powerful grip. That decided me. I went flat on my stomach and slid in after him.

I felt him crawl, and I followed. We had crawled for only a few yards when suddenly he wasn't in front of me anymore. If he hadn't grabbed me, I would have blundered head-first into a larger tunnel.

Here it was blacker than the inside of a devil's horn. You couldn't see your own hand in front of you, but at least you could stand upright.

'Follow me, and trail with your hand against the wall,' he said.

I did. We travelled this way for about a mile, and then we stopped. He groped for my hand and led me up four steps. Up here, he was forced to stoop, while I still remained upright.

That was how I first met the man who was responsible for my future life. It was a dog's life, but nevertheless a life.

I heard him going through his pockets, then I heard the rattle of matches. He struck one. The flame nearly blinded me. He got a lamp from somewhere, and lit the wick.

I gasped. I was looking at the cavern of Ali Baba and the forty thieves. Only that was fiction and this was real.

The walls were plastered with pictures of Tom Mix the cowboy. Strewn on the floor was what must have come fresh from a washing line. There were bed-sheets, pillow-cases, ladies' bloomers, men's underwear – all were still damp. There was a wheelbarrow, a gramophone and records, a stale wedding-cake, a police helmet, a pressure stove, pots, a red battered money-box, a guitar with three strings, and a horseshoe nailed to the entrance to keep away evil spirits.

But above all the prizes, my eyes kept straying towards the gramophone. He must have noticed this, because he went straight to it and started playing some records.

I looked around and saw that this part of the tunnel was V-shaped. Water couldn't come through here because he had placed a thick slab of cement to block the outlet that runs through to the main tunnel. One tunnel was then forced to share the water of the other. What really helped a great deal was that we were about three feet above the major tunnel.

After enjoying some of the records, we had our breakfast. Then my father started schooling me on the numerous small tunnels that start in and around Sophiatown and end up here in the big one.

I was taught when and how to take advantage of them, which one to use, and which one to avoid, where they led to, and what to do in case of rain. It was like a game of snakes and ladders with the ladders crossed out. We didn't need the ladders because they led up. All we needed was the snakes. The snakes swallowed us, and when we crawled out of their bowels we found ourselves back in our underground home with arms heavily laden with stolen goods. And no tail behind.

I looked with awe at my father when he was through explaining. He was an unusually short man. Because of this, it was difficult to determine his age. He could have been anything between twenty and forty.

He told me that his real name was Ga-ga, but because of his bandy legs, people referred to him as Kromie, 'Crooked' in Afrikaans. When I begged him for permission to refer to him as Ga-ga, which was his real name, meaning not to remind him of his bandy legs, he refused. He told me that in the American comic strips ga-ga means mad; he wasn't mad.

The dent in his forehead was frightening to look at. It was so big that you could fit a tennis ball into it. He told me that it was caused by the hoof of a farmer's horse. I started hating horses until this very day.

Kromie was bad through and through. He was more mischievous than troublesome. He could without effort cause a highly religious person to use vile words. Wherever he went he left grief and chaos behind. I honestly don't think that he could walk past a dry field of grass without setting fire to it. His pocket money came from children sent to the shops by their parents. My teaming up with him did not improve my relationship with the young population of Sophiatown nor the Main Road shop owners. There was a verbal prize hanging on our heads.

Take Honest Charley, for instance, from the Chinaman shop next to the bioscope. He was named Honest Charley instead of Black Market Charley. This Chinaman kept a big pocket watch in one of his waistcoat pockets. The man was attached to a chain.

I must have made a note of it unconsciously. One morning, after oversleeping and missing my usual bread supply on the road, I went into the shop to buy myself a tickey's worth of bread. I was suddenly struck by a mischievous brainwave.

'Charley,' I said, leaving out the Honest part of his name, and holding out the bread in my hand, 'will you please push this bread down the back of my neck? I'm afraid the other boys will snatch it and run into the bioscope with it.' Charley grinned, showing a row of golden teeth.

While Charley was busy pushing the bread down the back of my neck, I lifted the watch.

It was more through fate than anything else that I bumped into Ga-ga, my gutter father, as I was leaving the shop. Outside, I showed my father the watch. He whispered fiercely into my ear, then he dragged me back to the shop's entrance. He called to Charley who was busy scaling sugar into six-penny bags.

When Honest Charley looked up, Ga-ga said, 'Look, he's got your watch.' Honest Charley dropped what he was doing and grabbed a meat cleaver. If I had known that the watch meant so much to him, I wouldn't have pinched it. Maybe he had come all the way from Chinaland with it.

I wanted to run for my life, but Ga-ga held me fast. The cleaver was being brandished with murderous intent. I tried to pull free from Ga-ga, but he held on. It was only when the cleaver was lifted for the fatal blow that Ga-ga let go. I ran down Main Road as if the Devil was after me. Maybe he was, at that.

Then Ga-ga went into action. He darted into the empty shop, jumped over the counter, and emptied the till...

I was lying flat on my stomach, another morning, with my cheeks resting on the palms of my dirty little hands. A gramophone record was playing.

The voice in the record belonged to Jimmy Rodgers. He was singing a song called 'Waiting for the Train' with guitar accompaniment. The first time I heard that record, I took to it like a drunkard takes to drink.

I must have been really dreaming. Of what? Only my ancestors know. But what I do know is that I was dreaming, because Kromie had looked up from his comic strip and said,

'I'm talking to you!'

'What?' I asked.

He pointed a fat jam-stained finger at the comic strip. 'Do you think the Red Indians will catch him?'

To shut him up I said, 'Yes, he doesn't stand a chance.'

My Daddy chuckled gleefully at the plight of the pony express rider. As long as you agreed with him, nothing went wrong. I didn't want anything to go wrong. Not while I was listening to that record.

But something did. Good things don't last. My father trampled on my favourite record by accident.

A nightmare search for the record started. Every time I stole a record, it would turn out to be the wrong one. You see, I couldn't read. If I could, I would have saved myself a lot of trouble and the Jew a lot of grief.

It went on so long, that I was beginning to think that the old Jew at the bicycle shop didn't have that record.

But my will was as obstinate as the cracks on my mud-caked feet. I was in and out of that Jew's shop as if I owned it. At last I got the right record and six months in the reformatory. The youngest convict there.

When I came out, I was bitterly reprimanded by my father for stealing records instead of food.

One morning I went out as usual for our daily bread. When I came back, the gramophone was missing. My father had sold it during my absence. He claimed that it was spoiling me.

I felt as though my back was broken. My bowels wanted to work. I packed my guitar and left the tunnel for good to wander again in a world of uncertainty.

I didn't wander long. I soon found myself working for a circus, washing elephants' feet. Sometimes I wondered which feet needed to be washed most, mine or the elephants'. But seeing that I wasn't getting paid to wash mine, I didn't bother with them.

I travelled with the circus to Cape Town where for the first time I saw the sea.

In Cape Town I was mostly with a Coon Carnival group known as The Jesters. There was a guitar player that I greatly admired. He played almost like my Jimmy Rodgers. We were inseparable; I trailed behind him like a devoted young pup.

He sent me everywhere. I went daily to town for him to pick up cigarette stubs and empty wine bottles. Eighty empty wine bottles landed him a full one at the liquor store. In turn he taught me a few chords on the guitar.

I was so busy running errands for my friend that the circus left without me. I didn't care much. I was fed-up with the elephants' feet and getting tips instead of wages. I felt that if I kept on washing elephants' feet I'd never get around to washing my own.

I liked Cape Town because sleeping accommodation was no problem. I just slept where I felt sleepy. In corridors. On stairs. Balconies. Anywhere. I just lived, and lived, and lived.

My life was so free that I was just beginning to be convinced that this nice town had no reformatory. Then they arrested me for trying to steal a bus conductor's money bag.

My knife was too blunt, otherwise I would have gotten away with it. I had his money bag, which was hanging from a leather strap, with my left hand, while my right was slashing at the leather strap which was buckled to the bag. The damn-fool knife wouldn't cut the strap in one stroke. The white conductor tried to grab my knife hand. That made me forget the leather strap. Instead, I sank my knife through his hand. It's funny, the knife wouldn't cut the strap but it sank through his hand as if it was made of reformatory soap. That got me two years in Tokai, the Cape Town reformatory. The kind of work they gave me in the reformatory got me out of the reformatory. We were weaving fishing-nets. My nimble fingers were so good at it that in a year they gave me a 'hat' as promotion. I was now a monitor.

It was while I was a monitor that I learned about the fish train. The fastest train on the track. It travels non-stop from Cape Town docks to Johannesburg, with one water break at Bloemfontein so that the fish it carries shouldn't get rotten. The non-stop journey plus the chunks of ice with which they line the coaches keep the fish still fresh all the way to Johannesburg.

Maybe the fishing-net business was beginning to bore me. Or perhaps it was the fish train knowledge. I don't know. All I know is that I found my hands manufacturing a rope ladder instead of a fishing net, while the corner of my right eye kept straying towards the prison walls. It's a long time ago, but I can still hear the echoes of police whistles in my ears whenever I recall what I now refer to as the Tokai Break. They behaved as if I was forty instead of eleven.

Seven days after my escape from Tokai, a policeman was saying, 'Jump over his head and get to the other side, then work on the fingers of his left hand while I work on the right.'

A crowd of onlookers had gathered on both sides of the fish train. I was perched between two coaches. The white policeman on my right was grumbling and swearing as he struggled to release my frozen fingers from the wire cage of the coach. He was hurting me. The other policeman on my left was more gentle.

'Can't we light a fire and melt the ice around the little devil's fingers?'

'No, he'll get frostbite.'

'I wonder how the devil the little bastard got himself into such a mess.'

He gave one quick unexpected pull and my right hand was jerked free. Blood dripped from my fingers and tears spurted from my eyes as I examined my bleeding hand. The nail on my little finger was missing.

'Better do the same with that left hand, we can't afford to waste any more time with this little brat.'

'Hold on, I'm only left with the thumb.'

Pulling the baton from his belt, he knocked it several times against the wire cage. The ice cracked and fell away, and my thumb was free.

They hauled me off the train. At first, my knees wouldn't let me stand upright, but after the police gave them a good rub I was able to stand unaided.

'Pikannin!'

'Yes, baas.'

I looked up at the policeman with a dirty, tear-stained face.

'What on earth were you doing on that train?'

'I was trying to get loose, baas.'

'Yes, yes, I know. What I don't know is how the hell you found yourself hemmed in between two coaches and half-frozen to death?'

'I was coming home, baas.'

'Coming home from where?'

'From Cape Town, baas.'

'You mean,' spluttered the other policeman, 'you travelled a thousand miles from Cape Town like that?'

'I come from Cape Town with this train, baas.'

'Where do you stay, boy?'

'Sophiatown, baas.'

'What street, boy?'

'Good Street, baas.'

'What number?'

'No number, baas.'

'You mean there is no number at your house?'

'No number, baas.'

'Why?'

'Is not a house, is a bus garage, baas.'

'You mean you sleep in a bus depot?'

'Yes, baas. On the back seat of the last bus.'

'The back seat of the last bus, heh?'

'Yes, baas.'

'This is a case for the social workers...'

'Not social workers, please, baas.'

'Why not social workers?'

'Long time ago, they say I'm a head sore.'

'A what?'

'A head sore, baas.'

'You mean a headache?'

'Yes, baas.'

'How old are you?'

'Leben.'

'Eleven!' they echoed in unison.

As I was led through the gaping crowd, I fished out a half loaf of stale bread from inside my shirt and started biting into it.

I didn't care what they were going to do with me as long as I was back home. Familiarity is the kingdom of the lost.

They locked me up and only released me when they felt that I was old enough to look after myself. I could, too, if the police would only stop interfering.

Dugmore Boetie was a vagabond, thief, and a survivor. He was born in Johannesburg in the 1930s, and eked a life out of the urban sprawl by begging, borrowing, and stealing. Boetie's account, from borstal to living on the street, is a tough, no-holds-barred tale of life at the height of apartheid. While Boetie was meant to have died in the 1980s, there has been some debate over whether this work is a true autobiography edited by Barney Simon, or whether the editor in fact penned the book as a work of fiction. Even if that is the case, there is no doubting the colour, life, rugged reality, and quality of the writing.
Book Extracted: *Familiarity is the Kingdom of the Lost* (edited by Barney Simon, Arena Press, 1989)

A Season in Paradise
Breyten Breytenbach

... Bonnievale. That's where the big foul-up began. I was born and received in a thatched roof sharecropper's cottage, and was cut out for great things from the first wail. That's why I had barely turned six when they sent me to school! The village itself lies in a beautiful valley in the heart of the Boland and the Karoo. A river runs along it with the cheese factory on one bank and Uncle Red Daan's vineyards on the other. There's a station, and on the hill above the station where the road leaves the village for Swellendam, live Uncle Jors and Aunt Hanna. (Pretty poor, too.) At the other end is the graveyard and Grandpa and Grandma live just on the other side. I suppose Grandpa didn't want to have to walk so far. Then there was a lady who gave piano lessons close to Uncle Daan and Aunt Bettie Daan and a rich-in-earthly-goods Englishwoman in a huge house behind an avenue of bluegums who made us a present of a goose every Christmas. There is a road near the top dam where the dead horse lay rotting and where Pa hid from the water-bailiff. It also happened to be one of Antjie's hideouts. And nearby are a church and a vast rugby field where whistles can be heard blowing shrilly, and a vicarage and a church hall and the school where bells are continuously ringing and dusty kaffir plums trees along the street. Close by is our house with its verandah and its world. When I was leprous,* I was able to stare longingly in the mornings from the garden at my school friends as they walked, whooping-coughish from the frost, up to the koppies to search for kukumakrankas and to pick chinkerinchees. Then I would weep so bitterly that the tears would pour down my skin and burn the sores. In short, Bonnievale was an ordinary village with all the juicy white roots of evil well dug in.

Our home was a wonderful place where, among other things, miracles occurred. It had, as I have said before, a red verandah in front and a white one in the back. Also a kitchen, hallway, a bedroom for our parents, and a 'den' for the boys with beds which provided cover when

---

*Fact and fantasy are often indistinguishable in this book, and nowhere more so than in these reminiscences of early childhood. 'Leprous' may refer here to a time of real physical illness (though not leprosy), as seen through the eyes of both the man and the child, obsessed with transience. In any case, its metaphoric meanings are intended.

Ma was about to prod us with a cane or a broom handle, and where full piss-pots were kept as well. Between the bedroom and the 'den' was a bathroomy type of chamber. Covered with goose-bumps we would occasionally hear Ma walking around barefooted here, her feet making sucking noises as though they were sticking to the cement floor. Or we would hear Pa sneezing and wheezing as steam bubbled out through the door, clinging in tiny wet traces to the hallway walls. Here we were grabbed and scrubbed without fear or favor until our heels, rough as those of a kitchen fowl, were rough no longer. It was always dark in the house.

One evening a frog played the organ for hours in one of the rooms. We hunted him by candlelight and heard him moving plop-plop through the house – thus: plop, plop-plop-plop, plop-plop. But the frog was so large that it didn't even bat an eyelid at Ma's scolding.

In front of the house was a garden. That was where Ma buried Pa's liquor bottles. They were both keen gardeners. Surrounding the garden and the house was a fence with a gate. Pa had us believe that he was a Springbok, and to demonstrate this he would regularly leap over the gate each evening. Because we remained skeptical – he was our pa, after all – he hopped over the gate one evening, braced himself slightly, took a few long strides and then sailed effortlessly over the church. Not over the steeple, admittedly, only over the roof. He was as strong as an ox and afraid of nothing. Sometimes he would take us along with him on the front of his bicycle when he went to work, both B and myself up front on the crossbar between his knees, and then he would make the bicycle sing at fifty, sixty miles an hour, and you could no longer distinguish the individual stones beneath the wheels.

Years later he bought a car, a new one every year actually, since, sucker that he was, he also speculated because he was continually being swindled. Everyone was driving Mercurys then. It was Mercury left, right, and centre. Ours was a blue one, and where we drove, the dust was agitated. The older model had a rumble seat, and two or more of us always had to sit in the back with a travelling-rug around our legs, clutching our hats. In this car we travelled all over. I was always carsick, or thirsty, or I wanted to pee. It's hard to plead with your parents when you're sitting in the back in a rumble seat with your mouth full of dust. Sometimes we stopped the car so that I could be sick behind the bushes and suck an orange.

In the very same car we travelled one evening via Riviersonderend to Wakkerstroom where my second brother, B, was to play in the school band. He played the guitar and he was the youngest musician, the baby of the band. An hour ahead of schedule we were already seated, and every now and then he would poke his head around the curtain (this was still closed) from the bottom, to wave to us. When the curtains were drawn, he was sitting on the floor on a blanket. It was a heartrending performance and Hendrik Susan was present in person. There was even a Hawaiian guitar. As we rounded a bend on the way back that same evening, I tumbled out of my little seat just like a ball of dung released by a horse in full gallop, and broke my neck in two places. In the dark, no one had noticed my fall, and when they found me three days later, I was already dead and decaying and with baby Jesus. My mother was very sad.

At the back of our house were a see-saw, a couple of bricks used for barbecues, a cement patio, Dawid's small room, and a pear tree. Dawid, the brown man, was just as big and just as handsome as my father, but we were not as afraid of him. And under the pear tree I first discovered love. She was seventeen and an operator at the local exchange. In the evenings, around dusk, she would lift me onto her lap and hold me tightly, and I smelled the pear tree. There were other smells: the small fires beginning to crackle everywhere to cook supper, the lawns and flowers newly watered, the oil under Pa's Mercury, Dawid's working clothes, and my sweetheart's milkplump breasts. And sounds: the chirr-chirr of grasshoppers between lawn and hibiscus tree, dogs in the neighborhood barking at the smoke, the prayer meeting bell and the sexton's boots on the gravel path when he has emptied the bell of its peals, my mother puttering in the kitchen, the sucking and groaning as my father removes his Wellingtons, and my sweetheart's heart beneath my ears thud-thud thud-thud, just like the gurgling when my father secretly opens the sluiceways out of turn, or just like the plop-sounds of the frog. And the sky is the colour of mother-of-pearl like the palm of one's hand when one has spent a long time in the sea. That pear tree will never stop flowering again.

Uncle Niek and Aunt Joey's house was different from ours. They had a big orchard surrounding the house and a privy outside, painted red and with a seatboard opening shaped like a heart. Thus the heart is really nothing but a practical orifice. Next door stood the tall house owned by the professor with the hat. The professor had a sizeable fish pond filled with goldfish, red in colour. When he wanted to feed them, he sat down on the edge of the pond and tapped two pebbles together, and the fish would come to the surface with mouths wide open, so that you could count their rotten teeth. They were clever, those fish: one afternoon when I went on my own to look at the fish, I leaned too far over and fell into the pond. The professor was within hearing distance, but he was so preoccupied – he collected butterflies as well – that I called out in vain.

What with falling in and yelling, my teeth began to tap together like pebbles, and the fish were not going to allow themselves to be licked, they went for me and consumed me bit by bit. Nothing whatsoever remained of me, not even an eye or a sigh, and I was never found again. But for days the fish were too bloated to react to the professor's pebble-clicks. He was very worried about his little creatures, the poor old professor.

Grandma and Grandpa's house was something else again. Here everything was brown. The house was brown on the outside and blue and violet inside, the ridges along the upper part of the brown road running past the graveyard were brown, and for days on end Grandpa would sit on his brown chair on the back porch watching it all through and in his brown eyes. There were many fragrances in Grandma's house, all of them dark: cloves and biscuits kept in tins and Grandma's sad bed, because she was confined to it with the cancer, she had to keep the cancer warm. Grandpa Jan was strong and upright with broad spreading shoes and big hands. His hands were mostly fingers. I never heard him say a single word. He was already a hundred and fifty years old then, and a year or so before he had knocked a man out with one hand, though he had been out of practice for some time by that stage. Luckily, it was only a brown man. On Sunday mornings Pa would take Grandma to church, but Grandpa stayed behind on his brown chair to keep an eye on the graveyard. He was not taken in by the apparent peace. He was the best general in the Boer War and before that in the other wars along with Louw Wepener and Louis Trichardt and Majuba. He was a poor man, because he gave all his money to the needy and was not a bit interested in worldly wealth and opulence. (It's a family trait, this generosity.) His house in heaven will therefore be grand, with waterborne sewage and electricity.

One day, on our way home after having taken Grandma some soup, B and I came face to face with old Antjie. The horrible witch in her tattered clothes shuffled toward us with one hand extended, and B flung the soup bowl to one side, and we took to our heels back to Grandpa on the porch. He walked back with us, the whole ten miles, and before his bold and proud countenance old Antjie evaporated like snow in the sun. As far as I know Grandpa Swartjan Dirk Breytenbach never wore socks; nowadays this fashion is referred to as 'wearing Paul Krüger socks,' I believe. He was, of course, a family friend of Paul Krüger's, but his beard was neater.

It stands to reason that our village was also visited from time to time by natural and unnatural upheavals, events, and manifestations. We had earthquakes and unfaithfulness, hurricanes and adultery and threshing machines, shearers, holidays at the sea, christening Sundays, frost, visits from kings, centenaries, circuses, and so forth. Uncle Red Daan who suffered from diabetes – both his legs have since been amputated; when the second was amputated he was too weak for the gas so that he was given only a local anaesthetic, but apparently he is coming along nicely now – and his wife, Aunt Bettie Daan, who could talk at sixty miles an hour, would always have themselves photographed: both puffed out with pride and cheese, and with Daan Jr., Pietertjie, Sanna of Aunt Bettie Daan, Burgert – who in the old days would bleat like a sheep and now snaps like a dog – Kaspaas and Eben-this-is-the-limit squeezed in too, they may be seen sitting in a rickshaw, boots and all. The man wearing the feathers and the horns was presumably posing there only for fun, I take it he wasn't expected to pull them! But I state without hesitation that my childhood years were extremely uneventful and perfectly ordinary on the whole; in our village, and in my family in particular, there was very little squabbling, strife or discord, and never any question of violence.

One distressing incident, however, springs to mind clearly even now. I had just started school and B simply had to come along too, though his position as an economic liability at that time entitled him to lie around at home for another year. And then I became infected with mumps and whooping cough. As a matter of fact, I have never quite got rid of those mumps, actually, and in later years I cultivated a beard to keep the growths in check. All the same, B goes to school by himself, and I am left standing in the front garden, clutching my mother's dress, and the children emerge from the school gate in a long line – as there are so many absentees owing to the epidemic, the remainder are going to the veld for the day. And as they walk, old B waves to me, and I can see his bald head gleaming in the sun, and his tears are reflected on his cheeks like fragments of glass, and I weep and wave back, because they are marching in a column like convicts in the direction of the veld where Antjie is undoubtedly lying in wait for them – as it is, she's especially fond of B – and who will I have left now to knock around today in my state of quarantine? (Or did this grief manifest itself only later? A friend sent me a yellowed postcard recently: little young Amsterdam orphans, all sporting identical gray tunics and shaven heads – Jewish hostages behind the fence of a concentration camp.)

Thus all good things come to an end ...

Breyten Breytenbach was born in Bonnievale, Western Cape, in 1939. He studied art at the University of Cape Town, and is a writer, painter, and was a committed opponent of apartheid. This opposition lead to his exile in 1960, later settling in Paris with his Vietnamese wife. He returned to South Africa with a false passport in 1975, and was arrested and charged under the Terrorism Act

and jailed for seven years. After his release, he returned to France and obtained French citizenship. He currently divides his time between Europe, South Africa, and the United States of America.
Book Extracted: *A Season in Paradise* (Jonathan Cape, London, 1976)

Who's laetie are you?
Rrekgetsi Chimeloane

On some days students attended 'morning classes' and on other days 'afternoon classes'. This did not bother me, as long as I remembered which week I should be at school at what time. The times were either in the morning, starting at eight o'clock, or still in the morning, starting at eleven o'clock. Don't ask me why eleven o'clock was referred to as afternoon ... I liked both morning and afternoon classes as they both presented advantages to me. In the case of morning classes, I could play at the playgrounds after school until the afternoon pupils were let out, and then go home with them.

Walking home alone after morning classes had its problems. Especially for someone like me who was at Ikaneng Lower Primary School, which was about four kilometres away from where I lived. Having to walk back home with the streets deserted, except for the school-dodgers, drop-outs and bullies, was never an easy task. To make matters worse, there were not only boundaries between each of the suburbs or 'townships', as we called them, of Soweto, but there were also invisible boundaries between each of the zones which made up the different 'townships'. On top of that, in many cases there were invisible borders within the zones. Diepkloof had six zones, all of them, in one way or another, hostile to one another. In Diepkloof this meant that walking from Zone Four, which was where I lived, to Zone Three had certain hazards. The Zone Three boys, if they spotted you, would chase you all over the place and then beat the hell out of you – that is, if you were too slow or your tactics of manoeuvre were not up to scratch.

I do not think any person who grew up in a township can tell you how one distinguished between residents of one zone and another, given the large number of people who resided in the area. You could simply *see* the difference.

One day I saw doves flying low above my house. I was with my friends and I took a stone and was about to throw it at the doves.

'Ijo, ijo, ijo. O tla go gata Joe, ka majuba a gage!' One of my friends, Jimmy warned me that Joe would beat me into the dust if I hit one of his doves. How it was possible to distinguish between wild doves and local doves was beyond me, but it was, and distinguishing between people of different zones was a piece of cake by comparison.

One thing that I never understood, though, was the animosity we displayed towards things strange, especially animals. The mere sight of something strange translated into castigation of the highest order.

I recall how we used to stone strange dogs to death. There were even stone-throwing specialists when it came to stray animals. Dimros was one of them. He had a reputation of delivering a deathblow with a single half-brick thrown at a poor animal.

Coming back to boundaries, there were, as I said, even invisible borders within zones, and Zone Four, where I lived, was no different. It also had its territorial borders. There was 'ko Modise o Botse', which was the area next to a church called Modise o Botse; there was 'ko digroundeng', which was the area next to the Diepkloof soccer fields; … there was 'ko di olopreineng', which was the area next to Baragwanath Airport; and lastly there was 'ko maeneng', which was the area next to the mine dumps.

Ikaneng, where I went to school, was a stone's throw away from 'next to Zone Three', whereas I lived in Zone Four, next to the 'Baragwanath Airport' side. The most dangerous spots in any of the zones were 'passages' that made one's journey shorter. Passages were dangerous for everyone, including us kids, but mostly they were dangerous at night. That was when murders and robberies took place in and around passages.

There was this one passage which I had to use on my way to and from school. There were no viable alternative routes. For example, with the main alternative route you had to go by the shops first and then follow Immink Drive for about a kilometre, until you turned into the street where the school was; this route was very long and even worse than the normal short-cut I took when it came to unruly elements. Tactically, the worst part about this alternative route was that you did not have many ways out if bullies or territory-mongers gave you chase, because it was mainly one long straight street.

Also, what made the passage on this particular route painfully memorable to me was a series of accidents I experienced on it. I was knocked down by a bicycle three times in that passage. And on all three occasions I sustained head injuries. I really cannot explain how the accidents occurred. All I knew was that if I was on that passage and a bicycle entered the passage at the same time, it was certain that no matter which side I ran to, I would end up with my head graced by the spokes of the bicycle's wheels.

In such cases, whenever I reached home, I would go straight to the tap and pour water all over my head and face to disguise as best I could my injuries. I did not want my two sisters seeing me in that 'mess' for fear of being mocked. I also had to make sure that none of my four older brothers saw me, because I knew they would label me a sissy who could not stand up to his equals. So every time I came home after an 'accident' or a fight, especially if I had lost, I would head straight for the tap to rub away the marks, tears, and the red-hot prints that remained on my cheeks from the short, sharp, flat-handed blows to the face that were known to us as 'claps'.

The other obstacle along all of the alternative routes was my biggest nemesis, dogs. They really made my life hell. I had to remember all the routes I used not only for the potential bullies in the area but also for the dogs resident on those routes.

Yes, I was terrified of dogs.

I have no idea what I did to warrant such hostility from members of the canine species. The simple reality was that from as far back as I could remember, dogs did not like me. They seemed repulsed by my appearance. My friends and I could be walking down the street, less than a foot apart, but if there was a dog about, I would be the one who was attacked.

There was one dog in particular, five houses away from my house, a black and white little thing called Spotty, which made my life a nightmare. One of my mother's distant cousins, Mma Kumako, lived next door to the house where Spotty lived. Every time my mother sent me with a message to her, there was no other way but to pass by that dog's home. To make matters worse, where that dog lived was also at the beginning of my route to school and my route to the shops. This meant that I had to come into contact with Spotty almost every day.

Everybody always told me. 'That is a harmless dog and it will never bite you. Just don't run away when you see it.' The problem with those people was that they did not see the dog through my eyes. If they had watched the movie, The Doberman Gang, they would be keeping their ideas to themselves. I mean, how could I be expected just to stand there facing a set of shining, sharp white teeth, an unforgiving growl, and the wild glint in the eyes of that black and white dog?

Good as I was with stones, I could not stone Spotty. Stoning it would translate into a variety of undesirable repercussions, for example, the owners coming to tell my folks that I was abusing their dog, or Skumbuzo, their young son, retaliating by beating me up. Not that I was afraid of Skumbuzo by himself, but Skumbuzo and his cousin Muzi were inseparable, and if you added the dog to this duo, you ended up with a formidable opponent. My somewhat fragile, asthmatic body was a poor match.

One day, as usual, my mother sent me to her distant cousin, Mma Kumako's, to ask her where their next women's sosaete – social club –

would be. At that time there were almost no phones in black residential areas. I had only ever seen a phone in the movies. So a simple question could cost one up to an hour's walk or more – and usually it was the duty of the youngest, like me, to deliver the messages. Given the intricacies of territorial borders, and other considerations such as dogs, I did not like being sent to convey messages.

My mother did not want to know about these dilemmas. All she was interested in was for the message to be delivered and getting the feedback as soon as possible. If I ever complained that I was going to be beaten by other boys, her reply would be, 'Why don't you hit them back?' She did not know that it was not as simple as that. For one thing, you did not hit back in foreign territory; you humbled yourself even to the idiots and weaklings, with the hope that one day, if by some luck fate should deliver them into your domain, you would catch them and dish out revenge.

Another woman my mother used to send me to with messages, was Mma Mojapelo, who lived in Diepkloof Zone Three. Zone Three also had its subsections. She lived in the area called Ghost Town. This Ghost Town was not the kind of ghost town that had been deserted by its inhabitants. This one was different, because it was overcrowded with inhabitants. On top of which, Ghost Town was right next to an area called Jerusalem … yes, Jerusalem. Young people called the area Mjerujeru. If you never thought there could be anything holy around Soweto, especially in Diepkloof for that matter, think again. There it was, a mine dump called Jerusalem. How a mine dump in Diepkloof's backyard came to be blessed with the name of the Holy City, I have no idea. But there were those who claimed that there were freebies, meaning free sweets, at Mjerujeru. Us boys simply believed it when the older boys told us that they got a lot of sweets at the mine dump. Some boys even claimed they had stumbled onto a utopia of freebies and the best of all these freebies were the 'chunks of sweets'. It was not difficult to believe them after seeing Pitso and his friend returning from Mjerujeru with hand-loads of sweets and ending up selling them to us.

Among the different sweets they had for sale was this one monumental sweet called setabola-nnyoko, meaning 'the one that tears the gall apart'. The sweet, which boys like us loved to suck, was one big chunk of red crystal that was jagged at the edges but tasted sweeter and smoother than sugar. The adventurers to Mjerujeru had the sweet up for sale at five cents a chunk, which was way above what we could afford. All I could dream of was accompanying them on their next expedition so I could lay my hands on some free setabola-nnyoko. Of course I would have to do it without the knowledge of my mother. She always warned me not to eat too many sweets as my stomach reacted rather negatively to lots of sugar.

If my mother ever found out that I had been eating setabola-nnyoko she would not hesitate to give me castor oil. Castor oil was a thick, and I mean thick, oily laxative with an aftertaste that left me nauseous for a week. If there was one thing I hated among all the medications I had to take at that age, it was castor oil. My mother used to tell me it was good for cleaning my stomach, which was made dirty by all the sweets I liked to eat. On the other hand, though, it has to be said that castor oil was better than spyt – the syringe. Spyt was used for the same purpose as castor oil, only with spyt one did not have to wait before visiting the toilet. In fact it was administered as close to the toilet as possible, because after the mixture – of water and Sunlight soap – was injected up one's backside, everything would come gushing out at almost exactly the same time. With castor oil, one would have to stay in bed and drink black tea and eat soft porridge in order to help the castor oil do its work. Also with castor oil, my mother would not allow me to flush the toilet until she had made sure the castor oil had done its job. This was because I used to secretly race to the toilet to vomit it out. My mother had cottoned on to this practice, hence the inspection. If she found the castor oil had not done its work, the exercise would have to be repeated the next weekend. My mother always said, 'Gall will kill you, as it did Mma Mosweu's little boy.'

Anyway, to get back to Ghost Town. It was right at the top end of Diepkloof, next to Noordgesigt, and there was talk about paranormal activity in the area, including headless bodies that roamed the streets in the dark, and cars that sped along without drivers and caused havoc on the roads at night. What happened to Ghost Town at night was no concern of mine; what bothered me was the distance between my home and that of Mma Mojapelo, to whom I had to deliver my mother's messages. The distance was roughly six kilometres, which, as you can imagine, meant criss-crossing several foreign territories. Of course, at the time, public transport in the township was scarce. But even if taxis and buses were available, one of the main functions of children, especially young boys, was to be sent on errands. My mother used to say, 'You think you will stay at home and the only thing you do will be eating? Come on ... your work is to be sent anywhere we want you to go. Or do you want me to go there by myself?'

This was what I hated most about being the last-born. My four brothers and two sisters, as well as my father and mother, could send me anywhere at will.

Before journeys like the one to Mma Mojapelo I would first canvass for backup from among my friends. There was one friend among the dozens I had who was always there for me, and that was Levi. He and I went through an assortment of street fights and mostly came out right side up. I had enemies all over, across zones and within zones, but they were few compared with Levi's. I do not know if he was attracted to adversaries or whether he just enjoyed making enemies. But he must have had five enemies for every one I had. Acquiring enemies was the simplest thing in those years, especially when there was little in the way of police or other forms of protection. You could quite innocently look at someone and be accused of looking at that person in the wrong way. The next thing you knew you were being chased. If you managed to outmanoeuvre your attacker, he would hunt you from that day on until he had satisfied himself that he had punished you in one way or another. So Levi and I would always line our pockets with stones and ketis – pocket-sized catapults – as weapons and ammunition for the potential fights we might encounter along the way. One's enemies had a way of popping up in very strange places. Sometimes they even resided at your very destination. Can you imagine thinking that you had outsmarted all your rivals on a six-kilometre walk, only to find one of them sitting in the kitchen where you were sent, drinking black tea with slices of brown bread? Well, it happened. In such cases, you had to deliver your message as quickly as possible, standing in the doorway, and then run for your life.

But, anyway, back to the day I was sent to my mother's distant cousin, Mma Kumako, which was just a few houses away. I approached the yard carefully looking out for Skumbuzo's dog, Spotty. Luckily it was nowhere to be seen and I was relieved. I delivered my mother's message and then rushed out of the house. As I hurried out of the yard, happy that I had survived the dog this time, there it was charging straight towards me. You should have seen how I accelerated. 'Do not run away,' someone shouted. 'Just stay where you are,' another voice called out. I thought, to hell with your advice and ran like a bat out of hell. The next thing I felt was something stinging my backside. As I looked back, there it was, Spotty, with its teeth sunk into my buttocks. I screamed like a baby as people started shouting at the dog, 'Voetsek! Voetsek!'

Finally, scared off, the animal let go of me and strolled back into its yard, leaving me crying like a two-year-old until Kgorogo, Mma Kumako's young son, came and comforted me and led me back into their yard, where Mma Kumako administered her first-aid.

'Get the hair from the dog,' Mma Kumako shouted to her son, pointing to the little black and white dog next door which had nearly torn me apart. When he had returned, she said to me, 'Spit your saliva into my hand.' I obeyed. Then she said, 'Look that way,' and pulled my short pants down and applied the mixture of saliva and dog's hair to my sore bottom.

I was escorted home that day by Kgorogo. My brothers laughed at me when they heard that I was chased and bitten by a little dog.

Why did it have to bite me in particular? A lot of people said that I was a nice boy. Even my sisters often told me that they wished I was a girl because I was so cute. My mother's friends also said that they wished they had small boys like me because I looked so loveable. But no, not to Spotty. You would think a dog with a name like that would be a cute little fluffy thing that you could cuddle. Not this one. All Spotty wanted to do was sink its teeth into my behind. That was its opinion of me being cute. As I sat there on that day, thinking about what had happened, I grew more and more angry with myself as I thought about how I allowed such a little dog to scare me. At the same moment something hit me – Sophia. She stayed opposite Mma Kumako's house. She was the girl of my dreams. She was soft-skinned and light in complexion and was the embodiment of beauty to me. I wondered whether she had witnessed the whole debacle. How would I approach her and tell her I wanted her to be my girlfriend, that is, if ever I gathered enough courage to do that? But if she saw me and that dog, she would probably laugh at me too, just like the rest of them. Worse still, she would probably laugh at me together with her friends in class. I could just imagine her telling her friends: 'that stupid Alex was bitten by a little dog mo maragong' – on the buttocks.

I must get even with that dog, I told myself. Next time I walked near that house I would be carrying a half-brick concealed behind my back. One wrong move and I would strike it as hard as I could.

Since that day, Spotty never bothered me again. Could it be that it had just wanted to taste my backside?

Rrekgetsi Chimeloane was born in Diepkloof, Soweto in 1964. After high school he enrolled at a technikon, but student unrest interrupted his studies. He then went on to work as a maintenance operator in Sasolburg, staying in a men's only hostel for six years. During this time, he obtained a diploma in Comprehensive Writing, and became part of the African Writers' Association. His first novel, *To be like Sizwe*, was published in 1992, and he documented his stay in the men's hostel in his next book, *The Hostel-Dwellers – a first-hand account*. Chimeloane currently lives in Soshanguve.
Book Extracted: *Who's laetie are you? – My Sowetan boyhood* (Kwela Books, 2001)

Boyhood
JM Coetzee

He has never worked out the position of his father in the household. In fact, it is not obvious to him by what right his father is there at all. In a normal household, he is prepared to accept, the father stands at the head: the house belongs to him, the wife and children live under his sway. But in their own case, and in the households of his mother's two sisters as well, it is the mother and children who make up the core, while the husband is no more than an appendage, a contributor to the economy as a paying lodger might be.

As long as he can remember he has had a sense of himself as prince of the house, and of his mother as his dubious promoter and anxious protector – anxious, dubious because, he knows, a child is not meant to rule the roost, if there is anyone to be jealous of, it is not his father but his younger brother. For his mother promotes his brother too – promotes and even, because his brother is clever but not as clever as he, nor as bold or adventurous, favours him. In fact, his mother seems always to be hovering over his brother, ready to ward off danger; whereas in his own case she is only somewhere in the background, waiting, listening, ready to come if he should call.

He wants her to behave toward him as she does toward his brother. But he wants this as a sign, a proof, no more. He knows that he will fly into a rage if she ever begins hovering over him.

He keeps driving her into corners, demanding that she admit whom she loves more, him or his brother. Always she slips the trap. 'I love you both the same,' she maintains, smiling. Even his most ingenious questions – what if the house were to catch fire, for instance, and she had time to rescue only one of them? – fail to snare her. 'Both of you,' she says, 'I will surely save both of you. But the house won't catch fire.' Though he mocks her for her literal-mindedness, he respects her dogged constancy.

His rages against his mother are one of the things he has to keep a careful secret from the world outside. Only the four of them know what torrents of scorn he pours upon her, how much like an inferior he treats her. 'If your teachers and your friends knew how you spoke to your mother...' says his father, wagging a finger meaningfully. He hates his father for seeing so clearly the chink in his armour.

He wants his father to beat him and turn him into a normal boy. At the same time he knows that if his father dared to strike him, he would not rest until he had his revenge. If his father were to hit him, he would go mad: he would become possessed, like a rat in a corner, hurtling about, snapping with its poisonous fangs, too dangerous to be touched.

At home he is an irascible despot, at school a lamb, meek and mild, who sits in the second row from the back, the most obscure row, so that he will not be noticed, and goes rigid with fear when the beating starts. By living this double life he has created for himself a burden of imposture. No one else has to bear anything like it, not even his brother, who is at most a nervous, wishy-washy imitation of himself. In fact, he suspects that at heart his brother may be normal. He is on his own. From no quarter can he expect support. It is up to him to somehow get beyond childhood, beyond family and school, to a new life where he will not need to pretend any more.

Childhood, says the *Children's Encyclopaedia*, is a time of innocent joy, to be spent in the meadows amid buttercups and bunny-rabbits or at the hearthside absorbed in a storybook. It is a vision of childhood utterly alien to him. Nothing he experiences in Worcester, at home or at school, leads him to think that childhood is anything but a time of gritting the teeth and enduring ...

John Maxwell Coetzee was born in Cape Town in 1940, and educated at the University of Cape Town, as well as the University of Texas, where he gained a PhD. In 1971 he returned to South Africa and took a position within the Department of English at the University of Cape Town. His first novel, *Dusklands* (1974), is considered to be the first post-modern South African novel. Coetzee has won the Booker Prize on two occasions, first for his book *The life and times of Michael K* (1983), and, more recently, for *Disgrace* (1999). He was nominated for a Nobel Prize in 1988, and was awarded the Nobel Prize for Literature in 2003.
Book Extracted: *Boyhood: scenes from provincial life* (Vintage, 1998)

I Remember King Kong (The Boxer)
Denis Hirson

I remember white or khaki safari suits, and then the fashion for various pastel shades, with long socks to match.

I remember when the colour khaki was everywhere: school uniforms, socks, overalls, police, cadets, scouts, soldiers, farmers.

I remember garters, and combs stuck into the tops of long socks.

I remember M.E. Stores; woggles, sheath knives and broad-rimmed khaki scout hats with false leopard-skin hatbands.

I remember that Liberace had a costume fitted with epaulettes, electric lights and tassels that looked like the bottom of a theatre curtain.

I remember Ansteys, Stuttafords, John Orrs, Garlicks, Greatermans and Cleghorns in the middle of town; the haberdashery department, the lift-man on his seat and the lazy piano music in the tea-room on the top floor.

I remember Jeremy Taylor's song about the lift-girl who didn't even have time for a zizz (I thought that meant a pee).

I remember ladies standing around looking at dress patterns for hours.

I remember that you could take clothes home 'on appro'.

I remember capsules with shiny brass ends and a transparent middle, called 'dockets', sent off with documents inside them and then arriving back via overhead tubes at the sales assistant's counter with a satisfying pop.

I remember the X-ray machine in shoe departments where you could look down through an eye-piece and see the bones of your feet inside a new shoe.

I remember the problem of tying your own shoe-laces. Girls didn't seem to have this problem because their shoe-laces never came undone.

I remember my grandmother's fear that I would get my shoe caught at the end of the escalator.

I remember tram-loads of old ladies on the way from Yeoville into town, and their fierce reaction if you accidentally trod on their feet.

I remember the red nail of a big toe pushing through the front of a woman's shoe like a tortoise-head.

I remember old ladies in fox-stoles with the dried head and paws still there.

I remember when a house down the road from my grandparents' was sealed for fumigation, and imagining processions of very small creatures heading for cover.

I remember my grandfather's wooden truncheon on his bedside table.

I remember pink electric blankets, and candlewick bedspreads with matching bedside mats.

I remember that my grandmother's gardener Willie festooned one of the outhouses with meat hanging from hooks to make biltong.

I remember my grandmother and her maid working at a chicken, the smell of fresh raw chicken-flesh rising up from the stone sink, and then the bitter whiff of singed feather stubs.

I remember my grandmother's mince machine with discs of different sized holes, and feeding in bread to force out the last of the meat.

I remember the Indian sammy coming around with his horse-drawn cart of fruit and vegetables.

I remember going to the Newtown fruit and vegetable market on Saturday mornings with my father, the auctioneers standing on ladders above bags and crates of fruit and vegetables shouting a fast strange language that turned out to be prices.

I remember that I had to eat mangoes in the bath.

I remember going to a swimming pool at night to watch my plump uncles playing water-polo.

I remember the feeling of going hunting with my father when we examined all the things for sale at auction sales in private houses. And later the triumph of returning home to present my mother with the loot.

I remember mugs commemorating George V's visit to South Africa.

I remember:
   I'm the king of the castle,
   And you're the dirty rascal.

I remember being surprised to learn that the queen didn't wear her crown all day long.

I remember that I didn't go to school on the day South Africa became a republic, but the teacher kept a little flag and bronze medal for me anyway.

Denis Hirson was born in England in 1951, to South African parents. He lived in South Africa from 1952, and later studied anthropology at the University of the Witwatersrand. His father was imprisoned for political reasons for nine years. After his release in 1973, Denis Hirson moved to France. There, he has worked as an actor, teacher and writer. He has translated into English a collection of Breyton Breytenbach's poems. Hirson's first book of South African memories was entitled *The House Next Door to Africa*, a mosaic of memory including fragments on Eastern Europe and Johannesburg.
Book Extracted: *I Remember King Kong (The Boxer)* (Jacana, 2004)

Armed and Dangerous
Ronnie Kasrils

Johannesburg and the dun-coloured mine dumps of the Witwatersrand (the mining area to the east and west of Johannesburg) looked unreal as they rose from the flat highveld landscape and we descended out of a clear sky. The problem was that I had miscalculated the time of arrival. Instead of imbibing in a civilised way, strictly half an hour before arrival, I had to gulp down the scotch at the last moment.

As we disembarked I felt both tense and elated, as though I was about to appear on stage before an audience. I kept thinking of my opening lines for the passport official. I remembered to slow down my movements, as Eleanor had instructed and, with considerable relief, had my passport stamped, no questions asked.

'Welkom in Seth Efrika,' said the woman official, smiling sweetly beneath an elaborate hair-do.

I picked up my baggage, placed it on a trolley and moved through customs. A pimply-faced customs official stopped me. He was so young I thought it must have been his first day on the job. He motioned to my briefcase and asked what was inside. 'Just some papers and magazines.'

He looked carefully through the contents, a mixture of business and tourist literature. The question uppermost in my mind was whether this was a routine check, or whether a rigorous search was about to follow. If they were simply having a sniff at me, I reasoned, surely they would not use such an inexperienced kid? It was at this moment, my chest tightening while I sought to appear nonchalant, that I wished I had jumped the border fence instead. In the end, satisfied that I was not smuggling in banned material – I guessed he had probably hoped to uncover a copy of *Playboy* magazine – I was allowed to continue on my way.

I was soon in a taxi, aglow with excitement but glancing through the rear window for any signs of a tail. The city skyline, coming in from the airport along a busy motorway system suited my optimistic mood. In the distance was the phalanx of glass and concrete towers of downtown Johannesburg, framed by stony ridges and *koppies* (hillocks) and the mine dumps like sand dunes in the sunlight. With a sense of triumph, I picked out the Yeoville *koppie* where I played as a child. The speed of the traffic, the high performance cars, the dizzy interchanges, the gigantic power lines and impressive buildings that flashed past, indicated the development that had taken place. I looked from the mine dumps to the skyscrapers and thought how no other city in the world was so visibly tied to its economic roots.

At my out-of-town hotel I found a public telephone. I dialled a London number and reported my safe arrival on an answering machine. A call from London would be made to my undercover contacts in Johannesburg. This would trigger a rendezvous for the next day. In the meantime, I needed to check for surveillance to be as sure as possible that I was not being followed. The best way of doing that was to go for a long walk. I would kill two birds with one stone and look round Yeoville, my childhood stomping ground, which I was longing to see again.

After a rest and a change into casual clothes, I took a taxi to Yeoville. Away from the motorway system, many of the less fashionable parts of Johannesburg were substantially unaltered. The superstructure in Yeoville's narrow, main road, Rockey Street, was still much the same. The tramlines were gone, but not the municipal swimming baths. The nearby sports ground had been converted into a park, part of the surrounding wall still in place. For years that wall had borne the slogan: 'An attack on communism is an attack on you.'

I alighted at the park and paid the taxi. The art of counter-surveillance is never to look over your shoulder. You have to provide yourself with situations which naturally allow you to look around. Like stopping someone and enquiring 'Could you tell me the way to Rockey Street?'

I had a good view of the departing taxi as we half-turned to face one another. The young boy I had stopped readily replied: 'It's jist along thet way, sir. It's the striet with all the small shorps. O-kay hey?' It was the once familiar accent, an uncultured nasal whine, music to my ears. He could have been any one of my childhood pals. He could have been me.

I settled down on a bench to become accustomed to the people in the park. I needed to pay special attention to those who arrived after me. I found myself re-living the football games we had played when I was centre forward for Yeoville Boys' soccer team. Then there were the races I had run on the track that once formed the perimeter of this very ground. In those days the only black people to be seen in Yeoville, or any white suburb, were domestic workers. There were plenty of black people about now, some with children, enjoying the sunshine, sitting on benches which, in the not so distant past, had been reserved for whites.

A frumpy lady with shopping bags, in need of a rest, sat down beside me, sighing heavily. As one white to another, she complained: 'My aching feet, thank heffens, you know you cawn't always git a seat these days with all the *swartzes* (blacks) about.'

I made the mistake of catching her eye, which encouraged her. The words came out in a rush: 'And the kewz in the soopamawket? So many swartzes. And the gerl at the chack-out? Vot a cheeky *shiksa* (black woman). The mouthful she gayf me about my chaynch? From ver did they learn to git so obshtreperis?'

Her appearance on the scene was not unwelcome. If I was under surveillance, it could draw out whoever was tailing me. But nobody sauntered by trying to eavesdrop. After putting up with her grievances a while longer I took my leave. But I could not resist a bit of my father's homespun philosophy. 'Well, after all, madam, what can we do? We're on this planet together, so live and let live.'

Around the corner, the orthodox shul where I had my barmitzvah, once an unrivalled centre of Jewish life, appeared deserted. I walked away from the shopping area into the quieter suburban streets where any car or pedestrian following in my tracks would be easier to spot. I noticed that many fringe establishments had proliferated, catering for ultra-orthodox sects.

Most of these had been converted from ordinary houses. I walked into one of them. A young man in a dark coat and hat, with beard and long sideburns, *payas* in Yiddish, was seated at a desk. I pretended to be looking for the previous owner of the house. After a pleasant conversation in which he asked whether I was *baal te shuvah* – a repentant Jew wanting to return to the fold – and proselytised about 'the need to be sure of one's identity in these troubled times', I bade him *shalom* and left.

The street was quiet. My visit to the house would certainly have drawn anyone watching me. I could have expected a loiterer across the road, or another lurking at the corner. I was particularly on the look out for young men of any race, physically fit and casually dressed. Men, or perhaps young women, who would avoid eye contact and pretend to be engaged in some innocuous activity like tinkering with a car or window shopping. A car full of devout Jews drove by. Not the type to be conducting surveillance on behalf of the South African security police.

I made my way back to Rockey Street. Window shopping would provide other possibilities to uncover a tail. Shop mirrors and plate glass windows would obviate any need to glance over my shoulder.

Once unfashionable, the neighbourhood had become cosmopolitan with a shabby trendiness. The prim stores catering for lower-middle-class custom had largely vanished, to be replaced by a variety of scruffy craft shops, music dens, coffee bars, clubs and food outlets. Black and white couples, dressed in hippy style, ambled by as though apartheid had never existed. Yeoville might look seedy, but it was a pacesetter with regard to the collapsing race barriers.

On the corner of Rockey and Raymond Streets, a stone's throw from where I grew up, a motley crew hung about, looking like they dealt in dope. Nearby, street urchins sniffed glue. Just the kind of place that invited police scrutiny. I decided I had seen enough of Rockey Street.

There in Raymond Street was Albyn Court, the building where I had lived for the first 16 years of my life. Just two storeys high, but a full block in width, it was almost palatial in comparison to the jerry-built flats around it. Admiring the clean, functional lines of its 1930s design – certainly not regarded as special by the tenants of my time – I was flooded with memories of all who had lived there.

I visualised my mother and father in our first-floor apartment. Like all the other adults in the building, they were the offspring of Jewish immigrants who had arrived in South Africa at the turn of the century. My grandparents had come from Lithuania and Latvia fleeing from the Czarist pogroms. The family name, I believe, stemmed from a Jewish settlement in Lithuania called Kasrilevka, which is celebrated in many of the stories of Shalom Aleichem. My paternal grandfather, Nathan, was an early prospector on the Kimberley diamond fields, and brought his wife, Sarah (nee Sachs), out to South Africa in 1900, soon after my father's birth. My grandfather set up a jewellery business and later was the first owner of Albyn Court. By the time he died in 1938 – the *year* of my birth – he had lost his money on the stock market. Family recollections have revealed that Nathan Kasrils was an avowed anti-imperialist who had a loathing for Churchill and Cecil John Rhodes. It is said that he served on the side of the Boers as a sharp-shooter and possibly acted for them as a spy.

My father, whose name was Isadore – Issy for short – was a reserved, trimly-built man. Like most of the men in the building, he worked as a commercial traveller for a factory. He dressed conservatively in a suit and tie and always wore a wide-brimmed hat, the conventional style of the times. He drove a 1947 Plymouth and I sometimes accompanied him 'on the road' during school holidays. I saw how hard he worked, driving along dusty township roads, visiting the largely Indian or Chinese shopkeepers who were the factory's main customers. It was then that I saw the crowded shacks and squalid conditions in which black people lived. My father had a good relationship with his customers and the polite greetings he exchanged with them made me proud of him. In common with most of his friends he was a chain smoker, and his incessant coughing at the wheel of the car alarmed me. He died in 1963, shortly after I left the country.

Years later, in exile, I met the secretary of the Commercial Travellers' Union, Eli Weinberg. He had known my father and considered him a 'socialist'. This surprised me, as my father had not appeared to be interested in politics. Eli explained that the majority of the Union's members were highly individualistic Jews with an anarchistic temperament, who blew hot and cold and were difficult to handle. I recollected the tenants of Albyn Court – poker-playing, horse-racing gamblers. 'Your father was down to earth and understood the right course to follow in disputes with employers,' he said.

My maternal grandparents, Abraham and Clara Cohen, lived in a semi-detached house just around the corner from Albyn Court. They had run a grocery store when my mother was a child.

My mother, Rene, was a vivacious brunette, with a dazzling smile and fine figure. In contrast to my father, she was sociable and extroverted. They got on well together as long as she kept the rummy or canasta parties within limits. When my father met her she was doing secretarial work. Later, after the birth of my sister, Hilary, she took on part-time jobs in order to make ends meet. With the death of my grandmother, Clara, grandfather Abe came to stay with us. He became a commercial traveller too, and in the absence of his wife, who had been a restraining force, became the most popular gambler in Yeoville.

Although I was an energetic and somewhat unruly youngster, absorbed in sports and neighbourhood games, the attitude whites displayed to blacks did not pass me by. It was wartime and I constantly questioned my mother about the fate of the Jews in Europe. In many ways she was a simple, even naive, woman. But when I drew parallels between Jews in Europe under the Nazis and the way black people were being treated in our country, I found she was prepared to agree. This honest response to a six-year-old's questions left its mark.

Surveying the scene, I remembered the afternoon when I had been kicking a ball around in the street with my friends. One of the boys had embarrassed me by passing a foul remark about a black man who had been hit by the ball while walking by.

'Don't swear at me and don't call me "boy",' was the man's reply. 'In 20 years' time things are going to be very different in this country.' It was now 40 years later. The prediction, if delayed, was at last coming true.

Most of my generation of Yeovillites – or Yeoville boykies as we were called – went into the professions or business and had long moved on to the prosperous northern suburbs. Quite a few, like Ali Bacher, the Springbok cricketer, had become famous sportsmen. A large percentage, fearful of the country's future, had joined the brain-drain and emigrated. I wondered *if any* of those who remained would be prepared to help me if I came knocking on their door.

I had become so engrossed in the past that it was only when I noticed one of the present residents of Albyn Court peering at me from a second-floor window – where Jock Silver the bookie had lived – that I woke from my reverie. I had all but forgotten the other purpose of my stroll.

Ronnie Kasrils was born in Yeoville, Johannesburg in 1938. After high school, he pursued a career as a film scriptwriter, and then went on to join the African National Congress in 1960. A year later, he helped found the party's armed wing, Umkhonto we Sizwe. Kasrils spent a number of years in exile after being banned by the South African government in 1962. In 1963 he was sent to Russia by the ANC, where he completed a general military course and a specialist course in military engineering. Since the formation of the new democratic government of South Africa, Kasrils has held a number of government positions including Deputy Minister of Defence, and Minister of Water Affairs and Forestry. He is currently Minister of Intelligence.
Book Extracted: *Armed and Dangerous* (Jonathan Ball, Johannesburg, 1993)

Memoirs
Ahmed Kathrada

... My life as a young South African was smooth, marked by the joy of major celebrations, and the warmth and friendship, the sense of community, of small-town life. To celebrate Eid, we would hold a picnic at the dam, and all the Indian people of Schweizer came, bringing food and soft drinks, sweets for the children, tablecloths and umbrellas and all the other paraphernalia that made picnics colourful and joyous affairs. It was lovely, and I used to race around with the other children, doing the naughty things that children do, getting dirty and thoroughly enjoying myself.

For all our Gujerat origins and the emphasis on Arabic and the Koran, we grew up speaking more Afrikaans than anything else. It was almost my first language. The women in my family still speak Afrikaans, and *boeremusiek*, traditional folk music played on a concertina, still makes me nostalgic.

While I cannot claim that I was politically aware as a child, a number of things made an indelible impression on me. I have a vivid recollection of the 9 p.m. curfew bell being rung, signalling the hour after which Africans required a special pass to be on the streets. I also remember an incident when a white policeman tried to arrest an African on our business premises. My father angrily intervened and ordered the policeman out of the shop.

We had African domestic workers in the house and a Somali cook, Sayed, a tall, taciturn, pitch-black fellow, who used to conjure up the most delicious meals in our steamy kitchen. Because he was a Muslim, he lived in the house with us. My father was very religious, and therefore strict on the question of race. We were never allowed to be rude to any African staff or customers, but because of the religious difference, we did not treat other Africans with the same deference that we showed Sayed.

There was, somehow, a perception that, white or black, a Muslim was superior, different to everyone else, be they Indians, white or African, and though no one would ever say it in so many words, that is simply how it was. My father would never tell me that he, or our cook, was special because he was a Muslim, but we knew that was the case, and it was evident from the behaviour of people within the Muslim community.

Notwithstanding this intangible belief, the first non-family member that I encountered was not a Muslim, but an Afrikaner. The midwife who delivered me was known affectionately to everyone in town as 'Ouma' Oosthuizen, or 'granny'. I do not think she had any formal training, but she was experienced in bringing children into the world, and I was born at home. Ouma Oosthuizen was a daily visitor, a family friend, and she took a keen interest in the welfare of 'her' babies. Naturally, she and her entire family were also customers, and like many of our friends, they came from the poorer group of whites, the very people one would expect to be the most racist.

But Ouma was in and out of our house all the time, and no one ever detected the slightest hint of racism in her attitude and behaviour. She was almost part of the family, but if I were to speculate on her party-political affiliation, I would say without hesitation that, as a matter of course, she and her family would vote for the rabidly racist and oppressive National Party. High among its declared political priorities was making the lives of Indians so intolerable that they would willingly accept repatriation to India.

Ouma Oosthuizen was a sort of godmother to me, and later, when I was away at school and came home for the holidays, I always had to report to her on my progress. I had to show her my school report and answer numerous questions about my health, how I was adjusting to school, my teachers, and city life in general.

I must have been on Robben Island when she died. It is possible that at the time, our letters were so restricted in content and length that I might not have been able to write about her, or I might have deliberately chosen not to do so, because things had become so bad that her family could have been victimised.

The relationship between the Indian trader and the Afrikaner in the rural areas was, and still is, a very special one. Not even the supermarkets that can now be found in small towns have been able to put the Indian traders out of business, because they have always offered a personal touch to their customers.

It still happens that Indian shopkeepers send a truck to outlying areas on pay days, mostly to farms, because the distances are so great, to pick up the workers who want to do their shopping. At the end of the month, when the pensioners get their money, they, too, are provided with transport. Naturally, this is not altruism, it's business, but it is a service, and when the customers arrive at the shop, some are seated and given tea or coffee. When customers are short of cash, credit is extended, another privilege not available from a supermarket.

For more than fifty years, rural whites invariably supported the National Party. In some towns at election time, the party would borrow as many cars as possible from the Indian community, and the campaigners would ask their Indian friends, '*Vir wie gaan jy stem?*' [Who are you going to vote for?] This never changed. Even in the urban areas, the Afrikaners did not seem to know that an Indian could not vote. They could not understand this. They would go to a National Party meeting and applaud the most racist statements, yet be more than willing to act as nominees for Indians trying to get around the Group Areas Act.

When my nephew Enver opened his shop in Carletonville, it was among the first three or four owned by Indians. Today there are about a hundred, and until the Group Areas Act was scrapped, some ninety of them were registered to white nominees. Such arrangements were never formalised by means of written documents, and Enver's nominee, for instance, probably an Afrikaner, but naturally a white person, refused to even accept a Christmas gift, let alone payment for lending his name to the property. In some cases, nominees would accept monthly payments for the privilege, and if they were dishonest, they could claim the whole shop, but I never heard of a single instance where a nominee turned around and did so.

In 1940 or 1941, my father opened another shop on a little farm at Hessie, about twenty-seven kilometres outside Schweizer-Reneke, which was run by my sister's husband-to-be, a cousin and also a Kathrada. Two years later my father died, and my eldest brother Solly became the effective head of the family.

In the early 1950s, my brother Ebrahim also opened a shop, some twenty-two kilometres from Schweizer-Reneke at a place called London Farm. The original family businesses were run by the three other brothers – Solly, until he moved to Johannesburg in the early 1970s, Ismail and Essop, the youngest. Solly, Ebrahim, Ismail, my only sister Amina and her husband are all dead now, but Essop still runs the shop in Schweizer-Reneke.

Shopkeeping never held the slightest attraction for me, and when I was growing up, the family preferred me not to go anywhere near the shops, let alone work in them, as I knew nothing about the business and they thought I might simply give the goods away.

During the depression, there was tremendous hunger and poverty among the poor whites – and others, of course – in South Africa. Since Indians were prohibited from living or even spending the night in the Free State, residents of that province never saw them, unless they travelled to other parts of the country. Many Free Staters had no idea what an Indian even looked like, but this didn't stop them from perpetuating all kinds of myths, not least of which was that an Indian was someone you should run away from.

One such man, named Terblanche, arrived in Schweizer-Reneke after walking all the way from the Free State with his wife and children, seeking work, and food, all along the way. When they got to Schweizer, they went first to the homes of fellow whites, but found no help there. Eventually, hunger and desperation drove them to my father's shop, and he gave them food, not only for that day, but for several weeks, as well as clothes and other items for the whole family. Such action was not uncommon for my father, but Terblanche never forgot his generosity; and he became a lifelong friend of our family.

Among the non-Afrikaner whites in Schweizer-Reneke with whom we had an association was an eccentric old Englishman by the name of Mathias. He was a regular customer at the shop, and lived on his farm with an African woman. He fathered many children, and their relationship outlasted the Immorality Act and all the other discriminatory legislation. His fellow whites had long since given up on him, and so had the police. He was extremely well read and kept up with world events, receiving newspapers from England until he died, but he lived as an African.

There was also a Jewish man, who was a close friend of the family. Mr Slutzkin was a high-class leather worker, and pro-communist, especially after the Soviet Union entered the Second World War. I have no idea how he came by the literature, but throughout the war, he would go out of his way to give me reading matter that I found most interesting. Apart from our family, he had no friends, and I spent time with him whenever I went home, and he often came for a meal with my family.

Khanchacha was a fellow Indian, who lived on a farm outside Schweizer-Reneke. In his early years he had lived in Nylstroom, and was proud of the fact that he had been the barber of staunch National Party member and future prime minister JG Strijdom. When Strijdom died, he sent a letter of condolence to the family and received a very nice reply.

Apart from Irma Stern's family, the only other Jewish family in Schweizer were the Blooms, extremely wealthy and founders of Premier Milling. There must have been commercial competition between the Indian shopkeepers and the rich Jews, but beyond that, there was no relationship at all. I doubt that Slutzkin the shoemaker was any more welcome in the homes of the wealthy Jews than we would have been, so he spent most of his time with the Indians.

For all the racial harmony of my childhood and youth, small-town South Africa could not escape the complexity of the racist politics that characterised the apartheid era. In Carletonville, the mining town where my nephew Enver had opened a shop, a consumer boycott created much tension in the late 1980s. The town lay at the heart of a particularly conservative area, and the town council's decision to declare parks and various other public amenities reserved for whites sparked outrage among the established Indian community. The result was that a certain sector of the white community decided to stop patronising Indian shops. To add insult to injury; the boycott was led by a chap who was Enver's tenant!

On the other hand, during the latter period of my incarceration, the mayor of Schweizer-Reneke was my sister Amina's landlord at their farm shop and house in Hessie, and they had a good and close relationship. In fact, when he had guests, he would often ask my sister to cook a pot of biryani or make samoosas for them. He could have evicted her in terms of the Group Areas Act, but he refused to do so, despite the fact that he later became one of the biggest contributors to the right-wing Conservative Party. As for the fact that I was in jail, I was told that the subject never arose between Amina and her landlord. He certainly knew, but never allowed this to influence his dealings with other members of my family.

But, by the time I reached school-going age, I was forced to come face to face with an animal called 'segregation', as apartheid was euphemistically known before the National Party came to power in 1948.

As in the rest of the country, Schweizer-Reneke had schools for whites and schools for Africans. Being a tiny community, there was no school for Indians, and the law prohibited me from attending the existing schools. As soon as I turned six, my father arranged for the principal of the local African school, David Mtshali, to come to our house in the afternoons and give me elementary lessons in English, arithmetic and other subjects. I had no need of tutoring in Afrikaans, as I had grown up speaking the language.

My three older brothers were sent in turn to the school for Indians in Johannesburg, many hours' drive away. At the beginning of 1938, just a few months after my eighth birthday, I was packed off to distant Johannesburg to stay with a paternal aunt in Fordsburg, and attend the Indian school there.

I don't recall with accuracy how I reacted to this prospect, but it must have been quite traumatic. I do remember that in later years, my brothers teased me about how I quietly tried to hide my tears each time I had to return to Johannesburg at the end of the school holidays.

I suppose that was the first politically flavoured event that affected me directly and recognisably. My young mind simply could not comprehend these prohibitions. After all, our neighbours were white and my godmother was an Afrikaner; the man who taught me the ABC was black, and my playmates were both black and white. How could I possibly understand that I alone had to go to school in Johannesburg, and would only be able to spend time with my family during the holidays?

Ahmed Kathrada, one of the most important freedom fighters in South African history, was born in 1929 to Indian immigrant parents, in Schweizer-Reneke, a small town in the former Western Transvaal. He started his political work in 1941, when he joined the Young Communist League of South Africa, and formed the Transvaal Indian Youth Congress when he was sixteen. He was instrumental in the alliance between the African National Congress and the South African Indian Congress. Kathrada was one of several leaders arrested at Rivonia and charged for their part in the establishment of the military wing of the ANC, Umkhonto we Sizwe. He was found guilty, and spent twenty-six years in prison, including a stay of eighteen years on Robben Island, where he was detained with other senior members Nelson Mandela and Walter Sisulu. Kathrada was a member of parliament within the South African government from 1994, and is now Chairperson of the Robben Island Museum Council.
Book Extracted: *Memoirs* (Zebra, 2004)

Never been at home
Zazah Khuzwayo

The sun was already up when I went to piss behind one of the huts. We lived in a rural village on the south coast of KwaZulu-Natal. The family home was built on a hill. It was a large home with several round huts with grass roofs, a four-roomed building, a yard, a kraal and a place for chickens and pigs. If you looked downhill you saw a river that teemed with fish ... Everybody used to go there to fetch water, to do their washing or to bath. The cows, goats, pigs, donkeys, even the birds in the sky, used to go there. It was one of my favourite places in the village. There was not only a river but also hills, trees, and a big mountain.

My mom was in the kitchen lighting the fire. She was a very beautiful woman, with a light skin, long shiny black hair and a warm smile. But she did not often smile. She was very unhappy and always busy. The whole family called her Makoti ...

My father lived far away in a township on the north coast, where he was working as a policeman. He was very tall, dark and had a handsome face, but he was very fat and ate like a pig. He would demand food at any time. He had a black belt in karate and drove a white car, an old Volvo manual. The people in the village respected him. Everybody that came to visit my family said I looked like my father. This made me feel proud, because my father was educated, and he had a house in the township and everybody saluted him and called him *sayitsheni* which means 'sergeant'. I wanted to grow up and be like him. I wanted to live in the township and have my own car. I was very proud of my father.

He used to come home at the end of every month. Sometimes he came on special occasions, bringing his mother, my granny, a box of assorted cakes, sweets, fruits and a two-litre bottle of squash. My granny was very dark. She had long grey hair and was always very neatly turned out. She was a good member of the Roman Catholic Church.

The whole family went to church every Sunday. This was very boring for me. We had to travel a long way uphill on foot. On the way we passed a river and drank some water. Then, when we got to church, we washed the dust and mud from our feet. The church service started with hardly a smile on the shrinking face of the old priest. He made everybody pray on their knees for hours. I never believed that the priest was holy, but I kept it all inside. He repeated the same things every Sunday. To me he didn't look like a pleasant person. I used to think of him as a ghost that lived in the church.

After church we went home and had lunch. Then my mother would play with my sister, Thembi, and me. My mother always looked unhappy, except when she played with us. My sister was six years older than me. She was already in primary school. I was between four and five years old and couldn't wait to go to school, but I was still too young. I was able to count to ten though, and could draw in the sand.

Our family name was Khuzwayo. The Khuzwayo family was very proud and they were the most educated people in the village. The family consisted of my granny, three daughters and two sons. Her husband had died. One of her sons was my father; the other, the eldest, stayed across the road from my granny's home with his wife and four kids. Two of her daughters were happily married to rich and educated husbands. The other daughter was not married. She was a teacher and she was studying by night to complete her Bachelor of Arts degree. My mother was not educated and her mother was a *sangoma*, a traditional doctor and psychic. One morning, as I entered my mother's room, she was crying.

'Mummy, why are you crying and why are your eyes blue?'

'Zazah, you won't understand.'

'Please tell me.' I also wanted to cry.

She told me how my father beat her. She accused him of seeing other women and not considering her his own wife. She said she had slept outside that night. Everything was too difficult for me, a four-year-old, to understand.

When my sister came back from school my mother told her she was leaving: 'I'm sick and tired of this life.'

'Are you leaving us, mummy?' my sister asked.

'No, I will never leave you with these witches. I will come and fetch you.'

My sister started crying and I cried too, but I thought my father was a good man. Why did my mother want to leave him? How was she going to look after us when she didn't have a job?

My mother started telling us stories about the past: 'You know Thembi and Zazah, my first and second sons both died at birth because of this family and your father beating me up all the time. The Khuzwayo family does not like me because I'm not educated.'

'Mummy, why do people say that my father deserted you?'

'He left me when I was six months pregnant. He said you were not his child and he went to Jo'burg. But then, when you came out, you were the picture of him. He came back when you were three years old. Zazah, I had to go out and work as a maid with you on my back, because your grandmother wouldn't look after you. They blamed me for not having a son that would bear your father's name. They called me a witch. They also said I had no education and that I knew nothing about money. They convinced your father to give all his money to his mother, not to me. His sisters still want him to have a second educated wife. And I must be silent while they treat me like dirt. He is always right and I am always wrong. His mother and his sisters and brothers come first in his life.'

'What about us? We are his daughters.'

While my mother was talking, she was interrupted by a cousin who often visited her. She was a daughter of my father's brother. She said: 'Mamncane, I heard my mother and Tia (my unmarried aunt) talk about a child that your husband has from another woman. They say he must marry this woman because she is educated. Don't say that I told you. My mother will kill me.' There was silence in the room for few minutes. I saw a lizard on the wall staring at us and laughing at my mother's eyes that were full of tears.

'Did they say it's a boy or girl and who is the mother?'

'It's a boy named Mandla, but I forget the name of the mother. They say it must be kept secret from you, because you will kill the baby as both your boys died at birth and you can't have any more sons.'

My mother went into the kitchen to prepare lunch for the whole family. I could see the sorrow and pain in her eyes, although I still regarded my father as an honourable man. I didn't see anything wrong with what he did. He was doing what a man should do. I was too young to distinguish between right and wrong. After lunch my mother left for her family home 40 km away.

That evening I was lying on my stomach next to the fire while my auntie was preparing supper and everybody was in the kitchen. It was winter and the kitchen was warm as there was a fire in the middle of the room.

My grandmother started talking: 'Makoti didn't even ask for permission to sleep over at her family.'

'She must be missing her lovers,' my auntie answered.

'She forgets that we paid eleven cows for her to respect her husband, the whole family and even the dog that barks on these premises. I can understand why Mtholephi (that's my father) always beats her. She doesn't listen.'

It was the next morning. The herd boy was leading the cows to the pastures and a cock was crowing loudly. I went to piss behind the house; at the same time I looked out from the hill to see if my mom was coming back. I was missing her a lot. I realised how much I loved her. For the first time I felt lost. The place that I loved, that I thought of as home was no longer home to me. I stared at the trees. Two small sparrows were playing and their mom came and played with them. I started chasing the birds. Why didn't they allow me to play with them?

My sister called and I ran to her. At least I felt safe beside her. She loved housework more than schoolwork. We went to the kitchen to have breakfast. It was weekend. Everybody was going to the river to wash clothes. The river was a meeting place for the women of the village. I loved the river, but I refused to go as I was waiting for my mom to come back home.

Everybody went to the river except my grandmother and my auntie. They were complaining that if Makoti didn't come back, who was going to take her place? My mother was good at cooking, brewing beer and cleaning. I overheard from their conversations that there was going to be a party over the weekend. I was surprised that they needed her. So she was not as useless as they always claimed.

That winter afternoon I watched the sun go down. My mom did not come back and I turned round to go back inside the house. Without her everybody was a stranger except my sister. My auntie was dishing up chicken curry and rice. My grandmother asked me and my sister to step outside. Inside the kitchen was my grandmother, my auntie and her four kids. They were all having supper except me and my sister.

'Thembi, why aren't they giving us food?'

'If they don't like our mother, do you think they will like us? Zazah, don't start crying. No one will feel sorry for you. Our mother is going to come back, so stop asking so many questions. You are too young to understand everything.'

From that time I started getting answers. In my imagination I saw my mother's face that was always unhappy. Sometimes her eyes were shining with tears. She never allowed those tears to come out. She would pray with bitterness as if she was shouting, asking God to make things better in her marriage. And I asked myself why God didn't answer her, because she was a wonderful mother and a good wife. I started praying to God to bring my mother back.

That evening we had leftovers from the plates. We could only smell the chicken from the gravy. My sister had to do the dishes. Leftovers were better than nothing. I fell asleep hoping to see my mother come home.

Another day dawned. I was talking to my sister that morning about how cruel our family was not to give us food. I would tell my father what they did.

'Zazah, he won't believe you.'

'But he always buys food for us. He is our father.'

'Zazah, he always brings cakes, sweets, fruits and money for his mother, but never for us, never for our mother. He doesn't even know or ask us what we like.' So I kept quiet, knowing it was true what she said. Our grandmother would give us cake or something when she was in a good mood; maybe once a week. Every evening she would have tea, bread and cake before she went to sleep. She would eat sweets and refuse to tell us fairytales. 'What kind of a grandmother is she?' I thought to myself. I'd always thought that sweet things were for kids, but things were different here.

After breakfast I went to my usual place where I could sit on the hill and watch for my mother's return. I thought about how beautiful she was and the fairness of her skin; she was bright as the winter sun, with long shiny black hair and a warm smile. She could fit in well in a coloured community. I remembered her telling us that her father hadn't allowed her to go to school and he refused to let her work for white people or Indians. He strongly believed that she was going to sleep with them because she was very light in complexion and had long hair. He preferred to sell her for eleven cows, *ilobola*, with nothing in her hand except her heart that was too soft.

I sat there for hours alone. All I wanted was to see my mother coming back home. My cousins and my sister were at school. Everybody was like a stranger to me. My granny's house was like a cave. Nothing was the same without my mom. If my sister was not around I was going to run away. I sat there behind the house watching the people going their ways up and down.

Then suddenly I saw two figures coming downhill very slowly. One of them was my mom. I leapt up like a locust and ran up the hill like a mad dog. My heart was full of joy. I jumped into my mother's arms and held her and started to cry: 'Mummy, you are not going leave me again, *Hhe*!' She kept silent and held me tighter.

My mother was with her elder sister. I believed she had come to negotiate with my grandmother. We walked towards my grandmother's house. There she was, with a woman with a gravel face.

'Gogo, my mother is back!'

'Oh, *Nkulunkulu ngiyabonga*, thank God! Who was going to do all the work for the party?'

My mother and her sister entered the house and sat on the floor.

'Makoti, are you doing as you please in this house?'

'What do you mean, Ma?'

'First you went to your family without getting permission from me or your husband. Which means that we wasted all those cows that we paid for you.'

'But Ma, your son beats me all the time and you don't say a thing about it. He doesn't give me any money for my children.'

'Look at you, I am still talking and I didn't say that I am finished. You lost your two sons because you didn't listen and you made the ancestors very angry. If you want to have a son to carry on this family's name you must start to obey and respect even these premises when you walk on them. We have enough cows to pay lobola for another wife. You remember, Makoti, you went to look for a job without getting permission. You got a job and you started thinking you were a man.'

'Ma, what was I supposed to do? Watch my daughters die of starvation?'

'Makoti, you can't keep quiet, *washa nendlu, Hhe*. I want to finish.'

'Ma, I won't keep quiet. Your son went to Jo'burg leaving me when I was six months pregnant. He said my second daughter was not his. And you didn't even help me. You couldn't even look after my child while I was at work. Now I am sick and tired of this family. You never think of me as a human being. Why? Is it because I don't have a mother and my father is a sick man? Please tell me. Why?'

My mother burst into tears and she was shaking. Her sister was telling her to take it easy. 'Marriage is a difficult business,' she said. 'You must learn to overcome all situations with patience and perseverance.'

'No, Thoko,' she told her sister. 'I am taking my children and leaving for good. I will go and look for a job.'

'Makoti, you don't want to bring shame on yourself by failing to keep your marriage,' said my grandmother.

'Okay, then I will have to move to the township with my husband.'

'You want these kids to be nothing but bitches, to know nothing about their culture.'

'Why do you say that, Ma?'

'Because in the township they are going to shit inside the house. They won't fetch water from the river. They won't know how to get wood from the bush, how to make a fire, and then they will be worse than you in handling their marriages.'

The gravel-faced woman nodded, showing her teeth in her gaping mouth.

My grandmother went on: 'Maybe they won't even get married. Who wants a woman that cannot clean a house? You know, Makoti, if I were you I would obey. Your first two sons died at birth because you made the ancestors very angry with your stubbornness.'

'Yes, Ma, and nobody came to see me in hospital. They had to burn my sons. I didn't know their graves because of you. You all are like animals. And now you are busy turning your son to be exactly like you. I have a husband working as a policeman but he gives all his money to his mother and he spends the rest with the bitches in the township. What will you say to him? He is a man. So he has all the right to do whatever he likes, even if his own family has to suffer for it?'

'Makoti, that boy must give me everything. You don't have to be jealous. I raised him myself. Whatever happened in my marriage, I stayed and I persevered. And now I am reaping the fruits of that. You are a disgrace. I never argued with my in-laws. The world is going to laugh at you.'

There was silence in the room. Then my mom started talking. 'I am going to tell him that I am leaving for good.'

'*Hhayi bo*, Makoti. I am warning you!'

Suddenly a car hooted at the top of the hill. I was hoping it was my father's car. I thought he would sort things out as he was a policeman.

'Mummy, I am going to Daddy.' I ran up the hill to meet my father, who was tall and fat as a giant. He held my hand and walked to the house with me.

'Baba, my mom wants to leave and go to her family. Are you going to come with us?'

My father kept quiet and I did the same. As I was walking downhill holding his hand, I saw in my imagination a happy family sitting at a table having supper: my father, my sister, my mother with a newborn baby boy and me. We are all happy in my father's house. How I wished that dream could come true.

When we entered the house everything felt bitter inside. I fetched the small bench that was only for my father to sit on. I went to lean against my mother who was sitting on the floor, as in Zulu tradition a woman should sit on the floor on a special mat made from grass and cotton.

'Mtholephi, it's good that you came, we need you a lot,' said my grandmother.

The gravel-faced woman nodded as usual. She irritated me like hell. She didn't have a husband; all she could do was stick her nose in every family's business.

My grandmother said, 'Mtholephi, we have a problem. You have come at the right time. I don't even know how to say it to you.'

My mother started talking: 'BabakaThembi, I am leaving you and this hell that you have put me through. Enough is enough.'

'Ma, what has happened to MaHlengwa? Why does she want to leave?'

'I will explain to you, BabakaThembi,' my mother continued. 'These past two days I was not here. I went home, because I am tired of you and your family. It looks as if I'm married to your family and not to you. I also heard that you have a child from another woman. You kept it secret from me, thinking I am stupid.'

The gravel-faced woman said 'Makoti, let your mother-in-law speak. Nobody thinks you are stupid. Mtholephi is a man and he can marry ten women if he likes. At least the other women gave him boys – you have only girls.'

'Oh, so it is not just one woman? Now I don't understand.' My mom kept quiet and waited. Then she said, 'How can I keep quiet when there are so many things hidden from me? I didn't know that such good Catholics have so many secrets. So please tell me everything I don't know about.'

'Please, Sis, keep quiet.'

There were tears in my mom's eyes.

My grandmother said: 'Mtholephi, this woman of yours does as she pleases, as you can see. She cannot even keep quiet and let us talk. She went home without my permission. She also wants to go and live in the township with you. But what really makes me angry is that she says that you give me money and nothing to her. Just tell her how hard I worked to send you to school so that you can be what you are today.'

The gravel-faced woman joined the conversation. 'Who is going to bear Mtholephi's name if she can't have a boy? All she does is complain. Makoti, you came here to look after this family, not to tell them what to do. I think *ungukhanda limtshel'okwakhe*. You don't argue with your in-laws and your husband is your king. You have to bear with him in all situations.'

My mother started to cry. 'You are doing all this because I don't have a mother. Ma, please stop thinking that I am unfaithful to your son, because I am not. When I met Mtholephi I was a virgin. Everybody knows that. I am unlike your young daughter who had four kids before marriage and those kids have two different fathers.'

My mother was talking about my auntie Tia, the one who was studying for a Bachelor of Arts degree. She was a tall lady with big eyes; fat, and a lovely smile; but her heart was not so lovely, although she was a very good teacher and a music conductor at school. She used to be a nurse but was fired for falling pregnant without being married. Once she had a fight with my mother, so they didn't like each other. My aunt started the fight. My mother was very strong, so she didn't stand a chance.

After all this conversation in the kitchen my father came up with a solution: after the party that coming weekend we would be moving with him to the township. I was very happy that we were going to be a family again, staying far away from all the troubles that caused my mother to leave us. I couldn't believe that my dream was coming true.

That weekend there was *itiye*. *Itiye* is a cultural ceremony for ancestors. People came from different parts of the village to sing, drink Zulu beer, dance and eat. They did all sorts of things to be happy and a cow was slaughtered. The women wore dresses as colourful as a rainbow. Everybody took turns to dance according to their age groups. The teenage girls showed their legs and breasts, topless with colourful beads round their necks, arms and waists. Their bums showed when they swung up their legs. The cow-skin drum thumped and the older women wore beautiful headdresses to show they were married. The men went to the kraal where they slaughtered the cow. They braaied the parts of the meat that only men can eat. They joined the crowd afterwards to watch the women doing their best. The guys started fighting with sticks to show who was strongest. The winners were cheered and the losers were jeered by the crowd. My sister was one of the best dancers in the village!

My father promised to come and fetch us at the end of the month. My grandmother was very unhappy about my mother's decision to move to the township. I was very happy, as I didn't like housework, especially not fetching water and collecting firewood.

One night we were in the kitchen. My mother was cooking and I was on the mat next to the fire as usual when my granny said: 'Makoti, you must not send this child to school. She will waste my son's money. She is lazy, always lying next to the fire. She is even too lazy to talk.'

'Please, Ma, she is still young. Give her a chance.'

'Makoti, I wonder if you ever listen to anything I say. You forget that I am the one who paid lobola for you and I know what is best for you.'

'You were doing it for your son, not for me. Ma, you know I respect you, but you take advantage of me at times.'

It was the beginning of spring. Everybody was checking how much seed they had. If they did not have enough, they'd have to buy or ask friends if they had some to spare. In those days people helped each other. Those with an oversupply would share with their neighbours, but the Khuzwayo family was very proud.

I remember a poor man who used to go from house to house begging for food. He had no family and his clothes were torn and dirty. He used to come and ask food. My aunt and granny always told him to go away, because he stank. Only my mother would give him something to eat.

I asked my mother why she was always helping poor people. She told me this tale: There was a rich woman who had everything she wanted. One day she made a request: she wanted to see God. She called the servants to clean up the place. The house had to be absolutely perfect. But one servant was ill, so he failed to clean as the madam requested. She fired him. He pleaded that he had children, but she didn't understand.

The next day the rich woman was all dressed up like a queen. Everything she wanted she could get. Suddenly a man appeared at the gate. He was clean and shining and you couldn't look into his eyes. He looked poor; he had no shoes and a very long beard. The woman rushed to the gate to tell him to go away. She said she was tired of feeding the poor who couldn't help themselves.

Later a tall handsome guy appeared at the gate wearing a tuxedo and carrying a walking stick made of gold. His limousine was parked outside. The woman rushed to open the gate for him and let him in. The servants threw flowers on his way to the house and everybody bowed before him. When the man left the house he took a book out of his briefcase with the title inscribed on the cover: *Devil's servants*. The devil said to the woman: 'The man you chased away was God and now I can have you for myself.'

'Zazah, that is the end of the story.' I did not question my mother any further ...

Zazah Khuzwayo was born in rural KwaZulu-Natal, and, after matriculating in 1994, went on to study electrical engineering, later dropping out in order to find work. After completing her autobiography, *Never been at home*, she self-published it in 2001. Since then, it has become a modern classic in South Africa.
Book Extracted: *Never been at home* (David Philip, 2004)

Call Me Woman
Ellen Kuzwayo

... When I became aware of myself at the age of six or seven years in the early 1920s, I learned that I was one of four grandchildren of Jeremiah Makoloi and Magdeline Segogoane Makgothi, born Masisi. They owned a large fertile farm through which flowed the Leeuw River. It was approximately 2560 morgen (6000 acres) judging by the size of the farm my sister and I inherited in 1970. This was about 1 400 acres, a quarter of the farm inherited by my grandfather's four children.

The farm was situated about 50 miles south of a small village, Tweespruit, about 35 miles west of Ladybrand, 20 miles north of Hobhouse and some 30 miles east of Thaba'Nchu. Yes it was a beautifully cultivated farm, with plenty of rich grazing pasture as well as cultivated land which yielded abundant corn and maize in winter and equally abundant wheat in summer. It was also a very prosperous dairy farm. This is the farm which was wrenched from my family as recently as 1974. In that year, without any thought for human feeling, the authorities declared the area a 'black spot' – meaning not that black people should live there, but the very opposite. A stroke of the pen made it illegal for black people to own land in that area; white farmers were to take over. My maternal grandparents owned the farm in the 1880s; it was home to my parents and to us children. There had been close to 100 years of legitimate freehold ownership; it had been earned and maintained with hard work and toil by our elders for the benefit and welfare of their children and their families. Through iniquitous and inhuman legislation, my family was rendered homeless and wanderers in the land of our birth.

It had been a farm anyone could be proud of. There were all types of farm animals in large numbers: cattle, sheep, goats, pigs, horses and rabbits, as well as a variety of domestic fowl such as turkeys, ducks and chickens. About 25 yards from the homestead, there were two dams irrigating a large orchard which had a variety of fruit trees which yielded plentiful crops. It was surrounded on the eastern and southern sides by a thick hedge of quince trees, which are still there to this day.

Until I was about seven or ten years old, we ate, drank, roamed, played and went to school together as old man Jeremiah's grandchildren, moving as freely on the farm as the birds in the air. It was common practice for we children each to carry a mug and walk single-file to the barn where they milked the cows, in order to get our morning ration of fresh milk direct from the udder. We were not allowed to drink any other beverage, except cocoa occasionally. Adults always alleged that we children would grow filth in the tummy if we drank anything else. For the same reason girls of a particular age were forbidden to eat eggs or the kidneys of slaughtered animals. For a long time I believed all those stories though with some reservation.

As recently as February 1984, a friend and I took a flying business visit to Thaba Patchoa. I was moved to see the main buildings of that once dear homestead, erected with white stones and cement and given corrugated iron roofing, still withstanding the harsh weather with dignity. The ceiling and floors, finished with wood, are strong and intact after approximately 100 years. Other houses around that living monument sadly are beginning gradually to fall apart. At the homestead patches of hard earth floor are sagging under the fast growing reeds, where once our little feet moved swiftly. How sad. All these tell a story of a people who left footprints where they moved.

The church building was about three minutes' walk from the homestead. It was built with the same materials as the main buildings of the homestead; however, it had an earth floor and no ceiling. This building was used as a classroom from Monday to Friday. From an early age we took turns to clean the church on Saturdays to have it ready for the service on Sundays. During the week the students were allocated turns to clean it. As youngsters we enjoyed collecting cow dung and preparing it to smear the floor of the church in readiness for the service. It was in that church building that I started my schooling from Sub A to Standard 4.

Treasured memories come back to me now of the early lessons in the three 'Rs' which I received there, as well as the Bible classes and the catechism lessons – which often bored me. The highlights of the programme of those early schooldays were action songs and physical exercises which I was good at and loved. I recall the faces of some of my classmates, the playtime games and the meals we shared and so often exchanged. My cousins and I looked forward to the tasty sour porridge dishes brought by our schoolmates from the village; they in turn just loved the butter and jam sandwiches which we exchanged for their porridge. But treasured memories can never replace our fast-fading past.

I remember vividly the petty childish quarrels we often had; some ended with a fight on the sandy river bank not far from the school but certainly out of sight of any possible intrusion from adults. Once I got a good hiding from one of my classmates. She was a bully and a bullfighter all right. I lacked skill in fighting. Perhaps I had been 'tamed' by the Christian teachings of unending forgiveness and 'turn the other cheek' I received from home, in school, and from the pulpit.

Some very dear moments come back to my mind. I see the faces of the teachers who taught me in those years; and I hear the beautiful tunes we sang in that farm school in the late 1920s. Teachers Jacob Thepe, Michael Mokae and Julius Valtein all taught at different periods in this school. I recall a particular hymn we often sang at early morning prayers during teacher Valtein's time, 'Trust and Obey'. Yes, it was this hymn we sang to bid him farewell the day he left the school. We cried our eyes and our little hearts out. Now that I come to think of it, he must have been the favourite of the three because there was a song composed about his achievements by one of the pupils. There were great composers in that school in those years in the 1920s; they could easily match the young black composers of the present day – perhaps even their age-group from other race groups as well.

This is the song about teacher Julius:

    Tichere e na ea rona
    E tsoang koana Thaba'Nchu School
    (E tlilo ruta x 3) taba tsa Modimo
    Taba tse Molemo.

It means:

    This our teacher
    Trained at Thaba'Nchu School
    Has come to teach the word of God
    The good word.

It is very simple in music and words, but great in meaning to his pupils. Perhaps it was even so for our teacher.

Julius Valtein came later than the other two, who were his senior in age. Teacher Mokae was a jubilant chap, an entertainer and a disciplinarian. He insisted on quality performance in schoolwork and in recreational activities. Some of the favourite songs he taught were 'Swanee, How I Love You', 'The Wild Wild Women' and many others, which made our school concerts bright, popular, enjoyable and up to the mark.

Teacher Jacob Thepe, an older man who taught at the school earlier than the other two, had a great sense of humour and was very fond of teasing, particularly those of us whom he didn't consider to have distinctive good looks. I was pleasantly surprised some years ago to meet his daughter, Judith Matee, a nursing sister with the Cripple Care Association and a devout member of the Young Women's Christian Association here in Soweto where she has lived for many years. The surprise was greater when it dawned on me that Meriam Mothale, a typist I had interviewed and recommended to be employed by my office in November 1978, turned out to be Judith's daughter. This discovery after three months of working together with Meriam meant a great deal to me. I often taunted her about her ever-teasing, pleasant grandfather. She was more than taken aback to hear me tell her how well I knew him. Indeed this is a small world.

As a youngster, I looked forward to weekends, when I had two days without accounting for homework to my teacher. Homework was a real nightmare in those days. Sundays and Christmas Day were the times most welcomed. These were good days to display my homemade dresses to my friends; to relax and talk while we fetched water from the spring about 50 yards from the homestead.

It was one of our duties to ring the bell for the church service and to make sure that the chairs, benches and tables were well dusted and placed in their proper positions before the service. My grandfather conducted most church services on Sundays. His favourite hymn, 'Itsose Moea Wa Me', (*'Awake My Soul'* in English) is very dear to me. As I grew up, I realised more and more what a remarkable and impressive man Jeremiah Makgothi was, both inside and outside the church. Indeed, it is only within comparatively recent years that I have acquired any kind of a full picture of his life and I have been taken aback to realise the degree of respect and affection accorded him by many different people in all communities.

He was a graduate of Lovedale College near Alice in the Cape Province and very near to Fort Hare. In those years, Lovedale was one of the most renowned boarding schools in the country. It was run by the Church of Scotland Missionary Society for the black community. We got to know later in life from his only surviving child, my aunt Blanche Dinaane Tsimatsima, the youngest of his four children and now 83 years of age, that as a student, Grandfather travelled to college by ox-wagon over a distance of more than 500 miles, with all his provisions and belongings packed on the wagon. At the Orange River, the wagon crossed over to the Cape side and continued the journey to Queenstown. There Jeremiah transferred his belongings to a post carriage drawn by horses or oxen to Lovedale. He remained at Lovedale for the duration of his training from 1875 to 1883. At the end of his school career, Grandfather obtained the Junior and Teachers' Certificates. On graduation he returned to Thaba'Nchu, his home.

All these facts have been confirmed by Grandfather's own reports in a notebook I discovered in Blanche's bookcase, during one of my efforts to compile some authentic data on this stalwart of his age. In addition, I found a few of his textbooks. They include among others, *South African*

History and Geography by George N. Theal, *First Latin Reading Book* by William Smith DCL, LLD, *English Accidence* by Rev. Richard Morris. I ID, *Plain Geometry* by W. & R. Chambers, *Plain Trigonometry* by I. Todhunter NAFRS, and several others. Some of these books are dated 1879.

He became the headmaster of the first boarding school in Thaba'Nchu for African boys. In addition to this post, Grandfather taught in a day school attended by both black and white children. Among some of the students who attended school at that time from the white community were the children of the local Methodist pastor, Rev. Daniels, and one of his children became our family doctor when I was about eight or nine years old. Dr Daniels was commonly known as 'moroa monare', meaning 'son of monare', I cannot say why Dr Daniels was called so. My only guess is that Rev. Daniels must have made a lasting impact as a pastor on that community, to deserve the Setswana name 'monare' in recognition of his service.

During his years of teaching in Thaba'Nchu, Grandfather played a major role in the translation of the New Testament into Serolong, working on this project with Canon Crisp of the Church of England Missionary Society.

The archives at Lovedale contain the following entry on my grandfather, dated 1885:

> Jeremiah Makoloi was born at Thaba'Nchu, Orange Free State in March 1860. Both of his parents are church members, his father being a class leader in the Wesleyan Society. He was taught at the school there by David Goronyane, under whom he also acted for a year or two as monitor. He came here in November 1875, with fair attainments and attended the second and third years and student classes and, in 1878, he obtained a Government Teachers' Certificate of Competency, standing thirty-fourth in the list.
>
> While carrying on his studies he assisted in the evening preparation classes and in the office. He gained by competitive examination the Eckhardt Bursary for three years. On his return home in 1883, he was engaged in general work for some time, but latterly assisted in the translation of the New Testament into his own language (Serolong) by the Church of England Missionary, Canon Crisp.

The following is an extract from *The Friend*, the still surviving daily English newspaper in the Orange Free State, regarding Grandfather's work:

> We have been shown a copy of a new version of the New Testament in Serolong, which has been issued from the Church Mission Press at Thaba'Nchu, during

the past week. Nearly forty years have passed since Dr Moffat published his translation in the Setlhapi dialect. Since then much progress has been made in the knowledge of the language, especially with the assistance of the educated native helpers. The new translation is in the Serolong dialect of Sechuana and is issued tentatively, with the hope of obtaining as much criticism as possible before undertaking a stereotyped edition. Canon Crisp has been assisted in the work by Jeremiah Makoloi, who was educated at Lovedale Institution and of whose assiduity and ability the Canon speaks with much respect.

Grandfather was very active in the political life of his community at the turn of the century. He was the Secretary of the Native National Congress (later the African National Congress) and his brother-in-law, Moses Masisi, was the Treasurer. With several others, they worked closely with Sol T. Plaatje, the great challenger of the 1913 Land Act in the black community, and author of *Native Life in South Africa*, a book which powerfully denounced the new legislation. It is in this book that Grandfather is mentioned as an interpreter at the Dower Meeting held at Thaba'Nchu racecourse on Friday, 12 September 1913. There Barolong men and women had gathered to receive clarification on this traumatic legislation whose lamentable effects included the early up-rooting and dispossession of the black people. The meeting showed no way forward for the people and sent home those who attended feeling completely hopeless and thoroughly frustrated.

It should be noted, however, that early in this century in Natal, the Cape Colony, Transvaal, and the Orange Free State, there were already scores of men of Jeremiah's calibre in the Native National Congress, fighting on an intellectual and political battlefield to stop the colonists' iniquitous law-making. They laid the foundation for the unending struggle against these callous laws.

My grandfather subsequently became a court interpreter in the magistrates' court, working with the presiding officer and the black offenders, most of whom had not had the opportunity to go to school or to learn English. He became a very committed Christian, local preacher and church steward in the Wesleyan Methodist Church as well as a prosperous farmer. He died on 23 May 1920 at the age of 60.

Unlike my grandfather, who was a gentle person, my grandmother was outspoken and direct in her speech and dealings, to the point of being blunt. She had very fine features and was a woman with her own values and standards. I can never forget how on one of our many trips in the family Cape carriage (a covered four-wheeler) to Thaba'Nchu, she monitored and commented on Grandfather's driving for the whole of the journey. The bone of contention was that she felt Grandfather was giving too much space to any white farmer's cart, car or carriage travelling in the opposite direction. She repeatedly told him: 'Jeremiah, you must not go more out of the way for the other traffic than is necessary. You are entitled to your portion of the road as much as they are.' In a gentle way, Grandpa would reply: 'It is all right, Segogoane, do not worry!' He was unruffled by her remarks throughout the 30-mile journey. To use the modern expression, he kept his cool, and always with a slightly remote smile.

The climax of the journey came when we reached town and stopped while my grandparents did some shopping. As the couple were discussing their plans, and deciding what to do, a white lady, close to Grandma's age, approached the carriage and addressed herself to Grandma in Afrikaans, saying something like 'Ek soek 'n meid wat in my kombuis kan werk' ('I am looking for a maid to work in my kitchen'). My grandma gave her one look and without a moment's hesitation, replied: 'I am also looking for that type of person – can you help?' No one will ever know whether the Afrikaner woman simply expected my grandma to help her find a maid, or whether she was indirectly insulting her by asking her to go and work for her; your guess is as good as mine. If that was what she meant, she received an appropriate response. The white lady turned her back and left without a word. Grandpa was more embarrassed than hurt. He spoke firmly but softly to Grandma as if objecting to her reply. That incident shows just how straightforward Grandma was in her talk. It left a lasting impression on my mind.

Her housekeeping could not be faulted. She demanded the best from those responsible for household chores in the home. In short, she was a disciplinarian. She expected us to be clean at all times, even when we were out playing on our own. She insisted we returned promptly for meals, and that we sat down to a meal and finished it. She adhered to evening prayers and all children had to go early to bed. By bedtime Grandma *meant* bedtime. She accepted no giggles, silly or pretentious coughs or whispers after we were put to bed.

It was when she insisted we do something that we found it very difficult to suppress our playful tactics. We often ended up being spanked, and in tears. Despite her strictness, we loved our granny very dearly; she meant a lot to us, full of mischief as we were. It was common practice for us during the day to make fun of her prohibitions from the night before. We always ended up laughing our lungs out after going through the happenings of the night.

It was somehow an accepted fact that every time she went to Thaba'Nchu, we children went along with her. We invariably travelled in the Cape carriage, drawn by four beautiful stallions. The workers in the house took pains to prepare for that trip. Among the tasks to be accomplished was the sorting out of our attire, this included bonnets called by the Afrikaans word 'kappies'. These bonnets had two or three frills, starched and ironed smooth without a single crease. Our dresses were worn without a sash or belt. They had a high yoke and a well-gathered, full, knee-length skirt. All our dresses were made from the same pattern and were made from the same quality and colour material; only the sizes were different. We were really not thrilled with either the pattern or the uniform colour when we grew older. Our coats were white, made out of long silk – like mohair. Our whole costume made us look painfully different from the neighbourhood children. According to their standards and judgement (and ours) we looked odd, and we stuck out like sore thumbs. With my grandmother, however, there was no nonsense about clothes. We wore what we were told to wear.

On the long 30-mile journey between the farm and Thaba'Nchu we spoke very little or not at all, except to answer a remark or question from Granny. Like all children of that era, we were more seen than heard, and we accepted that state of affairs as law.

As I have said, although Granny was so strict we loved her very dearly. Proof of this was when we were on our own and playing, when we would relive the experience we went through under her care and drive away any hurt by imitating her and laughing at it all. Now, as I look back, I find it rather unusual that during that period in our lives we were more attached to her than we were to our own mothers. We addressed her as Mother and Grandpa as Papa. Only one of my cousins, Serekego, a little girl about three years younger than me, right through her life addressed Granny as Segogoane, never as Granny or Mother. As children we felt Granny was particularly fond of this little girl (indeed she was lovable). Apart from allowing her to use the name Segogoane, Granny always responded in a very intimate way to this little girl: she used to say to Serekego 'O no o reng Rakgadi'a mme?' ('What do you want, my mothers' aunt?') Serekego was named after my grandmother's aunt and she thus enjoyed the respect we did not. To this day, children named after an old person in the family are accorded respect and recognition. We often felt Serekego got away with what some of us would have received a spanking for.

As in any other family, we children played, ate and went to school together, and often even shared our clothes and food. We teased each other constantly, sometimes even to the point of telling tales to our elders, or fighting it out amongst ourselves. We roamed these beautiful hills over-looking the homestead; crossed the dongas (gulleys), from which we practised jumping; collected wild fruits we were forbidden to eat from the veld (open country); drank forbidden water from the dams; plucked fruit from the orchard, often before it was ready to eat; and occasionally went horseriding, to fetch the post from the local store. We became real experts in recognising the calls of different birds and in imitating them. It was easy to tell owls, wagtails, doves, and sparrows by their song without setting eyes on them. Our favourite pastime was playing 'house-house' and dolls.

We got a real thrill out of using mother's sewing-machine without her permission. We did this as often as there was need to make clothes for our dolls. The 'dress-maker', Aunt Elizabeth (my mother's much younger sister), would shake her finger at those of us who were notorious for tale-telling as she strongly warned us: 'Any one who tells Ausi Mutsi (meaning Mother) that I have been using the machine will get it from me and, what is more, I will never again make clothes for her dolls.'

These were the enjoyable days when we children grew up as one family at Thaba Patchoa Farm. Even after the death of our grandparents (they died within three months of each other in 1920), and we each went to our own parents' homes, we still exchanged visits during our school holidays. To this day when there is a happy or sad occasion in one of the families, it is always a very happy reunion for those present, regardless of the circumstances. This is how strong the bond of family ties was in that home ...

Ellen Kuzwayo is known as the 'mother of Soweto' and was born in 1914 in the Orange Free State. In 1930 she inherited her family farm, but it was taken away from her as it was located within a 'white area'. She studied to become a teacher and social worker but, after the Sharpeville massacre, she became more actively involved in anti-apartheid protests. She also fought strongly for women's rights in South Africa. In 1979, Kuzwayo was named Woman of the Year by a major newspaper (*The Star*), and also won the CNA Literary Prize for her autobiography *Call Me Woman*. She was elected as a Member of Parliament in the democratic government of South Africa in 1994.
Book Extracted: *Call Me Woman* (Picador Africa, 2004)

To My Children's Children
Sindiwe Magona

What then, of my childhood, child of my child of my child? Was it happy? Poverty ridden? Or plagued with trauma, crime, illness or some other malady?

No! To my child eyes, my childhood was stable and happy. It had a reasonable mix of tragedies, both minor and major.

My parents loved us, there was no doubt about that, most of the time. Their idea of raising children, however, was simple, direct and innocent of ameliorating influence of any theory – psychological, sociological, anthropological or any other such profundity. They were staunch adherents of the adage, 'spare the rod and spoil the child'. Often, a neighbour would intervene. A practice from which we learned to throw our embarrassment to the wind, screaming as loudly as we could, as soon as the beating began.

Corporal punishment was common practice when we were children. We got it at home, at school and even at Church on occasion. Therefore, we didn't take exception to it – which is not to say we liked it. Father, a man of very few and rather gruff words, would sometimes explain to us that such punishment was one of the ways parents showed their love for their children. Any child who was allowed to grow wild and was never punished for doing wrong was not as loved as we were and, upon reaching adulthood, would not know any better and would always be in trouble with the law, with other people, and worse, possibly even with God. We wailed often, for we were much loved.

If one word could summarize the kind of childhood I had, 'ordinary' would probably be that word.

Then, I had no idea of the link between the colour of my skin and the difference in life-styles; between mine and those of children of a lighter hue, 'coloureds', and those of a yet lighter shade, whites. The axiom, 'white best, coloured next, and black worst' was not yet in my ken. In fact, at that stage of my life, I had great difficulty identifying colour in people: for years, my eyes saw no significant difference between Indians, coloureds, or whites. Did they not all have long silky hair?

Although I can swear by all that is sacred that not a penny was ever spent on a toy by my family, we children were never at a loss as to what to do with ourselves. We played in groups, usually with both girls and boys participating.

A good deal of my waking day, I spent in happy play: there were games played by girls only and games for boys only. But when there was a shortage, a girl could find herself treated as an honorary boy, as long as there was need of an extra player; and boys sometimes, though rarely, deigned to play some girls' game. Of course, there were girls' games no self-respecting boy would even think of taking part in.

Any toys that came our way did so by way of charity: organizations such as the Cape Flats Distress Association (CAFDA) gave Christmas parties for children living in the locations.

We went to these parties for two reasons and two reasons only: to get toys; to fill ourselves with cakes, pies, cold drinks and sweets – things never on the grocery list in our homes. In fact, what list am I talking about? The parties were publicized via the location link – if one child knew, we all knew.

We did not question why it was the beneficent were invariably white, the beneficiaries invariably black. We had no way of knowing about the broader issues that had given birth to the organization itself, let alone understand its mission, to say nothing of the inadequacy and limitedness of its undertaking. How were we to know that many of these kind ladies were the wives and daughters of the men who paid our fathers peanuts; fed their dogs T-bone steak; and ensured our poverty by voting in a government whose avowed task was making certain we would stay servants, serf-like and docile? We were children. That these ladies were from another world, that they were giving us their time, showing us their Christian caring, alleviating our poverty, if for one day in a year, was completely lost on us: we did not even know we were poor.

Another source of toys was the white world where almost all the working women of my childhood were employed as nannies, housemaids, chars, and cooks. These women brought, into the black locations droppings off the white families they served. They returned with bags bulging with cold toast, stale bread, moulding cheese, milk, cake, and whatever other food was threatening to go off despite refrigeration. They came back with clothing – shoes, socks, hats, underwear, sweaters, dresses, raincoats, coats, gloves, blouses, skirts, pants, and anything else one can imagine, in various states of disrepair. Those who worked for families with children also brought toys to their homes. Books and comics were another offering.

Those of us who had working mothers, aunts, sisters, neighbours or family friends would run to welcome them long before they were anywhere near their destination, their houses. They would be forced to tell us what they had brought us from work. Those women who had stingy madams were forced to buy some delicacy such as fruit, sweets, or meat on their way home.

Whatever their own family composition, not one of those women was stupid enough ever to tell an employer they had no use for any gift. If one didn't have a child who could use a toy, a doll, a train, a dress, a slice of bread, a piece of cheese, a book, a pair of shoes, a raincoat, a comic book, old newspaper, or whatever else was being thrown out, one had enough sense to know there were scores of children and adults who could use anything, whatever state it was in.

So great was the need.

My own initial contact with the world of English books and comics, was greatly aided by a white family I would never know: a neighbour, Mrs Waya, would bring these, among other goodies, from her place of employment. There must, therefore, have been children my age in that family. Thus did I get introduced to characters such as Billy Bunter, his equally fat sister, Bessie, Roxanne and a host of other characters from *The Girls' Crystal* and *The School Friend.* Mickey Mouse, Minnie, Goofy, Scrooge, Donald Duck, Popeye and his sweetheart, Olive; Nancy, Sylvester and Puddy Tat, and even Bob Hope, I also met. Blondie and Dagwood are childhood friends I have passed on to my own children. I envy them their perpetual youthfulness.

Whilst I can vouch for the innocence of my family regarding buying any reading material, even the daily newspaper, I read books, granted mostly with limited comprehension. *Pride and Prejudice, Cry the Beloved Country, Great Expectations, Lorna Doone, The Mad Hatter, Treasure Island,* are some of the spoils Mrs Waya threw our way.

Nearly all the books and comics she brought were in good repair. However, I remember a few times, it did happen that I would be engrossed in a story only to have to stop short of experiencing the thrill of getting to the end because there were pages missing. Later, I learnt to make up my own endings.

Of my childhood friends, only Dawn had such things as nighties, shoes, socks and other not strictly necessary items of clothing. Years later, a group of us, comparing notes as adults, realized that those of us who, as children, had such things, had had mothers who were domestic workers.

Aunt Maria used to come to our home on Thursdays, her day off. With her own family a long way away in some remote rural area, she had adopted us as her family away from home. What did she not bring us! Pudding, toast, some clothing, fruit, and other gems.

I had occasion to recall Aunt Maria many many years later. My three children, beginning to be vocal about their deprivation, had appointed the youngest, Sandile:

'Sisi, can you tell us why you cannot have a nice job like the other children's mothers?'

A little puzzled, for although I was a humble school teacher, none of the other mothers in our street were brain surgeons either, I explained the job I was doing was very necessary to children as without it they would grow up ignorant. When I wanted to know what job they had in mind for me the prompt answer came from the most forward, the middle child, Thokozile:

'A job that gives you nice things to bring us. Look at the other children! Their mothers bring them cakes, cheese, cold meats, dolls...'

Thembeka, not to be left out, made the most telling observation, as befits the eldest,

'Sisi, your job is boring!'

The consensus was that my teaching job was altogether unattractive. I didn't blame the kids. The only thing I ever brought home from work was work to mark! Hidden benefits such as not being threatened with notices of eviction every other month, thanks to my unpretentious teacher's salary, did not begin to compare, to my offspring, with the tangible, visible, and heavenly goodies other mothers brought their children.

I had been as blind when I was a child. Our parents had faced a grim reality we knew nothing about. Mother, at some time or another, has sold sweets, vegetables, *vetkoek,* sheep-head, sheep-trotters, home-made ginger beer, cigarettes: all this illegally as she did not have a permit for selling anything from her home. On occasion, she has sold kaffir beer, *skokiaan*, and hard liquor, these illegal twice over: not only did she not have a licence to sell them, but possession, by an African, of these substances was illegal at the time. She has undertaken sewing, knitting, and domestic work as a way of earning some money. Never, in my mind, were any of these activities linked to father's wages; it was enough, for me, to know that father worked and got paid on Fridays.

Poverty datum line, making ends meet, cheap or uncivilized labour and exploitation; all these were concepts as foreign to me then as the language of the Martians is to me now. Organizations such as the Black Sash were compiling statistics about the plight of the disenfranchised in South Africa. I've often wondered whether some of the ladies of the Christmas Parties were also Black Sash members. Whatever the answer, even then, there were souls, white souls, who were perturbed by the treatment the darker races of the land were receiving. And such alarm had been voiced even before the first white foot stepped onto shore from the floating house that had been blown there (surely, by an ill-wind!) in 1652.

Ntsikane, a Xhosa Seer, had predicted the enslavement of the African at the hands of white people. 1948 saw the sealing of that struggle: the Afrikaner became absolute rulers. From then on, systematically, the African would be stripped of whatever little remained of what had once been his own.

We played cops and robbers and identified completely with cops, the good guys of comic and cinema myth. In our own lives, however, cops were feared, disliked, regarded with suspicion, the known enemy of our world. Cops caught our parents, our relatives and our neighbours for what appeared to us children as everything. Cops were bad luck. Cops were the only arm of government we experienced. And cops took people to jail.

To ward off misfortune – evil spirits, bewitching by another, job loss, cops and arrest – our parents lived by charms, herbs, and witchdoctor forecasts.

When charms, herbs, incisions, prayer and whatever other means of coping and protection had been enlisted failed, common sense prevailed. Once, mother became aware a liquor raid was upon her, a house or two away. She grabbed the aluminium tub that hung on a bent nail behind the door; onto the floor it went, into it went the water we kept in a four-gallon tin, into the water mother.

The first policeman who barged in let out a howl: *'Here God, die vroumens is kaal!'*(Good God, this woman is naked!), as he beat a hasty retreat, the others doing a right about turn without bothering to enter.

A nakedly pregnant black woman had, obviously, been the last thing these gentlemen expected. And for such an escape, what was the family's entire supply of water?

Sacrifice was also called for when visitors were expected. Our eyes preceded theirs and saw what they would see: the uneven legs of the table; the cupboard door stuffed with rags so it could close; newspaper table cloths and cupboard liners; the hasn't-been-polished-since-last-Christmas floor; all these and more, suddenly lay naked to our eyes, stripped of their comforting familiarity. Floor polish was not something one bought as a matter of course; there had to be a very good reason for that, the visit of some august person; an elder, the minister, or a teacher.

None of these people, however, provoked the frantic and frenzied cleaning that the doctor did. His stature was enhanced in our eyes by the fact that he was white.

A doctor's visit provoked a veritable panic attack! 'He'll take one look at the house,' we told ourselves, 'and pronounce: "No wonder you people are always sick. Look at this filth! You should all be dead, living like pigs!'"

To escape the condemnation we felt we richly deserved, the floor was scrubbed and polished, windows opened wide, sheets, night-dresses or pyjamas, and anything else we thought would help us hide our poverty from him, borrowed.

It was absolutely imperative, therefore, that knowledge of who had sheets, table cloths, towels, wash-basins, night-dresses and usable dishes be at the fingertips of all, the same way people elsewhere kept a list of all emergency telephone numbers.

Calling the doctors was a last resort: a frightful nuisance and expensive. It is understandable, therefore, that doctors were called only when it became obvious that a death certificate would soon be needed.

If anything frightened the community more than death itself, it was a certificateless death. Perhaps nowhere is the cultural difference, between African and white, more marked than in dealing with death: having to answer numerous hostile questions about the deceased is not our idea of mourning.

So, a doctor's visit, more often than not, spelled death literally. And 'we've sent for a doctor' had the same effect as the tolling of the bell I was to hear about in English Poetry: no bell tolls in the township.

The restless Mediterranean-summer days drove us out of doors, away from Mothers and away from chores. Outside, the problem was which pleasure to pursue. We swam dams, climbed hills, milked goats that were not ours, directly into our mouths, harvested vegetable gardens we had not planted, hunted rabbits of the veld and birds of the forest, played dolls' house, played weddings, church, school (I am at a loss now to explain this death wish. We all hated school but that did not stop us, apparently, from missing it during vacation), and a host of other games, pranks, and mischief besides.

Those greedy days! Instead of exhausting us because of their length and the vigour with which we hurled ourselves into them in earnest play, they only whetted our appetites.

We would walk half a day to get to the azure waters of Muizenberg. We braved streets and motor cars, a railway line, coloured residential areas, white neighbourhoods, long winding lanes on steadily rising terrain, the vineyards of Constantia and Tokai, our prize. There we would glean boxfuls of hanepoort, the sweetest grape in the whole wide world, pay sixpence or a shilling a box and set off to Blaauvlei with our entrepreneurial spirits soaring: the loads on our heads gladdening our hearts, making us light-footed.

With reluctance did we respond to our mothers' evening calls. More often than not, we had to be forcibly dragged indoors and to the chores, dull chores that did not begin to compare with the clamour, glamour and excitement of play.

Then there were the all-too-short winter days when play-time was stolen by the wicked rain that brought near havoc to our lives, mothers having designated it hazardous to the health of children at play. For it did not stop them from sending us to school, to the shop, or to a neighbour. Who needs to be protected against playing, rain notwithstanding?

Winter was fraught with danger. The cold, clammy, dank and dark shacks we lived in seemed to intensify whatever weather prevailed: ovens in summer; fridges in winter. For heat, we used coal. An inexpensive way to obtain this commodity was to pick coal along the railway tracks. This would be what had dropped from the goods-trains fuelled by coal. Of course, this was dangerous. But that was the least of our concerns; it was also illegal to enter the tracks. We were trespassing. I had never even heard the words 'beating the system' but doing something that I could be arrested for, for a reason I couldn't and didn't bother to fathom, had a definite allure for me. It never entered my (even then) thick skull that the fine my parents would have to pay would be a tragic setback.

Greater danger, however, came from this same source of heat. No, not the burns which are part and parcel of such means of heating. Among blacks, carbon monoxide poisoning is as constant a threat as drowning in white homes where swimming pools abound. In swimming-pool drownings the casualties are usually little children; carbon monoxide poisoning does not discriminate: it has happened that whole families have been discovered ice-cold in the morning, victims of their own attempts to keep from freezing to death.

Everyone knew that the brazier had to be taken out of the house before people went to bed. Unfortunately, many were seduced by the prospect of warmth throughout the night.

Our care-free, fun-filled days were punctuated by adult demands. The city chores were different from those I had been in the process of learning in the village. My brother often in fact fell foul of our parents because of his great reluctance to do housework. Mother and father explained there would be no more male or female tasks in Cape Town as there were no cattle for boys to herd. Thus, we were expected to take turns doing dishes, fetching water, and performing other household chores.

Floors, in the mud hut of the village, are smoothed bare earth. To keep the dust down, they are smeared with cow-dung, fresh cow-dung. This keeps the floor clean, green, and gives the room a fresh smell. In the tin shacks of the location, the floors are made of wood. I now scrubbed and, occasionally, even polished floors.

Where I had fetched water from the river, I learned to open and shut taps. We did not have running water in the house though. There was a communal tap. So I had to fetch water and since we paid for the water here, I had to learn, very early, to carry a four-gallon tin on my head. I learned to cook on a primus stove, using paraffin for fuel and methylated spirits to kindle it. In the village we had gathered twigs for kindling and wood and dry cow dung had been our fuel. I certainly had come a long way!

So fast was the pace, agility of mind had to be matched by nimbleness of fingers as fleas replaced lice in the daily onslaught on our bodies. Funds permitting, we bought DDT to strengthen our defence.

I learnt about products such as Vim, for scouring pots and pans. Our own Vim though, in the location, was ash and sand. I learnt to mind younger children; mother was to have five more children in Cape Town. I learnt these and many other time-consuming, petty, little, and annoying tasks without which, I am sure, families would perish and civilizations crumble! These tasks were learnt, practised and perfected, to the best of my youthful abilities and reluctant inclination. This is not to say I was never assailed with bouts of self-importance, as occasionally happened, when an adult gave praise for a job well done or when one's superior skills outshone another's. Such evidence of one's maturity would then be accompanied by a startled period of being a model child. Mercifully, that was short lived.

Our home became a home from home for people from our village (called homeboys and homegirls) who had been excised from their own families by the combined exigencies of their need for employment and the government's influx control policy, a policy aimed at keeping Africans away from the urban areas of South Africa. A policy that succeeded in wrecking African families in the villages. My home was a veritable gateway.

Like these migrant labourers, father had lived in bachelor quarters before his family came to join him. Now that he had a home, he also had a duty to his former 'roommates'.

As we ourselves lived in a single room in the beginning, a room that was bedroom by night, living-cum-dining room during the day, a bathroom and anything else room, any addition meant over-over-crowding. But we did what had to be done. Our visitors slept where we slept and ate what we ate.

Brides also came to get married to sweethearts whose contracts stretched months longer than their patience, threatening to put asunder that which burned to be together. Bhuti Phuphu, a bachelor, brought the young woman he was about to marry to our house. Living under a lay preacher's roof, she would qualify for a church wedding, whereas, had the groom-to-be taken her to his rooms at the hotel where he worked, the church would have refused to marry them.

Mzoxolo, Mandla's younger brother, took ill and his mother, Aunt Makhwange, brought him to Cape Town to be near his father and good doctors. Uncle Dyantyi would come to be with them every Sunday, his day off. And they stayed with us until Mzoxolo's health had been restored.

Occasionally, migrants were forcibly packed home: fears that they were becoming too attached to the women with whom they had liaisons in the city prompted such action. That kind of affair was not supposed to make one forget one's wife back home. Once, when such a person was being sent home, something got out of hand. I never got to know exactly what. Anyway, there I was, sound asleep when I was awakened by the noise of men at war.

Frightened, I sprang up crying. And at just that second, a blow aimed at another was deflected and the front end of the stick pierced my right thigh. To this day, I bear witness to that fight, five centimetres above the right knee.

Fights were not usual though when the going home was voluntary. It was the fact that a man was being sent home in disgrace, as it were, that inevitably caused blood to flow. That, and the home-brewed beer that, to amaXhosa, is part and parcel of any group activity.

Another group that went home through no will of their own were the truly and verily departed:

It is a Sunday morning: 'Nkqo! Nkqo-nkqo! Is this the home of Tolo from Umtata?' a voice asks. We freeze. Strangers in the location can spell big trouble.

'Who wants to know?' Father responds, going to the door. He opens it. Two men, strange men, stand awaiting admission.

'Come in. Where are the strangers from?'

'We are from Sea Point.'

'Yes?'

'Well, that is all.'

'I see.' And almost as an afterthought,

'Are you passing by or should the child get a chair next door?'

'We will be here a while,' reply the strangers.

'Sindiwe, go and borrow a *bankie* (bench) next door.'

When I returned the older of the two men was saying, 'He became cold; there and then. Cold. Now the police want a relative to come to the mopp (morgue) and point him out. That is why we are here.'

Tata then turned to us, to mother and to us children and relayed the news of the death of his cousin Sondlo.

Dear Bhuti Sondlo was no more. Felled by a hit-and-run car the night before. His wife and their four sons were, respectively, minus husband and father. The champion of *iintsomi* and tongue-twisters (the longest tongue-twister, according to the Guinness Book of Records, is the Xhosa one that goes, *'Iqaqa laseQawukeni laqabela entabeni, laziqikaqika kuqaqaqa, laza laqhawuka, uqboqboqbo!'** and I had learnt it from him). The master teaser lay silent. Never again (enjoying his day off) would he tell barefooted snot-nosed children reluctantly getting ready for school on a wintry morning, thick frost scrunchily shiny on the ground:

'Sleep! Is there anything more glorious on earth?

The poor, like the rich, get it.

The ugly, as the beautiful, enjoy it.

You, now, have to leave it and go to learn!

While I, like a king, remain under the blankets!'

His family would have had a very hard time. But his boss took on 16-year-old Simphiwe, Sondlo's eldest son, as replacement. Most African workers have no insurance, at work or privately, and Sondlo had been no exception.

In all this human activity, I as a child, was an observer, a minor participant, at most; a child looking on and watching adults doing adult things.

Sindiwe Magona was born in the Transkei in 1943, and grew up in Guguletu, Cape Town. She completed high school via correspondence, and later obtained a degree in psychology and history from the University of South Africa. She also holds a Master of Science Degree in Organizational Social Work from Columbia University. She went on to work in New York for the United Nations in the Department of Public Information, retiring in 2003, and settling back in the Cape in South Africa.

Book Extracted: *To My Children's Children* (David Philip, 2004)

---

*The skunk of Qawukeni went up the mountain, rolled itself over and over on the grass, and then his windpipe broke.

The Calling of Katie Makanya
Margaret McCord

She looked like a witch.

Her skin was as wrinkled and black as a dried prune, and her little red eyes peered through layers of wrinkles, half-foolish, half-wise, as though she had once known but had long since forgotten the timeless secrets.

The two little girls waited. In spite of the African heat, the younger child felt a shiver run down her back. She pulled at her sister's dress. 'Come away, Charlotte,' she muttered.

But Charlotte grabbed her arm and held her firmly at the edge of the wagon tracks. 'Katie, you stay here,' she whispered fiercely in her big-sister voice. 'Grandfather's coming.'

'Yes,' Katie said uncertainly, gazing down the hill at the short black man with streaks of grey in his hair and beyond him to the old woman huddled in the ox cart. 'But who's she?'

'Our old ancestor,' Charlotte said, tightening her fingers on Katie's arm.

As the cart approached, Grandfather raised one arm in greeting. '*Weu!* I rejoice to see you.'

'We rejoice also,' Charlotte called back.

Grandfather laughed and nodded towards the old woman. 'She gave me no rest. She did not want to stop to eat or even to sleep.'

Still laughing, he lifted the old woman gently to the ground and reached back for her walking-stick. While he outspanned the oxen, she hobbled forward, her bones rattling under her shapeless black dress.

'*Hawu*, my little Anna!' she said, tapping Katie's shoulder. Her mouth gaped open, empty of teeth, and her voice echoed the faint screech of an owl. Katie clung in terror to Charlotte's hand and again she tried to pull away. But Charlotte stood still, her chin held high, and stared back at the Old One. Charlotte was six years old and she was not afraid of anything, neither witches nor ancestors.

'She's not Anna,' Charlotte said firmly. 'She's Katie, daughter of Anna.'

'Not Anna?' The old woman shook her head in confusion, and suddenly tears glistened in her little red eyes and she wailed aloud to Grandfather. 'My son, the Zulus have taken Anna.'

'Anna's still working her fields,' Grandfather said. 'These are Anna's girls. They'll take you to the house and make you tea.'

'Tea? Yes, I want tea,' she mumbled.

Did witches drink tea and cry real tears? Witches knew everything. A witch would have known her name. Katie's fears eased.

Together the two girls guided the old woman over the clean swept earth, and steadied her walking-stick as she pulled herself up the steps of the verandah and seated herself in Ma's rocking-chair. The evening wind was already touching the hilltop. Katie ran inside for one of Ma's shawls to tuck around the old woman's shoulders, then turned to follow Charlotte to the cooking hut. But those wrinkled hands clawed at her dress.

'Katie, daughter of Anna, stay with me. Let that other one go.'

Charlotte hesitated. She did not like being thus dismissed. But her duty was clear, and after a moment she ran off alone to make the tea. The old woman beckoned Katie closer and stroked her cheek. 'Yes, you are Anna's daughter,' she said. Her voice dropped slyly. 'But that other girl? Who is she?'

'She's my sister Charlotte.'

'No. She's not like us.'

'She *is*,' Katie cried out. Of course Charlotte was her sister. Yet as she looked down at her bare feet and twisting hands, she saw that indeed the old woman spoke true. Her own skin was as black as the old woman's, as black as Ma's. But Charlotte was different. Like Pa, her skin was the colour of mealie tassels just before harvest time.

'But she *is* my sister,' Katie said.

Already the old woman had forgotten her question. 'I want my tea.'

Katie ran off quickly before she could change her mind. When she and Charlotte returned with the tray, Grandfather was squatting on his heels beside the rocking-chair, looking out on the hills which rolled down and down from the house like a great pile of green and red and golden calabashes. He was speaking gently to the old woman, pointing across the hills to other African homesteads, each protected from snakes by a patch of bare swept earth, and down to the valley where the river ran full, and beyond to the red corrugated-iron roofs and green trees of the white people in Uitenhage five miles away.

'Yes, it's good land my son-in-law has chosen,' he was saying, 'and a good house he's built for my daughter.' He stood up, reaching for the two blanket rolls he had unpacked from the ox cart. 'Where do we sleep?'

'I'll show you, Grandfather,' Charlotte said eagerly, leading him through the door into the two-room wattle-and-daub farmhouse.

On the veranda Katie managed to lift the heavy teapot and pour tea into a cup without spilling. As she stirred in two spoonfuls of sugar, she could hear Charlotte's voice inside the house: 'You'll sleep here in the room where we sit and study and work. The other room has Ma's bed, and the Old One will sleep with her.'

'My tea,' the old woman grumbled. Katie held out the cup but the old woman made no move to take it, just looked at it greedily until Katie raised it to her lips. She drank then, slowly at first, testing the heat, then gulped noisily. Suddenly she sat up straight and called out, 'Anna comes.'

Ma was moving up the hillside, a short, fat black woman with a basket of mealies on her head, and a hoe over one shoulder. 'Father! Grandmother!' she called out happily. 'I didn't think you'd come so soon.'

'Your grandmother was in a big hurry to see you,' Grandfather called back.

'Such a big hurry she even called me Anna,' Katie said, taking the hoe.

'Then she thought the Zulus had taken you away,' Charlotte added, helping Ma set down the basket of mealies. 'Ma, who are the Zulus?'

'We do not speak of them,' Ma said firmly.

'Our ancestor said –'

'Hush.'

But the old woman had already heard. 'The Zulus! They're coming back. Quick, my children, we must hide.' She tried to pull herself out of her rocking-chair but Grandfather held her down.

'We're safe here,' he said calmly. 'The Zulus are far away by the eastern sea.'

Still the old woman perched on the edge of the rocking-chair, wailing in despair. Knowing nothing, yet sensing her fear, Katie felt such a rush of pity that, without thinking, she patted her hand.

'Oy, my little one. You are with me. But I thought I buried you under the bushes.'

'I am here, Great-grandmother,' Katie said softly.

From that time forward until she went away with Grandfather in his ox cart, the old woman would not let Katie out of her sight. Sometimes the old woman thought Katie was Ma as a child. Sometimes she knew Katie as Ma's daughter. And sometimes she thought Katie was her own baby come back from the dead. But whoever she thought Katie was, she warned her constantly against those terrible Zulus. Time and time again she unwound the black scarf from her head to reveal the yellowed bone showing through the matted white hair.

Her thoughts were too mixed up to tell what had really happened. At last one evening after the old woman had been put to bed, and Ma, Grandfather, Charlotte and Katie were sitting on the veranda watching the purple shadows greying into night, Katie asked what the Zulus had done.

'We do not speak of the Zulus in this house,' Ma repeated.

'It's time, Anna,' Grandfather said. 'When the girls are old enough to ask their questions, they are old enough to hear.'

Ma sighed and reluctantly began to speak. 'It was long ago, when your ancestor was still a young woman. In those days our people were called the Mbo and they lived in Pondoland. They were happy there until they heard that Shaka the Zulu was eating up all the tribes around him and was still unsatisfied. And so the men sharpened their spears and made ready to defend themselves. But in that place there were too many trees and streams for the real sport of battle, so the warriors ran to look for a clear field in which to fight.'

Ma paused. From down on the hillside came the soft *hoo-hoo* of an owl, like the mournful echo of a child's cry.

'Go on,' Grandfather prompted.

'Before they left,' Ma continued, 'the warriors warned their women to flee, and leave the children behind so that their crying would not betray their whereabouts. Some did abandon their children. But your ancestor refused. She tied her baby on her back and took her little boy by the hand, and all three hid in the bushes.'

'You were that little boy?' Katie asked Grandfather.

'Yes,' he said. 'I remember very well. Those Zulus passed so close to our hiding place I could see the dirt under their toenails. But they did not see us. They were laughing too loud at a girl who was trying to hide in the river. This girl's head was under the water, but the current caught her skirt and her bare buttocks floated up in plain view. "That is a beautiful sight and we will return when the fighting is over," those Zulus called out as they kept running up the the path.'

'So you escaped?' Charlotte said.

'Almost. We crept out of the bushes, but too late we saw one last Zulu straggling after his brothers. As he passed us his knobkerrie swung down, crushing the baby's skull, and swung down again on my mother's head. He ran on supposing her dead, and why she did not die, I cannot say.'

'What happened then?'

'That girl came out of the river and pulled my mother to her feet and helped her bury her poor dead baby.'

'That's why we do not speak the name of Zulu in this house,' Ma said flatly.

'Let me finish,' Grandfather said. He smiled at the two girls. 'We walked for many days until we reached Matatiele. There we found my father with the other men of the Mbo, still waiting to fight and laughing at the Zulus who hadn't the courage to follow them so far. But they were afraid to return to their own country. Instead, they separated, some going to work for the Boers, others going another way to become the dogs of the Xhosas. That's why we are now called Fingoes – because we wandered about in a land that was not our own.'

'Don't you own your land in Blinkwater?' Charlotte asked.

'Yes. But how I got it is another story.'

In the days that followed, Charlotte listened to their ancestor. But she did not wait patiently when the old woman's thoughts wandered away from her words, and bothered her with questions. The old woman thought her disrespectful and more than once told her angrily to go away.

'I don't care,' Charlotte told Katie. 'I'm tired of hearing only about the long-ago.'

For the old woman, however, the long-ago was more real than today and the Zulus were the evil spirits that haunted her dreams. On the last morning of her visit she woke up very excited.

'Katie!' she called out frantically. 'Don't go with him, Katie.'

'Go with who?' Katie asked sleepily.

'That Zulu. That heathen warrior.'

Charlotte sat up on her mat, yawning. 'What's she yelling about?'

'She thinks she sees a Zu –, a bad man.'

'Yes, I see him.' The wrinkled chin trembled. 'Run, Katie, or he'll eat you up.

Katie slid across the floor and knelt by her bed, for she could see that the old woman was truly afraid. Her fear made Katie herself uneasy and she glanced over her shoulder half expecting to see some hideous, feathered warrior leaping through the door, but there was only Charlotte behind her giggling, and Ma and Grandfather crowding anxiously into the little bedroom.

'Don't worry yourself, Mother,' Grandfather called out. 'Katie is safe with Anna, and now you must rouse yourself. The porridge is hot and the ox cart is waiting.'

The old woman did not speak while Katie fed her the porridge, or when Grandfather carried her out to the ox cart and pulled the blankets over her shoulders to shield her from the cold morning air.

'Go well, Grandmother,' Ma said.

'Go well, Great-grandmother,' Charlotte repeated.

But Katie said nothing because of the tight sorrow in her throat. She could only nod when the old woman whispered, 'Remember what I told you, my little Anna.'

'But I'm Katie, daughter of Anna.'

'Yes, you too, Katie. You must remember.'

Grandfather cracked his whip and the oxen began to lumber slowly along the wagon tracks.

'Even now she doesn't always remember who I am,' Katie said, holding back her tears as the ox cart jolted down the hill.

'I know,' Ma replied. 'She's too old. No one knows how old she is. Only that she had already borne her children in the time of Shaka. You are more fortunate, Katie, because you know your birth date exactly.'

Yes, the girls were indeed more fortunate. Ma was not like the other mothers who told their children they were born in the time of this war or that war. Ma was an educated woman. She wrote everything down in the family Bible. First the record of Charlotte's birth, and then 'a second daughter, Katie, born on July 28, 1873 at Fort Beaufort in the Cape of Good Hope.'

Katie never knew why Ma called her Katie. First there was Charlotte, then Katie, Philip, Henry, John and finally Mary Ann. Pa was a Christian too, but not in his early years, and he did not altogether put aside the customs of his people. He called Katie by her home name, Malubisi – which means 'Mother of Milk' – because she was born at milking time.

On Saturday afternoons Pa came home from his work in Port Elizabeth and did not leave again until after the church service on Sunday. All day Saturday Katie could feel her excitement building. When the sun threw the shadow of the peach tree to the edge of the chicken run in the backyard, she started listening for the train's whistle and began watching for Pa to round a bend in the road. Then together she and Charlotte raced down the hill to meet him. Katie always reached him first, throwing herself into his arms so that he could swing her up to sit on his shoulders, while Charlotte skipped along beside him, chattering all the while about what she had learned in school that week.

'What did you learn, Malubisi?' Pa asked Katie when he set her down on the veranda.

Katie thought for a moment. 'My seven times multiplication table.'

'You learned that last week.'

'I learned it again,' Katie said stubbornly.

'But you must remember what you are taught one day so you can learn something new the next, or else you will grow up ignorant – as ignorant as I was when I was young.'

'You? Ignorant?' Katie laughed, unbelieving.

'Yes, I knew nothing. I was already grown before I saw any white people. They came into our country and shot us down before we could get close enough to throw our spears.'

Charlotte stilled her chatter and Ma, too, was silent as Father spoke, his voice like a river, sometimes swift and deep, sometimes quiet and shining with laughter.

'So my father called to me and some of my brothers and said: "I've heard these men with straight hair come from the south. Go, therefore, and search out their homeplace and find me some guns."'

He crooked his arm so that Katie could lean back with her head against his shoulder.

'I journeyed many days. When the food I took with me was finished, I killed a rabbit or buck. Nevertheless, I was often hungry and in time I grew thin and weak. But a Boer farmer in the Orange Free State saw me and gave me some trousers and put me to work. One day he gave me a box of figs and told me to take it to the storekeeper in the village some miles away. He also gave me a piece of paper which, he said, would tell how many figs there were and what the cost would be.

'But on the way I wanted to eat a fig, so I took the paper and said to it: "My *baas* says you can talk. We will see how well you talk today." Then I covered the paper with a big stone so it could not watch me, and I ate ten figs. When I was finished I removed the stone and put the paper back in the box. Yet when I delivered the figs the storekeeper grumbled because ten figs were missing and he would not give me all the money that was wanted.'

'Was your *baas* very angry?' Katie asked.

Pa laughed. 'I don't know. I ran away. I was afraid of his paper. I thought it was magic, because I covered it with a stone so that it could not see, and yet it saw and told the storekeeper how many figs I had eaten.'

Katie laughed at Pa's foolishness, but Charlotte did not think it funny that his people beyond the mountains could not read or write. 'Some day we'll go there to teach them,' she said. 'I'll go beyond this place, beyond Port Elizabeth, beyond the sea. I'll go to England to study what the white people are taught. Then I'll come back to teach our people.'

'Ho, miss, and where will the money come from?' Ma interrupted.

'Wait,' Pa said, 'perhaps all this will come to pass.' Always he encouraged Charlotte's dreaming, for God works in mysterious ways and perhaps He would guide Charlotte's feet as He had guided Pa's out of the wilderness until he came to the Cape. There he saw Ma and loved her. Because she was a Christian schoolteacher, Pa went to night school and learned the magic of the papers and the wonders of the Bible. In time he rose to be a foreman on the road gangs in Port Elizabeth and a lay preacher for the Presbyterians on Sunday. Then he and Ma were married. He never found the guns for his father or returned to his people beyond the mountains.

'Why doesn't your father come to visit us?' Katie asked.

'He lives too far.'

'Then can we go to visit him?'

'Some day,' Pa said. 'When you have finished your schooling.'

'But I don't want to go to school.'

'Why not?'

'Because my books are too heavy in my hands. They make my head ache and my eyes all red and watery.'

In this way she was different from Charlotte. Charlotte was never content to listen to what others told her but had to know a thing for herself out of her own thoughts or else find it written down in a book.

But for Katie, words in books had no more meaning than chicken scratchings in the dust. What she learned, she learned by listening – to Charlotte and Ma reading aloud, to the teaching of Mr Joba, to snatches of conversation overheard on the road. In time her ears caught the rhythm and melody of each different voice, each different tongue – the high clear notes of the English walking the streets of Uitenhage, the soft throatiness of the Boers driving their wagons up to the shops, the rippling lilt of the Xhosa language, all so similar yet each as different as the notes of a song. Sometimes she heard the words of the Europeans spoken, heard them repeated by her own people and, in the repeating, coloured and changed until the original sound was lost and a new word created. By the end of her second year in school she could speak English, Dutch, Xhosa and Pa's Sotho.

On their way home from school soon after the Christmas holiday, Katie and Charlotte saw the Redcoats drilling behind the courthouse in Uitenhage. Later when they stopped to rest themselves at the river, Katie listened to the chatter of the women who were washing their clothes. One of them was speaking of the Zulu king, Cetshwayo, who was threatening to drive all the white men into the sea.

'Is there really going to be a war?' Katie asked Pa when he came home on Saturday afternoon. He nodded his head.

'I'm told the Zulus are buying guns from the Portuguese.'

'Those Zulus!' Ma exclaimed angrily. 'Those heathen!'

Pa chuckled. 'You must blame their women. I'm told they are angry because of two women who ran away from their husbands and found refuge with the English.'

'This is no time for jokes,' Ma said. 'Those Zulus are always fighting.'

Despite Pa's teasing, he was not happy about Cetshwayo's war. After church one Sunday he kept shaking his head over news of the British defeat at Isandlwana where the Zulus had wiped out a whole regiment of white soldiers.

Many of the people, however, were excited by Cetshwayo's victory. Among the women on the road there was the gossip of this man or that who had run away to join the Zulus. But within a few weeks there was much weeping among those women, for only a few of the men came back, all of them sick and wounded.

When the church bells tolled out the news of Cetshwayo's surrender, there was rejoicing in the white people's houses in Uitenhage. In the kraals and African farmsteads, however, the news was received in silence. Even Ma felt sorry for Cetshwayo, who was banished from Zululand and sent down to Cape Town to live as a prisoner of the Queen. 'It would have been better for him to have died in battle,' Ma said, 'for how can the spirits of his ancestors watch over him when he is gone so far from his homeplace?'

Pa, too, did not seem happy. He was strangely silent when an old man whose son had gone away and come back with a bullet hole in his chest spoke out in anger. 'The white soldiers were not fair,' he said. 'They made no sport of battle. It wasn't enough that they had rifles and Maxims and machine-guns against us. They used a medicine also. This my son has told me. A terrible medicine which they sprinkled in a certain way so that when it touched the skin of a warrior it drove him to the river with a terrible thirst. Then, when he drank of that water, he died.'

'Yes, I have heard this too,' Pa said. 'In Port Elizabeth our people are saying "Basibulala ngetyhefu" – They are killing us with poison.'

'But I do not think it was the English who did this,' one of the deacons said. 'It was that Frenchman, Napoleon, because he was angry when his son was killed.'

'I have heard that also,' Pa said. 'But I do not know if it is true. In my daughter's history book it says that Napoleon is dead.'

'Perhaps that's why it is such a strong medicine,' someone suggested.

And so the talk went on and the rumours spread. Bitterness festered, especially among the Christians, for the Europeans had brought Christianity to the Africans and had preached against superstition and witchcraft, and yet they themselves had betrayed the Word by the use of magic potions. Katie found all the talk very confusing.

'Are some of the white people heathens also?' Katie asked.

'I have never heard a white man say he was not a Christian,' Pa said slowly. 'Yet I have seen some in Port Elizabeth whose wickedness would make our own heathen shudder. For among our own people evil comes out of ignorance and fear. But among the white people? Whence comes their evil I cannot say.'

But Charlotte knew. 'It comes from Satan. Those Europeans who are wicked are the messengers of Satan, sent to confuse us.'

'But how can you tell which of the white people are really Christians and which are Satan's messengers?' Katie asked.

'By prayer,' Ma said.

'By study,' Charlotte said.

Katie waited for Pa's answer, but he just shook his head and remained silent ...

Katie Makanya was born in 1873 at Fort Beaufort in the Cape of Good Hope. She grew up at a time when South Africa was being transformed by the influx of European settlers, and her courage and determination gave her the strength and will to triumph over poverty and hardship. She possessed a natural talent for rhythm and language, and she, along with her sister Charlotte, ended up touring Europe with the Jubilee Singers. When she returned home, she met up with James McCord, a white doctor who had come to treat the Zulus, and became his translator and assistant. Before her death, Katie related the remarkable story of her life to McCord's daughter Margaret.

Book Extracted: *The Calling of Katie Makanya* by Margaret McCord (David Philip, Cape Town and Johannesburg, 1997)

My Story
Miriam Makeba

I walk home from school with two girlfriends. The journey is five miles. It's hard making this walk day after day. This afternoon there is another problem: The skies are low and black, and raindrops, big and wet, begin to pelt us. My friends and I begin to run. There is thunder and lightning. We run faster. A bright flash lights up the ground. The thunder sounds like a bomb. My companion and I look back. Our girlfriend is not there. We see orange flames on the ground. A black thing is burning. We rush back. The remains of my friend's clothes are afire on a body that has been charred black. Her eyes are empty sockets and her tongue sticks grotesquely out of her mouth. For a moment I stand and stare in horror and disbelief. Then I turn and run. Some boys have come upon the scene, but I pass them without stopping.

I run all the way home. I have never known such fear. When I get to my grandmother's mud-brick house, the door is closed. I do not slow down or even notice. I knock the door down! I am going so fast that the door on its old hinges falls down when I strike it. Below me, lying on a mat on the floor, is my older sister Mizpah. She is covered with blood. Sweaty strands of hair fall over her face as she looks at me, too exhausted to speak. I am so terrified I cannot talk or even scream. A woman I do not know is here. A squirming, newborn baby is in her arms. The woman is a midwife. My sister has just given birth. The world has lost a life and has gained a life almost at the same moment. I have witnessed both. But the shocks are too great. Beside myself, I collapse. The boys who also witnessed the tragedy on the road appear and explain the reason for my delirium.

When clouds gather outside my window in the morning, I fear a rainstorm. My grandmother pampers me by letting me stay home from school when I tell her I have a headache. But there is something I have discovered at the all-black school that makes me overcome my terror of lightning. It is the senior chorus.

When she was in school, my sister Mizpah was a member, and I used to sneak into the school's little square auditorium after classes to listen. I liked the way the boys and girls were lined up on the stage, where the flag of the South African colony is posted on one side and the Union Jack is on the other. Whenever the teachers caught me peeking out from behind the seats, they threw me out. I was easy to find because I always sang along. Mizpah told me I shouldn't embarrass her, but I could not keep away. This senior chorus is much finer than the church choir that I was in. Listening to them, I got so stirred up inside that I had to sing along.

The teacher who leads the chorus is named Mr Molefe. He is very dark, and his large hands cut through the air as he conducts the music. It was a scary moment for me when those hands stopped conducting, and Mr Molefe turned and searched the auditorium to find the little voice that was singing behind him.

'You, there, little girl! What is your name?'

'Zenzi.' My voice is very soft and shy when I am not singing.

'You look too young to be a senior.'

'No, sir. I'm not even a junior.'

There was some tittering from the big girls. My sister gave me a dirty look. I guess she was thinking to whoop me.

Mr Molefe smiled at me. 'How would you like to join us?'

I did not know what he meant. 'Huh?'

'How would you like to sing with us? You can't seem to keep quiet down there. You might as well be on stage.'

I couldn't believe it. I got up and stood on the stage where he placed me. I looked like a skinny, big-headed midget surrounded by the big girls with their long legs and full chests.

Now Mr Molefe uses me as a surprise attraction. A novelty. During rehearsals he tells me I really sing well. All I know is I enjoy it. We go to competitions with other schools. We perform songs written by South African composers. They are in the tribal languages, and some are frankly seditious to the white rule. But since whites do not speak our tongue, we get away with it.

As a black child, just attending school is almost an act of sedition. Education is considered 'bad' for us, or, at best, unnecessary. The natives have been assigned the roles of servants to our colonial masters. We are not taught geometry because we will not be given a chance to use it. We are not taught geology. The less we know about the outside world the better. We are to live in isolation.

There is a child's book called *Black Beauty*. It is banned. The authorities do not read the book, so they do not know that it is about a horse. They think it is about racial pride!

What we are taught is the culture and history of England. Of our own tribal histories, there is nothing. Of the arts and accomplishments of our own people, not a word. We learn of Winston Churchill. I am told that he is a great statesman, and I believe that he is: for England, if not for us. I am told that Franklin Roosevelt is a great statesman. For America, we know he is, but not for us. The teachers talk a lot about Hitler. They say that if he ever gets to us he is going to make lamp shades out of our skin. I don't know why he is mad at us, because he is at war with England, and South Africa is just a colony, and, besides, what do we natives have to do with the colonial government here? But I do not want to have a lamp shade made from my skin.

We also hear of Mahatma Gandhi. He is making trouble for the British in India, but never to mind that, we are to study his message of pacifism. The authorities want us to be nonviolent, too.

I do not understand the war. I am only seven when it begins, and it is very far away. I'll be a teenager when it is over. My people have no rights in a country that has been taken from us, but we are still forced to die for it. My uncles are drafted into the army. Many of my friends' fathers leave. A long time passes, and some return to tell of fighting in North Africa. They return sick with malaria. At least they are alive. Two of my uncles never return. Their bodies are not shipped home for burial. We never see them again. The authorities do not let us live in dignity, and they do not let us die with dignity. No one can say that the British are not consistent.

It is illegal for a black to own a shortwave radio. We might hear things from the outside world that we should not, like how other people in totalitarian states are rising up against their oppressors. If you can afford one, you can have a regular radio, and listen all day to syrupy white-people's music and censored newscasts. There are two sets of newspapers: the ones for the whites and the ones for us. The authorities control the content of the black press, although natives staff the editorial positions. There are collaborators throughout black South Africa: rich people who grow fat off the sufferings of their brothers, and the strong men who are betrayed by a lack of opportunity and must find work in the police forces. And there are the spies and informers. Informers are discovered all the time amongst us. If they are lucky, they are beaten. If they are not lucky, they die.

I open up a black newspaper and look at the fantasy inside. Nothing is connected with real life. There are stories about witches casting spells on people. Every crime committed by a black is played up. The advertisements tell us that we are ugly, and the only way to obtain true beauty is to try to become as much like a white as possible. We are encouraged to conk our hair to make it straight. The ads for chemicals to bleach our skin fill a page.

The whites have to justify their rape of our land, and so they claim that we are inferior. We are not worthy of God's gifts. It says so in their Bible. They lay claim to our land and our lives and then, to add insult to injury, they patronize us. They say we are ignorant children. Our salvation and welfare are – alas! – 'the white man's burden.'

And after a while a terrible thing happens. For many of my people, the message begins to sink in. Day after day we are treated like dirt and told we are inferior. It is drummed into our heads. First, your self-respect disappears. You begin to hate everything that is black. The white culture is full of references to things that are black and evil. We are told not to let a black cat cross our path. With the war, there has come a thing called the black market, where money is traded illegally. But what black person ever heard of money before the white man came?

When you begin to hate yourself, you look at someone who is in your own image and you don't have any love for him, either. The streets in our township at night erupt with violent fights. Young people stab each other, kill each other. 'Why do you look at me like that?' a boy will shout, and then, stab! I see a knife fight almost every day. The authorities do nothing. They encourage this division among us. On weekends and at Christmastime the ghetto becomes a slaughterhouse. People kill each other, and the authorities say, 'Oh, it's just holiday drunkenness.' This way the authorities don't have to do anything. If someone wants to kill you, they just wait until a holiday, because they know they won't be prosecuted. Kill a dog or a bird in a protected area and you go to jail. Kill a white man and you hang. But kill a black man, it's all right.

I, too, fall victim to envy. You would have to be blind not to see that everything that is better or even good goes to the whites. You cannot help but think: I wish I was white so I might live well and not suffer the way I do. But if I am envious of white people as a little girl, I am only envious of the way they live. I do not want to *be* white. I will never bleach my skin, although I am dark. I will not straighten my hair. As time passes I begin to discover something about myself: I am not bad-looking. As my body grows, my head becomes more proportional. My mother says that I am pretty. Mothers are supposed to say that. But there are boys, certain boys, who also say I am cute. By the time I am a teenager I begin to believe them.

I don't have many girlfriends. Most of my friends, my best friends, are boys. I feel at ease with boys. They don't gossip like girls do. We go out to the field and fly kites. We talk about everything. They tell me about their girlfriends. I do have some girlfriends, and I get together with them every Sunday to play jazz records from America. We meet at somebody's house, make food, and sit for hours listening to Ella Fitzgerald and Billie Holliday on the wind-up record player. I like them a lot, these great jazz singers. My big brother, Joseph, gives me his records to bring. He is very musical himself. He plays soprano saxophone and piano. Joseph encourages me to sing. He taught me American songs before I even knew the language. When his friends come over he has me sing for them. Sometimes I don't even know what I am saying, but I put all I have into it.

... a man is a two-face:
a worrisome thing
who'll leave you to sing
the blues in the night!

Joseph is proud of me. His friends applaud.

When I am with boys whom I like I grow aware for the first time of how poor I am. When I was younger I didn't care if I had to go to school without shoes. But now I am embarrassed because the other girls have shoes and I don't. My mother buys me a pair, but I have to save these for Sunday to go to church. These are difficult days for my mother. Her work is not getting easier. I try not to complain. My older sister Hilda, who is my favourite, helps me. Usually I wear hand-me-down clothes. Hilda makes me some new dresses of my very own.

The World War comes to an end. Nothing changes for us, except that my uncles who are still alive come home. All the black war veterans have been promised pensions. The promises are not kept. Instead, each man is given ten pounds – and a bicycle ...

Miriam Makeba, one of the most renowned musical performers to ever come out of South Africa, and the first South African to win a Grammy Award, was born in Johannesburg in 1932. She first came to the public's attention when she performed with the Manhattan Brothers, then toured southern Africa with Alf Herberts' *African Jazz and Variety*. She was forced into exile in 1960 after the release of an anti-apartheid documentary in which she featured called *Come back Africa*. She went to America where she was invited to sing at President Kennedy's birthday party, and worked in New York with noted musician Harry Belafonte. She also testified to the United Nations about apartheid, leading to her records being banned in South Africa. After marrying a leader of the Black Panthers, she was harassed by the US government, and her concerts and recording contract were cancelled. Makeba and her husband moved to Guinea, and she later returned to prominence when she performed with Paul Simon on the *Graceland* tour. After the release of Nelson Mandela from prison, she returned to her homeland as a free South African.
Book Extracted: *Makeba: My Story* (Skotaville, Johannesburg, 1988)

My Traitor's Heart
Rian Malan

… We lived in the city, but every year or so we'd go on a pilgrimage into the heartland, into Afrikanerdom. It started in Calvinia, where my grandmother, the widow of Stephanus Jacobus, lived in an old-age home. My father had converted her from a SAP to Nat, and she became a party stalwart in her old age, always turning out to flip pancakes for the apartheid-supporting faithful at National Party rallies. She was a nice old lady. She smothered me in the lavender-smelling folds of her huge bosom and pressed treats on me – pancakes with cinnamon and sugar, and *koeksisters*, twists of deep-fried dough saturated with golden syrup.

From Calvinia we trekked south to the Sandveld, where my Uncle Ben farmed sheep on the shore of a cold gray sea. It was a barren and lonely place, the Sandveld, charged with an ominous and forbidding power. Ben's farmhouse stood all alone in a desolate, dun-gray landscape, shuttered against the harsh light, the heat and drifting sand. The house was dark and gloomy inside, the heavy Victorian furniture sinister under dust drapes never removed unless the Calvinist *dominee* was due to visit. At dusk, an old crone in a long black dress came hobbling across the sand dunes to fetch food at the kitchen door. She was a *bywoner*, one of Ben's white vassals, too old to work now and living out her life as the master's pensioner. Her name was Tannie Jeanette, and she terrified me. She had hairy warts on her face and a hunchback, and I took her for a witch. She once bought a portable radio from the Jewish peddler who made the rounds of those lonely farms. When the peddler returned, months later, Tannie Jeanette tried to claw his eyes out, claiming he'd sold her a radio that spoke only English. She had never owned a radio before. She didn't know it could be tuned.

There was an Afrikaner for you. Almost all of us were that way, three or four generations ago. In fact, everyone on Ben's farm was a throwback in some sense or other. The Mongolian cheekbones of the brown-skinned shepherds recalled the Hottentots, a race long extinct. Ben's speech was haunted by the *brei* – a roll of the *r* that harked back to French, a language unspoken in South Africa for almost two centuries, and his white *bywoners* spoke an archaic dialect called High Dutch.

Indeed, the *bywoners* themselves were archaic. There were three of them in all, Tannie Jeanette and men named Nic and Evert. They were unlike any other whites I had ever met, standing in virtually the same feudal relation to their master as the brown shepherds. They lived in bare rooms whose whitewashed walls were hung with the skins of trapped animals. The men often went barefoot, wore beards that hung to their chests, and sawed through the throats of kicking sheep on a bluegum stump in the yard of the farmhouse. They were the last of their kind, but then Ben's way of life was dying, too. It seldom rained on the Sandveld, so he drank from a brackish well. His wife cooked on one of those old cast-iron stoves with balled claw feet and lighted her house with paraffin lamps. At night, they slept under karosses made of jackal skins.

I think Uncle Ben was happy in the nineteenth century, but his wife Millicent aspired to better. She wanted tiled bathrooms, pop-up toasters, eye-level electric ovens and other trappings of white civilization. She was my father's youngest sister, and very beautiful, with raven hair and skin as dark as a Spaniard's. She was stern, pious and prone to fits of shrieking: at children, at Ben, at the ragged colored girls who slaved over the cast-iron stove in her kitchen. Ben, on the other hand, was a quiet, goodnatured fellow. He smoked a pipe and wore khaki shorts. There were lines around his eyes from squinting at the sun, and he seldom felt the urge to speak.

His farm was big and trackless, and he traveled it in a prototypical beach buggy, an old car stripped down to its engine and steel skeleton. It took half a day to cross the farm, and Ben always brought his rifle along in case he saw a buck for the pot, or a lynx; the lynx took lambs, so he shot them on sight. In the far corner of his land there lay a *vlei*, a marsh that was home to one of Africa's largest breeding colonies of flamingo. As we drew near, the sound of the engine startled the birds into flight, and there would be streaks of pink and gray across the sky, as if the sun was rising at noon.

At day's end, we drove over the sand dunes to watch the gray-green Atlantic breakers rolling onto a lonely, windswept beach. There was always a gale on that beach. It picked up sand and blasted it at your legs, and it stung so sharply it made you want to cry. Sometimes a defenseforce Shackleton flew by at rooftop height, patrolling against the Russians. Ben knew they were out there, lurking, because a Russian lifejacket had once washed ashore on the beach. The Russians were the enemy. That was already known. Ben's only son grew up to be a professional soldier, and went off to fight Russia's Cuban surrogates in darkest Africa. His daughter also joined the army, and married a very famous South African soldier indeed – Captain Wynand du Toit, shot and captured by Cubans in 1985 while trying to blow up Gulf Oil's installations in Angola.

When we returned to the farmhouse in the evening, the brown shepherds would be lined up in the courtyard, tin beakers in their hands, waiting for their 'tot'– their daily ration of *vaaljapie*, a crude white wine that came from a town two hours' drive to the south. Ben kept the stuff in a stack of leaky old barrels, in a room where the sandy floor had remained damp with wine for generations. As the door of the wine room swung open, the pungent smell of *vaaljapie* permeated the yard, and everyone's mood seemed to lighten. The tired shepherds drew their daily tumblerful and settled down along the walls of the barn, talking softly. Sometimes I sat with them. The wall at my back was still warm from the sun, golden dust hung in the air, and the evening was filled with the heady fragrance of cheap wine. It was the best time of day on that farm. When I went back twenty years later, the farmhouse was empty and abandoned, its shutters flapping in the wind. Ben was dead, his wife had moved into a condo, and all the *bywoners* and brown shepherds had vanished. But I picked up a handful of dust in the old wine room, and it still smelled of *vaaljapie*.

From the Sandveld we travelled inland to Nieuwoudtville, home of Tannie Aletta, my father's elder sister. Her husband, Jooste, was a sergeant in the South African Police. They lived in the stone police station. When we visited, they put us in the whites-only section of the adjoining jailhouse, where we slept under rough blankets on bare wooden bunks. This seemed very exciting to me. I shivered deliciously at the thought that my bunk might once have harbored a murderer or bank robber. I once asked my aunt if this was at all likely. 'Oh no,' she said, 'it's very quiet here. There has never been a murder here. It's only the coloreds who kill each other.'

Nieuwoudtville lay within the Bokkeveld Mountains, high and dry and sometimes very cold at night. Through the barred window of my cell, I saw a dusty street, a post office, a general-dealer store, a church, and distant mountains. The town was a speck in a vast ocean of arid scrub and dust. Its emptiness was frightening. Even more frightening were my cousins, tough little fellows with brush-cut hair who ran barefoot over thorns and played rugby to maim on fields of dust and stone. They called me *Rooi Jan*, or Red Rian, a play on my name that embodied a scornful reference to the Boer term for a foreigner who turned pink and peeling in the blazing African sun. They were barbaric little tribesmen, those cousins of mine. I was always relieved when we moved south to Clanwilliam, where my uncle Etienne taught farmers' sons in the village boarding school.

My uncle Etienne was a gregarious fellow, darkly handsome, with a flashing gold tooth in his easy smile. Decades later, I opened a book called *The Super Afrikaners* and discovered his name in it. In fact, both my father's brothers were in it. They were both *Broederbonders*, members of the Brotherhood, the secret society of Calvinists and apartheid zealots that constituted the spine of the Afrikaner power structure. The prime minister, his cabinet, most Afrikaner MPs, and all senior civil servants were Brothers. The Brotherhood's invisible hand controlled the state broadcasting corporation, the censor board, the police, the education system, and probably the army too. The Brotherhood was a sinister organisation, ruthlessly dedicated to the aggrandizement of Afrikaner power and the imposition of doctrinal purity on South African minds.

Even in retrospect, my Oom Etienne seems a most unlikely Brother. He had none of the trappings – no Mercedes Benz with tinted windows, no lucrative government contracts, and no secret bank accounts bulging with the profits from crooked land deals, at least as far as I know. My Oom Etienne even had a sense of humour, not a quality for which Brothers were known. He owned a movie projector, and when we visited, he'd show us Laurel and Hardy shorts or Al Debbo's lunatic Boer farces. He had a Wagnerian passion for rugby, but as for apartheid, I never heard him mention the word.

And that was Afrikanerdom for me. Those pilgrimages marked me, to be sure, but they were not enough to make me a true Afrikaner. Even my father failed in that. I was always sceptical or disdainful of those things that lay closest to the Afrikaner heart. I used to stare up into the eaves of the church while the *dominee* droned on, wondering how on earth God tolerated such boredom. I flinched when the brush-cut Boerboys came in for the tackle, and struggled to breathe in the oppressive Calvinist atmosphere of their homes. I was intimidated by the immensity of the landscapes in which they lived, and horrified when they shot wild animals out there.

Once, crossing Ben's farm in his buggy, we flushed an aardvark on the sun-blackened plain. Aardvark were harmless and inedible, but Ben was tired of breaking axles in their burrows, so he gave chase. The creature disappeared down a hole in the ground. Ben leapt from the buggy, rifle in hand. The aardvark was trying frantically to dig its way out of sight. Ben put a bullet or two into its scrambling hindquarters before it dragged itself around a bend. He shrugged and climbed back in the buggy, but I was traumatised for weeks by the thought of that wounded creature, dying slowly in its dark tomb. It was an unworthy reaction for a Boer, but I was never much of a Boer anyway.

I didn't even enjoy playing war with my brush-cut cousins. They always wanted to play Boer War, and stalk imaginary British invaders around the outbuildings and barns of various farms. It seemed a stupid and backward game to me. I came from Johannesburg, you see, and my imagination had already been colonized by foreign influences. In Jo'burg, we always fought the Japs or Jerries, like the heroes in Hollywood movies or imported war comics.

Johannesburg lay in Africa, but that was more or less incidental. Johannesburg had skyscrapers, smart department stores, cinemas, and theatres. It was part of a larger world. There was no TV in my boyhood, because the Brotherhood feared it would cause what Mao termed 'spiritual pollution'. We had radio, though, and all the characters in the boys' serials were British or American. Randy Stone was the night-beat reporter in an American city. Ricky Roper, the Sunrise Toffee Junior Detective, lived in an ambiguous someplace where everyone had BBC accents. Chuck drove a cab in Brooklyn. Mark Saxon came from outer space, but even his world seemed more immediate than Afrikanerdom to me.

I mean, I didn't realise *Reader's Digest* was a foreign magazine until I was at least ten. I have no recollection at all of the Sharpeville massacre, in which sixty-nine black people were shot dead while protesting against the pass laws; only the vaguest memory of Nelson Mandela's trial and jailing. I remember the day John F. Kennedy died, though. It was a Saturday morning in South Africa. I was helping my father in the garden when Mrs Pretorius came scurrying across the street to say President Kennedy had been shot. She'd just heard it on the radio. My mother gasped, clasped her hand over her mouth and said, 'Shame.' My Afrikaner father shook his head regretfully.

Even he was somehow detribalized – by education, by urbanization, maybe just by inclination; all that was left in him of the mythic Afrikaner was the peasant cast of his features and an instinctive desire to plant things. He was an Afrikaner Nationalist and a supporter of apartheid, but above all he was a personnel manager, and his overriding preoccupations were insurance, the mortgage, the garden, the car, the family, and the job. The shelves of his study were lined with American tomes on management and motivation. He even bought *I'm O.K., You're O.K.*, thinking it might be useful in his line of work. He subscribed to *Die Huisgenoot*, to be sure, but he also got *Time* and *Life* and *National Geographic*. Those American magazines brought news of a world that seemed infinitely more alluring than my own – a world where people a few years older than me were growing their hair long, smoking dope, and rioting in the streets.

In 1967 or thereabouts, *Life* carried a story about a Frenchman named Regis Debray who went off to Bolivia with one Che Guevara. Their mission was to help oppressed Indians in their fight for freedom. I gathered from the text that Che was a disreputable something called Communist, but he cut a pretty dashing figure in the pictures, with his long black hair, combat boots, beard, and beret. I thought, whoa, Communism, that's for me. The plight of Bolivia's Indians seemed rather similar to the wretched lot of the blacks in my own backyard, so I put two and two together, and bingo, I was the Just White Man, champion of the downtrodden, sworn foe of racism, and ardent proponent of Communism, whatever that was supposed to be.

No, that's not all there was to it; there was more to it than that. I'd better go back to the beginning and see if I can dredge it up.

Rian Malan, the grand nephew of the former Prime Minister of South Africa and architect of apartheid Daniel Malan, was born in Johannesburg in 1954. Rian Malan fled his homeland in 1977 in order to avoid compulsory military service. Describing why, he said he '... would not carry a gun for apartheid, and would not carry a gun against it.' He went to Los Angeles where he worked as a writer, returning to South Africa eight years later, where he now works as a journalist.
Book Extracted: *My Traitor's Heart* (The Bodley Head, 1990)

Long Walk To Freedom –
The Autobiography of Nelson Mandela

The village of Qunu was situated in a narrow, grassy valley crisscrossed by clear streams, and overlooked by green hills. It consisted of no more than a few hundred people who lived in huts, which were beehive-shaped structures of mud walls, with a wooden pole in the centre holding up a peaked grass roof. The floor was made of crushed ant-heap, the hard dome of excavated earth above an ant colony, and was kept smooth by smearing it regularly with fresh cow dung. The smoke from the hearth escaped through the roof, and the only opening was a low doorway one had to stoop to walk through. The huts were generally grouped in a residential area that was some distance away from the maize fields. There were no roads, only paths through the grass worn away by barefooted boys and women. The women and children of the village wore blankets dyed in ochre; only the few Christians in the village wore Western-style clothing. Cattle, sheep, goats and horses grazed together in common pastures. The land around Qunu was mostly treeless except for a cluster of poplars on a hill overlooking the village. The land itself was owned by the state. With very few exceptions, Africans at that time did not enjoy private title to land in South Africa but were tenants paying rent annually to the government. In the area, there were two small primary schools, a general store, and a dipping tank to rid the cattle of ticks and diseases.

Maize (what we called mealies and people in the West call corn), sorghum, beans and pumpkins formed the largest portion of our diet, not because of any inherent preference for these foods, but because the people could not afford anything richer. The wealthier families in our village supplemented their diets with tea, coffee and sugar, but for most people in Qunu these were exotic luxuries far beyond their means. The water used for farming, cooking and washing had to be fetched in buckets from streams and springs. This was women's work and, indeed, Qunu was a village of women and children: most of the men spent the greater part of the year working on remote farms or in the mines along the Reef, the great ridge of gold-bearing rock and shale that forms the southern boundary of Johannesburg. They returned perhaps twice a year, mainly to plough their fields. The hoeing, weeding and harvesting were left to the women and children. Few if any of the people in the village knew how to read or write, and the concept of education was still a foreign one to many.

My mother presided over three huts at Qunu which, as I remember, were always filled with the babies and children of my relations. In fact, I hardly recall any occasion as a child when I was alone. In African culture, the sons and daughters of one's aunts or uncles are considered brothers and sisters, not cousins. We do not make the same distinctions among relations practised by whites. We have no half-brothers or half-sisters. My mother's sister is my mother; my uncle's son is my brother; my brother's child is my son, my daughter.

Of my mother's three huts, one was used for cooking, one for sleeping and one for storage. In the hut in which we slept, there was no furniture in the Western sense. We slept on mats and sat on the ground. I did not discover pillows until I went to Mqhekezweni. My mother cooked food in a three-legged iron pot over an open fire in the centre of the hut or outside. Everything we ate we grew and made ourselves. My mother planted and harvested her own mealies. Mealies were harvested from the field when they were hard and dry. They were stored in sacks or pits dug in the ground. When preparing the mealies, the women used different methods. They could ground the kernels between two stones to make bread, or boil the mealies first, producing *umphothulo* (mealie flour eaten with sour milk) or *umngqusho* (samp, sometimes plain or mixed with beans). Unlike mealies, which were sometimes in short supply, milk from our cows and goats was always plentiful.

From an early age, I spent most of my free time in the veld playing and fighting with the other boys of the village. A boy who remained at home tied to his mother's apron strings was regarded as a sissy. At night, I shared my food and blanket with these same boys. I was no more than five when I became a herd-boy looking after sheep and calves in the fields. I discovered the almost mystical attachment that the Xhosa have for cattle, not only as a source of food and wealth, but as a blessing from God and a source of happiness. It was in the fields that I learned how to knock birds out of the sky with a slingshot, to gather wild honey and fruits and edible roots, to drink warm, sweet milk straight from the udder of a cow, to swim in the clear, cold streams, and to catch fish with twine and sharpened bits of wire. I learned to stick-fight – essential knowledge to any rural African boy – and became adept at its various techniques, parrying blows, feinting in one direction and striking in another, breaking away from an opponent with quick footwork. From these days I date my love of the veld, of open spaces, the simple beauties of nature, the clean line of the horizon.

As boys, we were mostly left to our own devices. We played with toys we made ourselves. We moulded animals and birds out of clay. We made ox-drawn sledges out of tree branches. Nature was our playground.

The hills above Qunu were dotted with large smooth rocks which we transformed into our own roller-coaster. We sat on flat stones and slid down the face of the large rocks. We did this until our backsides were so sore we could hardly sit down. I learned to ride by sitting atop weaned calves – after being thrown to the ground several times, one got the hang of it.

I learned my lesson one day from an unruly donkey. We had been taking turns climbing up and down its back and when my chance came I jumped on and the donkey bolted into a nearby thornbush. It bent its head, trying to unseat me, which it did, but not before the thorns had pricked and scratched my face, embarrassing me in front of my friends. Like the people of the East, Africans have a highly developed sense of dignity, or what the Chinese call 'face'. I had lost face among my friends. Even though it was a donkey that unseated me, I learned that to humiliate another person is to make him suffer an unnecessarily cruel fate. Even as a boy, I defeated my opponents without dishonouring them.

Usually the boys played among themselves, but we sometimes allowed our sisters to join us. Boys and girls would play games like *ndize* (hide and seek) and *icekwa* (tag). But the game I most enjoyed playing with the girls was what we called *khetha*, or choose-the-one-you-like. This was not so much an organized game, but a spur-of-the-moment sport that took place when we accosted a group of girls our own age and demanded that each select the boy she loved. Our rules dictated that the girl's choice be respected and once she had chosen her favourite, she was free to continue on her journey escorted by the lucky boy she loved. But the girls were nimble-witted – far cleverer than we doltish lads – and would often confer among themselves and choose one boy, usually the plainest fellow, and then tease him all the way home.

The most popular game for boys was *thinti*, and like most boys' games it was a youthful approximation of war. Two sticks, used as targets, would be driven firmly into the ground in an upright position about a hundred feet apart. The goal of the game was for each team to hurl sticks at the opposing target and knock it down. We each defended our own target and attempted to prevent the other side from retrieving the sticks that had been thrown over. As we grew older, we organized matches against boys from neighbouring villages and those who distinguished themselves in these fraternal battles were greatly admired, as generals who achieve great victories in war are justly celebrated.

After games such as these, I would return to my mother's kraal where she was preparing supper. Whereas my father once told stories of historic battles and heroic Xhosa warriors, my mother would enchant us with Xhosa legends and fables that had come down from numberless generations. These tales stimulated my childish imagination, and usually contained some moral lesson. I recall one my mother told us about a traveller who was approached by an old woman with terrible cataracts on her eyes. The woman asked the traveller for help, and the man averted his eyes. Then another man came along and was approached by the old woman. She asked him to clean her eyes, and even though he found the task unpleasant, he did as she asked. Then, miraculously, the scales fell from the old woman's eyes and she became young and beautiful. The man married her and became wealthy and prosperous. It is a simple tale, but its message is an enduring one: virtue and generosity will be rewarded in ways that one cannot know.

Like all Xhosa children, I acquired knowledge mainly through observation. We were meant to learn through imitation and emulation, not through questions. When I first visited the homes of whites, I was often dumbfounded by the number and nature of questions that children asked their parents – and their parents' unfailing willingness to answer them. In my household, questions were considered a nuisance; adults imparted such information as they considered necessary.

My life, and that of most Xhosas at the time, was shaped by custom, ritual and taboo. This was the alpha and omega of our existence, and went unquestioned. Men followed the path laid out for them by their fathers; women led the same lives as their mothers had before them. Without being told, I soon assimilated the elaborate rules that governed the relations between men and women. I discovered that a man may not enter a house where a woman has recently given birth, and that a newly married woman would not enter the kraal of her new home without elaborate ceremony. I also learned that to neglect one's ancestors would bring ill-fortune and failure in life. If you dishonoured your ancestors in some way, the only way to atone for that lapse was to consult a traditional healer or tribal elder, who communicated with the ancestors and conveyed profound apologies. All of these beliefs were perfectly natural to me.

I came across few whites as a boy at Qunu. The local magistrate, of course, was white, as was the nearest shopkeeper. Occasionally white travellers or policemen passed through our area. These whites appeared as grand as gods to me, and I was aware that they were to be treated with a mixture of fear and respect. But their role in my life was a distant one, and I thought little if at all about the white man in general or relations between my own people and these curious and remote figures.

The only rivalry between different clans or tribes in our small world at Qunu was that between the Xhosas and the amaMfengu, a small number of whom lived in our village. AmaMfengu arrived in the eastern

Cape after fleeing from Shaka Zulu's armies in a period known as the iMfecane, the great wave of battles and migrations between 1820 and 1840 set in motion by the rise of Shaka and the Zulu state, during which the Zulu warrior sought to conquer and then unite all the tribes under military rule. The amaMfengu, who were not originally Xhosa-speakers, were refugees from the iMfecane and were forced to do jobs that no other African would do. They worked on white farms and in white businesses, something that was looked down upon by the more established Xhosa tribes. But the amaMfengu were an industrious people, and because of their contact with Europeans, they were often more educated and 'Western' than other Africans.

When I was a boy, the amaMfengu were the most advanced section of the community and furnished our clergymen, policemen, teachers, clerks and interpreters. They were also among the first to become Christians, to build better houses and to use scientific methods of agriculture, and they were wealthier than their Xhosa compatriots. They confirmed the missionaries' axiom, that to be Christian was to be civilized, and to be civilized was to be Christian. There still existed some hostility towards the amaMfengu, but in retrospect I would attribute this more to jealousy than tribal animosity. This local form of tribalism that I observed as a boy was relatively harmless. At this stage, I did not witness nor even suspect the violent tribal rivalries that would subsequently be promoted by the white rulers of South Africa.

My father did not subscribe to the local prejudice towards the amaMfengu and befriended two amaMfengu brothers, George and Ben Mbekela. The brothers were an exception in Qunu: they were educated and Christian. George, the elder, was a retired teacher and Ben was a police sergeant. Despite the proselytising of the Mbekela brothers, my father remained aloof from Christianity and instead reserved his own faith for the great spirit of the Xhosas, Qamata, the God of his fathers. My father was an unofficial priest and presided over ritual slaughtering of goats and calves and officiated at local traditional rites concerning planting, harvest, birth, marriage, initiation ceremonies and funerals. He did not need to be ordained, for the traditional religion of the Xhosas is characterized by a cosmic wholeness, so that there is little distinction between the sacred and the secular, between the natural and the supernatural.

While the faith of the Mbekela brothers did not rub off on my father, it did inspire my mother, who became a Christian. In fact, Fanny was literally her Christian name, for she had been given it in church. It was due to the influence of the Mbekela brothers that I myself was baptized into the Methodist, or Wesleyan Church as it was then known, and sent to school. The brothers would often see me playing or minding sheep and come over to talk to me. One day, George Mbekela paid a visit to my mother. 'Your son is a clever young fellow,' he said. 'He should go to school.' My mother remained silent. No one in my family had ever attended school and my mother was unprepared for Mbekela's suggestion. But she did relay it to my father who, despite – or perhaps because of – his own lack of education, immediately decided that his youngest son should go to school.

The schoolhouse consisted of a single room, with a Western-style roof, on the other side of the hill from Qunu. I was seven years old, and on the day before I was to begin, my father took me aside and told me that I must be dressed properly for school. Until that time, I, like all the other boys in Qunu, had worn only a blanket, which was wrapped round one shoulder and pinned at the waist. My father took a pair of his trousers and cut them at the knee. He told me to put them on, which I did, and they were roughly the correct length, although the waist was far too large. My father then took a piece of string and drew the trousers in at the waist. I must have been a comical sight, but I have never owned a suit I was prouder to wear than my father's cut-off trousers.

On the first day of school my teacher, Miss Mdingane, gave each of us an English name and said that thenceforth that was the name we would answer to in school. This was the custom among Africans in those days and undoubtedly was due to the British bias of our education. The education I received was a British education, in which British ideas, British culture and British institutions were automatically assumed to be superior. There was no such thing as African culture.

Africans of my generation – and even today – generally have both a Western and an African name. Whites were either unable or unwilling to pronounce an African name, and considered it uncivilized to have one. That day, Miss Mdingane told me that my new name was Nelson. Why she bestowed this particular name upon me I have no idea. Perhaps it had something to do with the great British sea captain Lord Nelson, but that would be only a guess.

One night, when I was nine years old, I was aware of a commotion in the household. My father, who took turns visiting his wives and usually came to us for perhaps one week a month, had arrived. But it was not at his accustomed time, for he was not scheduled to be with us for another few days. I found him in my mother's hut, lying on his back on the floor, in the midst of what seemed like an endless fit of coughing. Even to my young eyes, it was clear that my father was not long for this world. He was ill with some type of lung disease, but it was not diagnosed, as my father had never visited a doctor. He remained in the hut for several days without moving or speaking, and then one night he took a turn for the worse. My mother and my father's youngest wife, Nodayimani, who had come to stay with us, were looking after him, and late that night he called for Nodayimani. 'Bring me my tobacco,' he told her. My mother and Nodayimani conferred, and decided that it was unwise that he have tobacco in his current state. But he persisted in calling for it, and eventually Nodayimani filled his pipe, lit it, and then handed it to him. My father smoked and became calm. He continued smoking for perhaps an hour, and then, his pipe still lit, he died.

I do not remember experiencing great grief so much as feeling cut adrift. Although my mother was the centre of my existence, I defined myself through my father. My father's passing changed my whole life in a way that I did not suspect at the time. After a brief period of mourning, my mother informed me that I would be leaving Qunu. I did not ask her why, or where I was going.

I packed the few things that I possessed and early one morning we set out on a journey westward to my new residence. I mourned less for my father than for the world I was leaving behind. Qunu was all that I knew, and I loved it in the unconditional way that a child loves his first home. Before we disappeared behind the hills, I turned and looked for what I imagined was the last time at my village. I could see the simple huts and the people going about their chores; the stream where I had splashed and played with the other boys; the maize fields and green pastures where the herds and flocks were lazily grazing. I imagined my friends out hunting for small birds, drinking the sweet milk from the cow's udder, cavorting in the pond at the end of the stream. Above all else, my eyes rested on the three simple huts where I had enjoyed my mother's love and protection. It was these three huts that I associated with all my happiness, with life itself, and I rued the fact that I had not kissed each of them before I left. I could not imagine that the future I was walking towards could compare in any way with the past that I was leaving behind.

We travelled by foot and in silence until the sun was sinking slowly towards the horizon. But the silence of the heart between mother and child is not a lonely one. My mother and I never talked very much, but we did not need to. I never doubted her love or questioned her support. It was an exhausting journey, along rocky dirt roads, up and down hills, past numerous villages, but we did not pause. Late in the afternoon, at the bottom of a shallow valley surrounded by trees, we came upon a village at the centre of which was a large and gracious home that so far exceeded anything that I had ever seen that all I could do was marvel at it. The buildings consisted of two *iingxande* (or rectangular houses) and seven stately rondavels (superior huts), all washed in white lime, dazzling even in the light of the setting sun. There was a large front garden and a maize field bordered by rounded peach trees. An even more spacious garden spread out behind it, which boasted apple trees, a vegetable garden, a strip of flowers and a patch of wattles. Nearby was a white stucco church.

In the shade of two gum trees that graced the doorway of the front of the main house sat a group of about twenty tribal elders. Encircling the property, contentedly grazing on the rich land, was a herd of at least fifty cattle and perhaps five hundred sheep. Everything was beautifully tended, and it was a vision of wealth and order beyond my imagination. This was the Great Place, Mqhekezweni, the provisional capital of Thembuland, the royal residence of Chief Jongintaba Dalindyebo, acting regent of the Thembu people.

As I contemplated all this grandeur an enormous motor car rumbled through the western gate and the men sitting in the shade immediately doffed their hats and then jumped to their feet shouting, '*Bayete a-a-a, Jongintaba!*' ('Hail, Jongintaba!'), the traditional salute of the Xhosas for their chief. Out of the motor car (I learned later that this majestic vehicle was a Ford V8) stepped a short, thickset man wearing a smart suit. I could see that he had the confidence and bearing of a man who was used to the exercise of authority. His name suited him, for Jongintaba literally means 'One who looks at the mountains', and he was a man with a sturdy presence upon whom all eyes gazed. He had a dark complexion and an intelligent face, and he casually shook hands with each of the men beneath the tree, men who as I later discovered comprised the highest Thembu Court of Justice. This was the regent who was to become my guardian and benefactor for the next decade.

In that moment of beholding Jongintaba and his court I felt like a sapling pulled root and branch from the earth and flung into the centre of a stream whose strong current I could not resist. I felt a sense of awe mixed with bewilderment. Until then I had had no thoughts of anything but my own pleasures, no higher ambition than to eat well and become a champion stick-fighter. I had no thought of money, or class, or fame, or power. Suddenly a new world opened before me. Children from poor homes often find themselves beguiled by a host of new temptations when suddenly confronted by great wealth. I was no exception. I felt many of my established beliefs and loyalties begin to ebb away. The slender foundation built by my parents began to shake. In that instant, I saw that life might hold more for me than being a champion stick-fighter ...

Nelson Mandela, born in the Transkei on the 18th of July in 1918, is one of the most influential political figures of the 20th and 21st centuries. He was one of the founding members of the ANC Youth League, and was elected its national president in 1950. In 1952, he and Oliver Tambo opened the first and only black law firm in South Africa. Mandela, who had always promoted using passive resistance to the apartheid regime, eventually realised that violence would have to emerge if their struggle was to be successful. An armed division of the ANC, Umkhonto we Sizwe was established in 1961, and its presence was announced with bomb blasts in three cities. After this, Mandela left South Africa in order to gain international support for the ANC. On his return, Mandela was sentenced to five years in prison and, following the Rivonia trial, he and a number of his comrades were sentenced to life in prison; most of this time Mandela spent on Robben Island. He was finally released from prison on the 11th of February 1990, a week after F W de Klerk unbanned political organisations. In 1994, Mandela became the first democratically elected President of South Africa. He has received more than fifty honorary degrees, including one from Harvard, and shared the 1993 Nobel Peace Prize with F W de Klerk.
Book Extracted: *Long Walk to Freedom: The Autobiography of Nelson Mandela* (Macdonald Purnell, 1994)

Part of My Soul
Winnie Mandela

The part of Pondoland where I come from is still totally tribal; tribesmen still congregate on the hills, wearing their traditional blankets. I went to a country school and my political enlightenment was very vague at that stage.

My father was a history teacher in the government service; he was supposed to be some little tribal chief, but he refused to take up that position (which I couldn't understand at that time). It was only in the classroom that I learned about the background of my country.

My mother, a domestic science teacher, was a religious fanatic. When I was only eight years old we used to get locked up in a room with her and my little sister, and she forced us to pray aloud. When my father was there, she would take us – two or three times a day – to a corner in the garden. It had high grass and formed some kind of protective shelter and she would pray. We had to follow her in these religious rituals, which we didn't understand. This has always been so ingrained that my own rebellion against the Church later, in high school, I think was a rebellion against that kind of petticoat government from her. In all her prayers she prayed for her children. She must have been crazy for a boy. I remember her asking God every day for a son. This also developed in me the feeling, I will prove to her that a girl is as much of value to a parent as a son. Also, my belief in God had been shaken in my childhood, when mother, who prayed three times a day for my gravely ill sister, one Sunday returned from church and found 'Sisi Vuyelwa' coughing blood – bleeding to death. I was standing behind my father, a little girl of seven, when he pulled a white sheet over my sister whilst mother knelt in a starched white petticoat next to her bed, exhorting God to send his angels to save my sister. She must have had TB.

From then on, mother was never the same. I watched her wither away, sitting in the dark corners of the house and praying silently. I think she could have had cancer. She lay there, just diminishing daily; for me as a little girl, she was literally disappearing, and she was in great pain, that's all I remember. She had probably had too many children for her age – we were nine – and she must have been about forty when she died.

As I watched her lips move and her tear-drenched face, I hated that God who didn't respond to her and who instead came for her when she was breastfeeding a three-month baby boy – my brother Thanduxolo. I battled to prepare his feeding bottles for him at the age of nine and spent hours at night cuddling him and trying to put him to sleep with sugared water.

We had to find our way in life after mother's death, disciplined by my father's sisters, who were ruthless and hard. Children had to be taught the hardships of life!

When my mother died, I had to leave school for half a year to work in the fields; I milked cows and looked after our own sheep and goat, and I had to harvest the crops, our mealies – that's where the bulk of the muscles comes from. It was a miracle that I passed Standard 6.

Father battled to keep the family of nine children well fed with a putrid teacher's salary that hardly differentiated him from the rural peasants, my people, who lived from the sweat of their brows, tilling the arid land with no farming tools but the crude plough and with emaciated cattle which I took to the 'dipping tank', where the white man tried to kill the ticks for the tribesmen.

When my father taught me history, I began to understand. I remember distinctly, for instance, how he taught us about the nine Xhosa wars. Of course we had textbooks, naturally written by white men, and they had *their* interpretation, why there were nine 'Kaffir' wars. Then he would put the textbook aside and say: 'Now, this is what the book says, but the truth is: these white people invaded our country and stole the land from our grandfathers. The clashes between white and black were originally the result of cattle thefts. The whites took the cattle and the blacks would go and fetch them back.' That's how he taught us our history.

And then he would say, for example, 'Adam Kok whom they refer to as a Hottentot, he was one of our leaders. His people were perhaps more robbed than any other little tribe in the area. They went so far as to exchange cattle with table knives!' And my father warned us: 'When your fathers go to the mines, they will be regarded as "boys", even by the white children, and when your mothers go to town to work for your education, they will be called "girls". It's a white man's way of insulting a black man.'

At least during that time there was not yet a difference between white and black education. It was before the rubbish Bantu education was brought in in the early fifties. There was a common syllabus and we were doing academic subjects like Latin, English, chemistry, physics and mathematics. There were strict standards. With the introduction of Bantu education standards dropped, the horizon became narrow and provincial. We still learnt about America and China. The children who came after us learnt the distance from Brandfort to Bloemfontein and what they grow in the homelands. They know nothing about the world and can't even speak English properly.

So I became aware at an early age that the whites felt superior to us. And I could see how shabby my father looked in comparison to the white teachers. That hurts your pride when you are a child; you tell yourself: 'If they failed in those nine Xhosa wars, I am one of them and I will start from where those Xhosas left off and get my land back.'

Every tribal child felt that way. That was the result of my father's lessons in the classroom.

There is an anger that wakes up in you when you are a child and it builds up and determines the political consciousness of the black man.

There was a song, for instance, the Bloemfontein song, which we used to sing – my father taught us music too – and I still remember its beginning: 'When our black leaders came together in Bloemfontein,* there was a big *indaba* and the leaders called upon the black people to unite and fight the common enemy.'

My father taught us other songs which dealt with events in the history of our people. They were songs from the tribesmen, by traditional composers.

And my brothers at home sang the songs they had learned from the elders up in the mountains of Pondoland, where I come from. They were songs about the mineworkers: how the men feel about having to leave their homes and their children, when they go far away to work as contract workers for the white man.

I still know the words today. The white makes a mistake, thinking the tribal black is docile and subservient.

When I went to Shawbury High School, I saw the white toddlers in town wearing beautiful dresses. We were nine in our family, my father could never afford to clothe us all. The white kids had buses to school; we had to walk barefoot many miles a day. I wore shoes for the first time in secondary school, and that was only because it was part of the school uniform. I never even questioned whether we could afford shoes or other things.

There was one teacher I loved very much. He had his own way of teaching us about our struggle and he idolised Bismarck. We had a long corridor and before he came to our class, he started at the far end, shouting: 'The unification of Germany, Bismarck believed, could not be attained through parliamentary speeches and debates, but by means of bl-o-o-o-d and iron.' By the time he said 'bl-o-o-o-d' he had reached our classroom. It was so funny. And he continued: 'And so is our

---

*The conference which founded the African National Congress in 1912.

struggle in this country.' He was so obsessed with it, that there was not a single examination paper which didn't have that and all of us sang that quotation. That is how I came to believe that my own struggle is to be won by means of blood and iron. (*Laughs*).

By the way, my father always had the greatest admiration for the German people and their industrial achievements. That's why he insisted on that terrible name 'Winifred', which subsequently became 'Winnie'. He also believed in the Christian names, because of the missionaries. Whenever he disciplined us he would refer to the hard-working and industrious Germans. He wanted us to become as strong as they are. As if I had my fighting spirit from them!

But since I became internationally known under that name, I'll have to continue with it. After all, it is a constant reminder of our oppression! My African name 'Nomzamo' means in Xhosa 'trial' – those who in their life will go through many trials – also in the sense of court trials ...

Winnie Mandela was born in the Bizana district of the Transkei in 1936. She completed a Bachelor of Arts degree, majoring in International Relations, at the University of the Witwatersrand, and went on to work at Baragwanath Hospital as a social worker; South Africa's first black social worker. Early in her political career she met a young lawyer named Nelson Mandela, and the two were married in 1958. Following her husband's arrest and imprisonment in 1962, Winnie was banned and jailed repeatedly. In 1969 she was detained for 491 days, most of which was in solitary confinement. Winnie was appointed Deputy Minister of Arts, Culture, Science and Technology in the first post-apartheid government but dismissed eleven months later. In 1996, she and Nelson Mandela were divorced. Today, she retains a powerful influence within the ANC Women's League.
Book Extracted: *Part of My Soul* (Penguin, 1985)

Final Postponement
Cecil Margo

I was born in Johannesburg on 10 July 1915, the fifth child of Saul Lewis Margo and Amelia Hilson, Jewish immigrants of Eastern European stock. My father's family hailed from the Russian port of Odessa. In the mid-1800s they emigrated to the United Kingdom to avoid compulsory service in the Tsarist army and further exposure to the brutality of anti-Semitic pogroms.

My father was trained as a mechanical engineer. His younger brother qualified as a dentist. The other members of the family (there were 11 children) were still too young to be enrolled for such training. In England my father won a scholarship to Leipzig University and furthered his training to a higher level.

After becoming employed he was sent to South Africa on an assignment. In Johannesburg he ascertained that his qualifications were sufficient to be enrolled on the register of architects. (He later obtained a diploma in quantity surveying from the University of the Witwatersrand.) He took advantage of this and his name remained on the register for upwards of 70 years. He established a substantial practice in South Africa and was well known for his professional services.

While in Johannesburg during the early stages of the Anglo-Boer War (1899–1902) he met my mother's family, the Hilsons, who were establishing themselves prominently in the furniture trade. Driven by the same pressures facing my father's family in their homeland, the Hilsons emigrated to South Africa from Dvinsk. My mother, Amelia, had commenced training as a dentist, an unusual achievement for a young woman at the time, but did not complete the course.

Shortly after the Anglo-Boer War my parents were married by the distinguished Rabbi JN Hertz, later Chief Rabbi of the United Hebrew Congregations of the British Empire. They had six children and set up home in a large house at the top of Munro Drive, which my mother named 'Berloga', the Russian word for a bear's den. Those who knew the family would have been able to verify the aptness of the name. The house has recently been declared a national monument.

In 1917 I was two years old and dimly aware of the titanic struggle for survival between good and evil that was being fought out over the horizon on the other side of the world. Against this background of fear and anxiety gleaned from adult conversation, a terrible foreboding of disaster had built up within me, and suddenly there it was: what I assumed was the image of Death itself, in the form of a woman being consumed from her feet to her hair in the fiercest of fires, while she rushed towards me, screaming in an agonised crescendo for God's mercy, and in a later shock wave becoming recognisable as my mother, the person I needed most to love and protect me!

I did not then grasp how it had happened: the apparently harmless flames from the candelabra on her dresser, bent by a sudden gust of wind, had reached out to her skirts, and in an instant had wrapped her in a blazing inferno. I still see, as a snapshot of terror, my mother dashing from me into my father's arms, and how he tried to beat out the fiercest of the flames with his bare hands. I remember how my sister, Deena, known to everyone as Dickie – the eldest of our family of six children and by then already a responsible ten-year-old – appeared wielding a travelling rug to smother the smouldering remnants of my mother's garments; and how two men in white linen coats with red crosses took my parents away on stretchers. After what seemed like an eternity, during which Dickie and our much-loved Mauritian nanny tried to comfort us, my father returned with his arms and hands heavily bandaged.

The days, weeks, months and birthdays passed and mother slowly recovered, but not without extensive scarring. We, as a family, have never escaped from the horror of that day.

I recall another traumatic episode from my childhood. We had been taken by our nanny to Seeff's Shopping Corner in Observatory, Johannesburg, near to where we lived. A crowd had gathered around a blinkered and bloodied carthorse, trembling as it stood mutely on three legs. Its fourth leg had been torn off in a collision with a grocer's van, so Nanny had been told.

An elderly man in a policeman's uniform (most young men were absent on service in the Great War) was waving the crowd away with what must have been a service revolver in his hand. Then, without warning, he pressed the gun against the horse's head and fired two shots, each of which sounded to my unpractised ears like a major explosion. The horse stumbled and fell, its three remaining legs twitching violently in convulsive, decerebrate movements, until death supervened. At the time, I was severely shocked, but Nanny answered all my questions and I put aside the disturbing scene I had witnessed.

Years later, in 1942, in the Western Desert in North Africa, during a raid by enemy aircraft, I saw and heard a man repeatedly kicking the door of a vehicle in a vain effort to open it. In a flash, I was back at Seeff's Corner with an elderly policeman pumping bullets into a shattered horse.

No doubt what triggered my recollection of the horse episode, which had lain forgotten in some remote corner of my brain, was the apparent similarity in the darkness of the noise of the later occurrence to the earlier one. How useful it would be if such powers of storage and recall by the brain could be trained to be available at will!

I was about ten, in 1925, when our family had another tragedy associated with fire. My two clever cousins, Leah, aged 13, and Nathan aged 14, the children of my mother's brother Harry Hilson and his Swiss wife Freda were setting up a room in their house in Blackwood Avenue, Parktown, as a home laboratory. It seems that there was no supply of municipal gas for a Bunsen burner and the children had used a methylated spirits burner instead. While Leah was pouring methylated spirits from the supply bottle into a small container, there was an explosion followed immediately by fire everywhere. They had locked the door to prevent their younger siblings from coming into the room and with the intensity of the fire they were unable to escape and were burnt alive.

Today, more than 70 years later, the memory of these events has been softened but I shall always remember answering Uncle Harry's phone call and handing the phone to my mother, only to see her collapse in a dead faint.

In 1967, tragedy again visited our family. One Sunday afternoon, near Johannesburg, my cousin Leo, together with his two young sons, were passengers in a twin-engined Beech aircraft, piloted by a friend, to enjoy a 'flip'. In flight the left engine faltered and then failed altogether. The pilot promptly feathered the propeller of that engine changing the pitch of the propeller so that the chord lines of the blades were in line with the airflow and applied full power to the right engine, but in the thin air of a hot summer afternoon, at 5 500 feet (1 676 metres) above mean sea-level, he had difficulty in maintaining height. He then committed the cardinal sin of allowing the aircraft's speed to drop below the safety margin for asymmetrical flight. He was unable to control the consequent vicious stall of the left wing, and the aircraft rolled onto its back and dived into the ground. All on board were killed. In my memory, these events will never be effaced.

Let it not be thought, however, that my childhood consisted only of a series of horrific traumas. On the contrary, my recall of these events in the family history is balanced by the recollection of a childhood and youth that, in the main, were relatively tranquil and secure.

Johannesburg in the 1920s was a small city, but it had already outgrown its first frontier brashness. Our place in the constellation of the British Empire appeared immutable, and whilst on the Johannesburg Stock Exchange events could occur and in the boardrooms of the great mining houses decisions could be taken, which could affect the far-flung reaches of the Empire, life in the upper middle-class suburbs was peaceful and leisurely.

Our family lived comfortably enough, except during the years of the Great Depression (1929-32), when university fees had to be found for five children, two of them studying in England.

We were a close family and we children grew up in the love and security which our parents gave us in full measure. The three older children and the three younger ones formed two musical trios of piano, violin and cello, and relatives and friends who were received by our parents were forced to listen to the works of Mozart and other great composers being mercilessly tortured and left unrecognisable by our performances. In this happy environment we enjoyed an abundance of fun and more than our fair share of adventures.

At the eleventh hour of the eleventh day of the eleventh month of 1918, the Armistice ending World War I came into effect. It was said that eight million men lost their lives in that war, compared with 30 million men, women and children in World War II. I was three years old. Riding on the shoulders of my eldest brother, Lionel, then aged eight, I waved my Union Jack at the dense crowds celebrating in the streets, singing, cheering, dancing and drinking.

I had three brothers and two sisters. My brothers and I were sent to King Edward VII School in Johannesburg, where we were educated in the finest traditions of the British Empire, with 'God Save the King', 'Land of Hope and Glory', Sir Henry Newbolt's 'Vitae Lampada', Rudyard Kipling, Rupert Brooke and similar sources, as the cornerstones of our patriotism and the watchwords of our faith.

At the age of six, in 1921, I was permitted by a neighbour's son, aged nine, to join his 'gang'. Seven of us met in a field nearby and the leader of the gang, a boy called Charlie, lit a cigarette, from which each of us was allowed one puff only before it was carefully extinguished and put away for future use. Then, on the grass, with Charlie leading, we wriggled forward on our bellies towards the vertical flap in the wall of an earth closet. In those days there were no flush toilets; human waste fell into a bucket below a toilet seat. At night municipal sanitary workers would lift the flap giving access to the bucket from outside, and replace the used bucket with a fresh one. Having arrived at the flap, we were instructed by our leader to keep silent. With his finger to his lips and much muffled 'shshing', Charlie raised the flap gently, and we saw a pair of testicles, the colour of Spanish onions, and the bare buttocks of some unsuspecting individual sitting on the toilet seat. The leader called in whispers for his magic willow wand, an old cricket bat, which was then thrust at the genitals of the unfortunate occupant of the toilet seat.

There was a startled squeal of pain and dismay, whereupon the gang dispersed with alacrity and with the same sense of achievement as an army patrol withdrawing from a successful operation. I did not continue my membership of the gang, more out of fear than disgust.

My first taste of illness, aside from the usual childhood maladies, was in Form 4. I had twice been moved into a higher grade, which resulted in my being younger than my peers by two years, and consequently the only boy in the class in short pants. I remember the form master remarking, 'You must have been born during injury time.' The academic pressure over-stressed my physical resources and I was plagued with boils and styes, the one following the other, causing not only distress but also severe distractions from my school curriculum. This was in the time before antibiotics and nothing seemed to help. The fourth doctor my parents consulted was a Dr Garrun, who made the confident diagnosis that I was run down and would benefit from a seaside holiday as soon as possible. My elder sister, Dickie, was obliged to give up her musical career to take me to the Cape and feed me on cream and other fattening foods aimed at improving my state of health and overcoming the infestation of boils. Looking back, I now see that the diagnosis and the remedy prescribed were ridiculous, and served only in costing me two months' attendance at school, with a consequent loss of valuable learning time.

I recall an occasion involving my brother Max, a medical student and a member of the Transvaal Air Training Squadron (TATS), an air force unit that trained selected university students full-time during college vacations and part-time in the early mornings in term. In breach of all regulations, Max flew over our house at six o'clock one morning in a DH9 aircraft, a relic of World War I, not noted for its quietness. He succeeded in arousing the entire neighbourhood with a series of badly executed stall-turns. My mother's reaction was to dash on to our tennis court in slippers and robe, calling rather ludicrously through cupped hands: 'Max, Max do you want some more of those biscuits? Have you any washing? My darling son, do be careful!'

One of our neighbours, Mr Sand, tried to out-shout the combined noise of mother and aeroplane by a bellow of protest but had to be content with alternately blocking his ears and shaking an impotent fist. My mother asked of the entire gathering of neighbours why it was necessary to fly so early in the morning. 'Surely the sky is there all day,' she said. We were all convinced that her performance had brought irretrievable disgrace upon the family.

An event in which my mother was obliquely involved took place in the early 1920s when a woman resident of the koppies behind the very respectable suburb of Observatory in Johannesburg phoned the Yeoville

Police Station to report that there was a wild leopard on her verandah. The police sergeant on duty took this as a huge joke. 'Why don't you put some salt on its tail, Madam?' he quipped.

The woman persisted until eventually the sergeant instructed a Constable Van der Merwe to 'have a look'. Constable Van der Merwe took his bicycle and rode off to the woman's house. As he was pedalling up the drive a fully-grown leopard lunged straight at him. Constable Van der Merwe had however been prepared for any contingency, and his loaded and cocked .45 Colt revolver was aimed directly in front of him. He managed to shoot one shot between the eyes and the leopard dropped dead, right in front of his bicycle.

My mother, who was a lovable busybody, set about collecting signatures in support of a petition to the Prime Minister, General Smuts, to have Constable Van der Merwe promoted to the rank of sergeant. With the help of my father, who drove her from house to house in his Model 'T' Ford, she collected around 300 signatures in support of her petition, which she then took to Pretoria to be laid before the prime minister. Of course Constable Van der Merwe was promoted and for years thereafter, just before Christmas, his entire family would turn up at our house with gifts of fruit from their farm to thank her once again for her efforts.

It is of interest to note that, as recently as September 1996, a wild young leopard was run down by a car in Observatory when it darted out of some thick bushes.

We seemed to have been fated to become involved with animals other than those of the domestic variety. In about 1936, a friend, Cecil Wulfson, brought us four lion cubs to be raised. He had been a member of a hunting party in the Rustenburg area and was present when another member of that party had shot a lioness, leaving her cubs motherless. He rescued the cubs and gave them to us in the hope that we could raise them. They spent much time on the tennis court and attracted considerable attention, but, despite veterinary help and a special diet, they all died of rickets.

Then there was the camel saga. The Administration of South West Africa, now Namibia, advertised in 1932 in the *Sunday Times* (which had the widest circulation of any newspaper in southern Africa at that time) that its Camel Corps was being mechanised, and that camels would be available at no charge to suitable applicants, who were invited to apply on a prescribed form. South West Africa was a mandated territory under the then League of Nations, and for all practical purposes it was administered by the South African government.

My close friend, Alan, and I, both students, resolved to apply for a camel, and to pitch the application in the strongest possible terms. At our home there were two spacious riding stables from an earlier era among the outbuildings on the property. Moreover, St Patrick's Road, on the northern boundary of our home, in those days ran into a large area of open veld owned by the municipality and was entirely suitable for grazing. Indeed, our nearby neighbours in St Patrick's Road, the Bradlows, kept a cow that grazed on that open veld. Alan and I took every possible advantage of these favourable factors to urge the merits of our case.

Time passed with no acknowledgement of our application, until one afternoon when a policeman arrived in the yard, wanting to inspect the amenities we had claimed we had for the care of a camel. We satisfied those requirements easily enough, after which there was a long period of silence, followed by the arrival of a second policeman who notified us in writing that our camel had arrived at the railways goods yard at Kaserne. He demanded to know the date and time at which delivery was to be made to our home.

By now my father had sensed trouble. He explained to me that there was a substantial risk of third-party liability for a camel bite or kick, and that he could not allow us to keep the beast without a suitable insurance policy. Imagine the reception accorded us, then little older than schoolboys, on inquiring at the counter of successive insurance brokers: 'Please Miss, can you insure my camel against third-party liability?'

Meanwhile, the second policeman had been pestering us for a date and time for delivery of the camel. In the course of his latest visit he casually asked my mother, 'Ma'am, have you ever smelt a camel? I promise you, you won't believe that anything can stink as strongly as that!'

That was the end: we were beaten by my mother's unshakeable prohibition, to say nothing of the insurance brokers' total lack of enterprise. The Johannesburg Zoo obligingly took over the camel and the feeding as well as the accommodation charges at Kaserne.

A few absurd rumours had gained ground, however. For example, the camel was said to be uncontrollable unless orders were given to it in German, that being the official language of SWA where it had been trained. In later times my friend, Bobby Hahlo, Dean of the Faculty of Law at the University of the Witwatersrand (Wits), was perhaps responsible for further fiction when using the camel story in his lectures to illustrate the liability of a parent and guardian for the wrongful acts of his or her minor child. Subsequently, about 12 years ago, I was having a drink in London with Professor Jim Gower, the eminent authority on company law and investor protection, who had spent a sabbatical term at Wits during Bobby's era. In the course of reminiscing over his spell at Wits, Jim inquired gently, 'Was it not you who rode to lectures on an elephant or a dromedary or some such beast?'

The camel story seems to have survived to this day, perhaps as part of the legacy of lecture notes passed on originally from Bobby Hahlo.

From time to time, when asked if the camel story is true, I do not trouble to inquire which part, but affect an air similar to that of Lawrence of Arabia and answer simply: 'Of course.'

My brother Max, having saved some money, bought a 1926 (or thereabouts) model Dodge saloon car for £10. As may be inferred from the price, it was a wreck. It had no doors or windows and no windscreen. It had no cover against the weather, no silencer or exhaust pipe, no self-starter, and had to be started by means of a crank handle. The one virtue that was consistently praised was its economical petrol consumption. On the other hand, my father's Chrysler was very heavy on petrol. He complained to the mechanic who serviced it that the car seemed to be giving only five miles to the gallon, but repeated tests revealed no leak or other fault.

The mystery was solved when it became known that Max had salvaged, cleaned and reconditioned some discarded enema tubing acquired from the hospital and had used it to siphon a good supply of petrol from my father's car. After this revelation my father's petrol consumption returned to normal and our Dodge lost its phantom fuel supply.

The tale of the Dodge moved towards a peaceful end when Max drove it to the home of a well-known stockbroker, whose daughter Sheila was holding a tennis party. Max parked the car on the driveway, on a fairly steep slope, but took the 'precaution' of placing some stones in front of the wheels.

Later, while Max was giving all his attention to the mixed doubles game in which he was playing, Sir Isaac Newton's law of gravity asserted itself. The stones were pushed aside, the car ran forward, crossed over a terrace and launched itself onto the tennis court, leaving deep grooves in the playing surface.

Max, with the best of intentions, at once announced that he would have the damage repaired and without delay called in a garden repair contractor, who promptly dragged the car out sideways, thereby inflicting further damage on the court, the terrace and the garden. When Sheila's father returned that evening he was aghast at the picture of devastation that confronted him. Sheila and Max have both passed on, and I cannot recall how the matter was eventually resolved.

My mother, always anxious that we should do well in our study of physical culture, had heard of a Swiss form of gymnastics known as eurythmy, classes for which were conducted by a Swiss lady called Miss Zetterquist. We boys were enrolled for a course in these exercises, for which we had to go to Miss Zetterquist's classes at the bottom of Harrow Road, which ran steeply downhill.

My oldest brother, Lionel, devised a method by which all four of us could ride to Miss Zetterquist on his bicycle. He occupied the saddle, Max sat on a carrier at the back, Hal sat on the crossbar between the handle bars and the saddle, and I sat in a basket carrier above the front wheel. Mounted on one bicycle, with one rider controlling it, the four of us travelled down Harrow Road at a speed of 40 miles per hour. How the bicycle withstood these grossly unreasonable demands made upon it, and how we boys survived these perilous trips, are not matters easily capable of explanation, even by reference to the linguistic resources provided by Miss Zetterquist's Schweizerdeutsch.

With abounding confidence, at a Scout evening at the Scout Hall in Yeoville, I was applying for my musician's badge, for which I played on my violin what I thought to be a superb rendition of Dvorak's 'Humoresque'. At the end of my performance, which I was convinced was a musical triumph, the Scout Master called out, 'Is Scout Martin here?' Martin nodded and I was then asked to lend my violin to him. I refused at first, explaining that it was a very delicate instrument and that only experienced and expert violinists like myself could be trusted to play it. I was eventually persuaded otherwise and gingerly handed my violin to Martin, who tuned it in a flash. I knew at once from his expert tuning of the strings that there was trouble ahead. And so there was! Martin proceeded to present a magnificent rendering of the work – a positive *deus ex machina* – of which I had never heard the likes before. I dearly wished for an opening in the stage to swallow me up, such was my embarrassment.

Of all the triumphs and disasters that accompany the maturing of boyhood to manhood, I have had a magnificent share. My boyhood passed with vivid and largely happy memories, guided through the pathways of knowledge and experience to the richest temples of strength, courage, intelligence and love of my fellow man.

Cecil Margo was born in Johannesburg in 1915. He was a pilot during World War 2, and fought with the Allied forces in East Africa, the Western Sahara, North Africa, and Italy. He was awarded the Distinguished Flying Cross and Distinguished Service Order for his achievements in the war. His career as a judge in South Africa is just as illustrious. Margo was appointed a Judge of the South African Supreme Court in 1971, and also presided over the Commission of Enquiry into the loss of the SAA 'Helderberg' which crashed off Mauritius in 1987. Margo died in 2000 after a long illness.

Book Extracted: *Final Postponement – Reminiscences of a crowded life* (Jonathan Ball, Johannesburg, 1998)

Memory is the Weapon
Don Mattera

... Where did it all begin for me?

We stood in a long queue inside a state-owned courtyard waiting our turns to be classified or reclassified either as 'pure' coloureds or as 'natives' – as Africans were officially dubbed in the forties and fifties. As a flower or tree would be classified into a certain species, so were the coloureds grouped and regrouped until they stopped believing they were just humans. For it is in the nature of men to create pigeon-holes. When I left the classroom at the Vrededorp High School, in the company of several of my standard eight classmates one day in August 1955, it was by order of an Act of the white parliament which decreed that all 'coloureds' or even so-called coloureds were to report to specially set up reclassification courts to determine our 'race'.

William 'Lovely-boy' Bokera, a very yellow-skinned boy, who like me had an African mother and a coloured father, tugged nervously at my jacket sleeve. The sweat of the fear of the unknown glistened on his forehead like oil. 'Hey Don, are we going to tell the fokking Boere that our old ladies are darkies? I mean it's not their bloody business who our damned mothers are; I mean we didn't tell our *toejappes* (fathers) to grab darkie *ousies* (girls).' I didn't answer. There's no way I was going to reply; one never knew who else was in the yard, keenly watching and recording speeches and events.

'Hey, are you listening bra? Are we going to tune them about our old ladies?'

'I don't know, Lovely-boy but it shouldn't really matter because as I understand it you are what your father is, and in our cases, both our fathers are half-white and they have not been classified native or African,' I said, trying to allay his fears.

'Never! In this country you are what they think you should be, what they want you to be, and all that through the stroke of a pen. Since this reclassification shit, everyone is changing his surname.'

I nodded. How widespread it was this conversion of surnames. Sonnyboy Letlapa (Stone in Tswana), who was a fair-skinned Morolong changed his surname to Kleppers derived from the Afrikaans word *klippe* (stones). Direct adaptations were Maybee from Mabe; Radbee from Radebe; Cummings from Khumalo and McKwenna from Mokwena; the list is endless.

Some people actually adopted our surname. Once a policeman called at our home to inform us that one of our relations – one B Mattera – had been arrested for a pass offence. I hurried down thinking it was my father because his initials were B.G. I saw a man called Basil inside the prison courtyard. I enquired whether he had seen my father because our information was that a B Mattera had been arrested. He smiled sheepishly, almost remorsefully, and said: 'I hope you don't mind Donny, but I gave them my name as Basil Mattera.' I shook my head. 'You do recall,' he added, 'that I used to work for your folks. Please tell that Boer over there I'm your uncle!' His voice fell to a pleading whisper.

'*Meneer*,' I said to the obese desk sergeant, 'that man over there is my uncle. He's a coloured; can you please release him?'

The policeman shook with derisive bursts of laughter. 'That kaffir your uncle? Don't tickle my arse. Since when do Hotnots slice open their ears? Just look at that blerry *houtkop* (wooden head); a real *fokken* Zulu with only painted wooden plugs missing in his ears. If he's your uncle, then I was the blerry midwife!' His laughter rang through my ears, into my stomach and fell deep into the soles of my feet.

Lovely-boy Bokera's father, who was also known as Bokeer, had won respect as an outstanding golfer and a man who had a way with women. His wife Nana was a simple, buxom Tswana who had not lost her rural traditional traits nor ever hid or was ashamed of her blackness. This, apparently, was the cause of Lovely-boy's uneasiness – that he might, like hundreds before him, be reclassified African. The queue was shortening; some men emerged in tears and others smiling. A tear and a smile; out of one 'race' and into another by the stroke of a pen and through the scrutinous eyes of Afrikaner officialdom. I shuddered at the thought of being made a 'native' overnight without having a say in the matter although, because of my close connection with my Tswana relatives, I felt no shame about being an African.

Suddenly a group of men in front of Lovely-boy and me moved out of the queue to speak to a man at the exit point of the reclassification office. Amid quiet whispers and the shaking of heads, I detected concern on their faces. One by one they moved towards the huge gates, all of them touching their hair.

I approached one of them. 'Excuse me big man, what's happening? Why are you guys all pulling your hair like that and where are you going?'

'To the barber-shop, boy; we're all dashing out for a haircut!'

'Why?'

Pointing over his shoulder with his thumb, he said: 'Those bastards in there, those dogs are using matchsticks and pens to classify us!'

'Matchsticks? Pens?'

'Yes,' came the quick response. 'Matchsticks and *fokken* pens, which they run through our hair! And when the pen or matchstick gets stuck, the Boers shout: "Go to Room 47 and get a pass!" Like we were *fokken* natives. What the hell do they take us for?'

His words stung everyone into silence. People began looking at each other's heads. Those with soft, straight hair smiled confidently and one or two actually combed their heavily-greased hair to the open envy of some of the more curly-haired, who were now vanishing from the queue. A very dark-skinned man smiled quietly. He had shaved off all his hair: matchsticks and pens cannot get stuck on a bald head. A tear or a smile on the way to pain and humiliation or to the joy and satisfaction of being a 'real' coloured.

Lovely-boy emerged a 'pure' coloured. He had passed all the tests without a single hitch: he could recite both the Lord's Prayer and Psalm 23 in Afrikaans; exclaimed *'eina!'* (ouch) and not 'aychoo' as a 'native' would when inflicted with sudden pain. Lovely-boy was a few inches taller as he walked through the heavy gates. My turn came.

'And what do you want to be, *boetie?'* said meneer Lotter, my classifier. 'A Hotnot or an Italian? I see your whole family has already been issued with identity numbers; yours must be in the batch.' There had been no matchsticks or pens; no blood tests, no scrutiny. I was the Italian's son, and the last-born of the family. If the Boers believed I was my grandpa's son, I was not going to be the one to shatter that belief. My number was 331-591697C; the 'C' stood for coloured but the birth certificate read 'mixed' in the column denoting race. It was the first I knew of a race called mixed. Mixed, though, was far far better than native, and being called kaffir, as many reclassified coloureds were to discover. Heart-rending stories, filled with biting humiliation and anguish, daily made newspaper headlines in the late fifties. Some victims of the reclassification trauma chose suicide to bail them out of their absurd misery. Whole and stable families were shattered overnight as brothers, sisters, sons and daughters were ripped apart by the cruel laws of race separation. Relentless pass raids netted in hundreds of 'borderline' cases; those bordering between African and coloured, not between white and coloured. The latter species would be dealt with only later as the 'other coloured' grouping.

In one sordid instance of reclassification insanity in 1955 Thomas Wentzel an elderly man in Noordgesig, Johannesburg, was also reclassified native when he approached the authorities to ask why his son William had been reclassified. Old man Wentzel had fought against the Germans in two wars, a coloured soldier in the Cape Coloured Corps.

The dark- and fair-skinned Gabriel brothers were split; one to 'pure' and the other to 'native' pigeon-holes and never the twain to meet in the same township or the same house. This was the Law.

A comb once stuck in the hair of a man called Maynard in a reclassification office in 1955, and presto, a 'native' was born. His cranium, the shape of his nose and lips and forehead, were minutely scrutinised and compared against the government-approved human charts and genetic diagrams; their authenticity, power and finality were indisputable.

And where there is power there is corruption. The two are inseparable, like twins joined in the womb. There was no price too high nor gift too expensive to bend and twist laws that forced people to live lies and demean themselves in the land of their fathers. Men and women hid in fear of pass arrests, tasting for once a small measure of the anguish and the shame that were part of the lives of the millions of Africans throughout the country.

And, as the law of the white man would have it, many of these unfortunate creations of God – in a way creations of the god apartheid – have accepted the categorisations without any real protest. Into this group called coloured, this cultureless genetic enigma, was I classified 'for the purposes of the South African Population Register'. But in their heart of hearts the Boers know this is only one of the many offerings they make at the altar of their god.

With the stroke of a pen, my Africanness and the acquired Italian tradition of my paternal grandfather were obliterated. Apartheid decided my race and my destiny on that dusty August day of 1955 in a government courtyard, where men stood in long queues to be branded and pedigreed with the hot iron of humiliation and scorn. Second-class citizens with a second-class future and destiny; South Africa's dirt-heap race; or so the people were made to see themselves...

Don Mattera was born in the Western Native Township in Johannesburg in 1935. He spent his youth as the leader of a gang known as the Vultures, and oversaw the gang's metamorphosis from a defence unit for street kids into one of the most violent and feared gangs in Johannesburg. He also spent time in the racially mixed, and soon to be destroyed, suburb of Sophiatown. Mattera went on to become a founding member of the Black Consciousness movement, as well as an acclaimed poet and journalist. At present, he is involved in 143 community organisations, and is a patron of over fifty trusts.
Book Extracted: *Memory is the Weapon* (Ravan Press, Johannesburg, 1987)

Blame me on History
William Bloke Modisane

Whatever else Sophiatown was, it was home, we made the desert bloom; made alterations, converted half-verandas into kitchens, decorated the houses and filled them with music. We were house-proud. We took the ugliness of life in a slum and wove a kind of beauty; we established bonds of human relationships which set a pattern of communal living, far richer and more satisfying – materially and spiritually – than any model housing could substitute. The dying of a slum is a community tragedy, anywhere.

It was especially true of Sophiatown, the most cosmopolitan of South Africa's black social igloos and perhaps the most perfect experiment in non-racial community living; there were, of course, the inevitable racial tensions, which did not necessarily flare up into colour-caste explosions. Africans, Coloureds (mixed-bloods), Indians and Chinese, lived a raceless existence. It is true that as racial groups, we were placed, socially and economically, on different levels of privilege; white was the ultimate standard and the races were situated in approximation to this standard: the Chinese were nearest to white, they were allowed into white cinemas and theatres and some restaurants; the Coloureds, nearer white, and the Indians, near white. Social mixing was difficult, but community spirit was high.

As children, mixing was easier, and together we had our normal – by South African standards – racial skirmishes with the white boys from the adjoining working-class white area. There was a mud pool in the buffer strip which divided Sophiatown from Newlands, and as a lad I joined in the fights for the right to swim in the mud pool. Whichever group got there first imposed its right to use, and continue using the pool; we threw stones at each other. The white boys usually dominated the contest in the end, invariably resorting to pellet guns. At the beginning it was for the right to use the pool that we fought, but this rationalisation soon lost its validity – it was for the sake of fighting that we went to the pool.

I was in the water when one of these fights started, and they threw stones at me and trying to ward off the stones I was drawn deeper into the water, until suddenly the earth under my feet gave way. I struggled against drowning until I preferred death to the agony. My hands searched for a weight to keep me down. During the struggle to stay down I was grasped by a hand and guided out; and once out of the water I threw stones with one hand, at the same time as trying to pull my trousers on with the other. I have never learned to swim.

The African children, as a race group, did not fight Indian, Coloured or Chinese children, as race groups; but we fought each other in gang wars in which opposing factions would be made up from individual members of the group units. Yet we would unite as a Sophiatown gang – a non-white group – to fight the white boys from Newlands or Westdene; children divided by the race attitudes and group conflicts of our society.

Like America, South Africa has a frontier or voortrekker mentality, a primitive throw-back to the pioneering era, the trail-blazing days, when the law dangled in the holster and justice was swift, informal and prejudiced. Instant justice, lynching and horse-whippings are deep in the traditions of these countries; both are compulsive addicts of horse operas, we are always playing cowboys and Indians. The mud pool was the Wild West of America or the dark interior of Africa; and to us, out there in the pool, the white boys were the Red Indians, and we were the cowboys. The symbols were undoubtedly reversed in the white camp; and in the rivalry for the mud pool we ravaged each other, desecrating the sanctity of the body of our society; we, the colour pieces of a colour society, inflicted festering sores on each other, and on the society; rehearsing our roles, arranging and dividing ourselves into the colour groups determined by our society. We were the warriors of Dingane, commemorating, celebrating the victory over the wiles of Piet Retief; we were the heroes of Africa: Tshaka, Hintsa, Moshoeshoe and Sekhukhune.

As a boy growing up in the Sophiatown without playgrounds we improvised our own games, the games of the children of the streets; our repertoire included games like dodging traffic, stealing rides on horse-drawn trolleys, getting on and off whilst in motion, and the more proficient we became the more ambitious we got, graduating to the green Putco buses. During riots we would be in Main Road stoning cars driven by whites, and the red tramcars which carried white commuters between Johannesburg city and Westdene and Newlands. We were part of the riot programme, stoning the police and being shot at, and hit, like everyone else. I learned early in life to play games with death, to realise its physical presence in my life, to establish rapport with it. The children of Sophiatown died in the streets, being run over by the Putco buses and the speeding taxis and were shot during riots.

Standing over the death of Sophiatown, another death came into my consciousness; I remembered the room in Gold Street, the all-in-one room which was kitchen, bathroom, bedroom, maternity room and a room for dying; thoughts of my sister, Nancy, who died of starvation, delicately referred to as malnutrition. For twenty-four hours a day, every day for the days of one week, relatives, friends and neighbours mourned over the body, the hymnals were sung as a kind of religious ode to death. I was impressed by the ceremonial of the wake, by its symphonic solemnity; the women were wailing a chant of mourning, seemingly talking to each other, throwing phrases at each other; one group stating the melodic line of sorrow, the other singing the harmonic complement, a consolement almost causing a sort of unintentional counterpoint.

There was solemnity about the lighted candles over the body; they moved my sister, Suzan, to tears and she was permitted to cry because she was a girl.

'A man does not cry,' an uncle stressed.

Seeing Ma-Willie, as my mother was called, crying was unbearable, and trying to be a man was difficult; the sight welled up that tear which I brushed off so discreetly; but death failed to horrify me, except that I hated it for what it did to my mother and perhaps blamed Nancy for dying. On the day of the funeral Ma-Willie was overcome with grief; the aunts, the other women and the girls broke down into weeping fits, a cousin became hysterical, seized by epileptic spasms, shrieking aloud and writhing on the ground and fainting. She was carried to another part of the yard and laid on a rug and fanned by a neighbour. The plain white coffin with silver handles left our house, irrevocably, and I was never to see Nancy again; it was this fact, alone, which emphasised the permanency of death.

If my father had not walked up to me at that precise moment I would have most probably disgraced my masculinity; he took me into the house of a neighbour; and thus death had made his first personal intrusion into my life.

I switched off the memory machine, but there was another kind of death gaping at me; I turned away from the ruins of the house where I was born in a determination not to look upon this death of Sophiatown. I removed my hat and stood still while a modest funeral train drove past; it was an open lorry carrying a small white coffin and not more than a dozen people.

Another child victim, another Nancy. Those of us who survived the clutches of malnutrition, the violence of the streets, lived with another kind of ugliness; the dry-breast barrenness of being black in white South Africa. There are times when I wish I had been born in a bush surrounded by trees, wild flowers, vales, dongas and wild life; to have grown gracefully like the seasons, to have been spring's simplicity, the consciousness of summer, but I became, as they say, a man before I was a Boy.

My father, Joseph, was always the signal of authority, unapproachable, the judge symbol; the only time he came close to me was to administer the cane or lay down the law of Moses, and this six-foot-two giant towered above my world, the only real force I ever feared, the authority I respected; perhaps I should have loved him too. One afternoon he came carting a rough bird-cage with seven pigeons and leading a dog which he presented to me, then wrung from me a pledge impressing upon me the seriousness of my responsibility for the protection, the maintenance, the sustenance of the pets.

I was excited and together we constructed a kennel for Rover, the dog, and a compound cage, the top half for the pigeons and the bottom for the fowls Ma-Willie wanted to keep; the working together brought us close and all through that time he became a friend I could touch, even if I pretended, with calculated casualness, that it was accidental. After the construction he retreated into his tree-top tower, to become again the symbol of authority. I prepared the feeds for the dog and the pigeons, and was punished if I fell behind with the schedule.

I resented having lost him, felt enslaved to the pets because the schedule made encroachments into my playtime; friends would whistle signals for me to join them in play, but the house duties: fetching water from a communal tap fifty yards away and having to fill two ten-gallon drums; washing dishes, the feed for the dog, nursing the baby, kept me away from the streets, away from my friends until just on sunset, and after sunset I was not allowed out of the yard.

I risked the cane, disobeyed my mother, disappeared from home, neglected my duties and was away until an hour before sunset; then I hurriedly started the fire in the mbaula, brazier, fetched the water, cooked the dog's food and washed the dishes, and by seven o'clock my dog would be fed; the tight schedule worked except that the time for my school work was wasted, all my energy would be sapped. This arrangement was disorganised the afternoon my father returned from work earlier than expected, and I was playing in Good Street when I saw the dread figure, a whip in his right hand; I disappeared into the nearest yard, jumping fences and cutting across to Gold Street, round into Victoria Road and into the yard. I preferred to be whipped at home.

I loaded three four-gallon tins on to my push-cart and hurried to the tap, rehearsing excuses, selecting the approach most likely to soften my father, the appropriate manner of apologising, begging for forgiveness; when I returned with the first load he was in the room with Ma-Willie who was ill in bed, and Suzan, realising the trouble I was in, was trying to start the brazier fire.

'Thanks, Suzie, I'll do it,' I said. 'Is he very angry?'

Little Suzan was too terrified to speak, she was biting her bottom lip, signalling with her head. I started the fire and rushed out to the tap again; when I returned I lighted the Primus stove and boiled water for tea which I served to my parents. My father remained silent. I heated more water and washed the dishes, and Suzan drank her tea between wiping dishes. Whilst the supper was cooking, the fowls locked in and Rover whining for his feed, I knocked on the door.

'I've done most of the work, father,' I said, with all humility. 'I'll wait in the kitchen.'

He joined me ten minutes later, locked the door and administered to me a whipping to remember, a whipping I took without a squeak, but with plenty of tears; and when it was over I dried my eyes and went into the bedroom to collect the cups.

'Would mama like another cup of tea?'

She shook her head, I looked at my father and he said 'No,' then I started for the door.

'He's not a bad boy,' Ma-Willie said, as I closed the door behind me.

It was the statement which was to blackmail me all my life; I wanted to live up to it, to embrace the responsibility implied in that statement. It became important for me to have it changed to: he's a good boy. When my friends were pilfering I would conveniently be on an errand for my father, I chickened out of street fights, concentrating my efforts into being a 'good boy'. But one afternoon during winter vacations I fought Uncle Louie, the Gold Street strong man.

We had been playing marbles and I had won all his beautiful coloured marbles which we called 'glass eyes'. Then suddenly he demanded them back and they had been the most beautiful I had ever owned; he was the street bully, so I gathered them into my marbles bag and handed them to him. He had hardly closed his fingers round the bag when I snatched it and dashed for home with him on my heels. About five yards from the gate where I lived he tripped me and I fell flat on my face, when I looked up Ma-Willie was looking down at me; the humiliation was unbearable, I lashed out at Uncle Louie flaying him with fists from all directions. He was so surprised that he put up a clumsy fight and when we were separated I kept my winnings.

There was a glint of pride in my father's eyes when the story was related to him; we began to grow closer, he spoke to me directly more often, and his image took on another stature. One afternoon he defended me when I had been punished unjustly by a stranger at the tap; I went home to report to him and without another word we returned to the tap together, me carrying a fighting stick.

'I agree that a naughty child should be punished,' my father said, 'but my son says he was not impolite.'

'He tells lies,' the man said.

'My son does not lie,' my father emphasised. 'And if he has deserved a beating it is I who will give it.'

This demonstration of faith in my integrity filled me with pride and admiration, and almost as an objection to being called a liar I struck out against the man with the stick I had, and drew blood with the second blow.

'Don't do that,' my father said, taking the stick away from me.

My father apologised for me and the man apologised for having punished me; the image of my father ennobled itself in my mind. Our relationship grew stronger, he seemed to grow fonder of me, we talked about my school work, what I wanted to be, and when I informed him that I wanted to be a doctor his mind fastened on something else.

'A doctor is a man,' he said, with an abnormal emphasis on the word 'man'.

He had in the past punished me, not so much for what I had done, but for the lies I had told in the desperate attempt to escape the cane, and it took me a long time to understand this. I was seldom punished if I told the truth; we discussed what I had done, and I would usually be filled with a sense of shame, not a guilt complex. He insinuated into my consciousness the separation between the emotion of shame and the sense of guilt which he said was a sterile and introversive form of torture which dissipated itself rather than focused on the enormity of the wrong; guilt swamps the individual while ignoring the deed itself. My father fastened on the deed, exploiting the emotion of shame, and in this way I turned away in disgust because of the shame, and it was this sense of shame which has motivated me from hurting people by word or deed.

Then the walls of my world came tumbling down, everything collapsed around me, wrecking the relationship. My father shrunk into a midget. There was a Pass raid and two white police constables with their African 'police boys' were demanding to see the Passes of all adult African males.

'Pass jong, kaffir,' demanded the police constable from Uncle George, a distant relation of my father. 'Come on, we haven't all day.'

He would not dare to address my father in that tone, I bragged, my father is older than he.

'And you, why you sitting on your black arse?' the constable bawled at my father. 'Scratch out your Pass, and tax.'

I was diminished. My father was calm, the gentleness in his face was unruffled, only a hardness came in his eyes; he pulled out his wallet and showed his documents, an Exemption Pass certificate and a tax receipt for the current year. My hero image disintegrated, crumbling into an inch high heap of ashes; I could not face it, could not understand it, I hated the young constable for destroying my father; questions flashed through my mind, I wanted to know why, and I think I resented my father, questioned his integrity as a man. I turned my face away and disappeared into the bedroom, searching for a parting in the earth that I could crawl into and huddle up into a ball of shame.

In my little prejudiced world of absolutes my judgement was cruel, imposing upon him the standards of my own world of fancy; we lost each other from that moment, and in his own way he tried to recover his son, but I was hard and monstrously unjust, and so he again became the harsh hand of authority, the authority I could no longer respect. I began to fear him, keeping out of his way and in the end I saw only the cruelty never the man. I grew closer to Ma-Willie and the four of us, Suzan, Marguerite and I arranged ourselves against him, united by our fear of him; he must have been the loneliest man in our little black world; I knew very little about him, never got to know whether he had parents, brothers and sisters; I knew vaguely that he came from the Pietersburg area, that there were some kind of relations in Medigan.

Once when Ma-Willie pushed me he became very angry and threw a chair at her, and watching my mother shrink away from him filled me with a loathing for him and a sympathy and closer attachment for Ma-Willie who was the only parent that was real to us; she took us on shopping expeditions to town, supervised and bought all our clothing, the school uniforms, the school books, took us on our first day to school and helped with the homework.

Walking up Toby Street I passed the beautiful house of the Mogemi family, they had not yet sold their property to the Resettlement Board, but everything else around it was levelled with the dust; the Lutheran Mission Church, Berlin Mission, stood erect among the ruins, and a hundred yards up the road was the palatial home of Dr A B Xuma with two garages. I turned south at Edward Road and stopped at Bertha Street and the sight to the east was deadening, my eyes spread over a desert of debris and desolation. Suddenly I needed my father, to appeal for his protection, to say to him: Do you see, my father, do you see what they have done to our Sophiatown? But he was only a patch of earth with a number at the Croesus cemetery, he was a number I had burned into my mind that day we buried him.

It was on the afternoon of February 16, 1938, that he died, and I was at school unable to help him that moment when he needed it desperately; he had lived alone in himself and died so, alone and lonely, the children were at school and Ma-Willie had gone to visit her relations in Alexandra township. It was shortly after the lunch break when I was summoned to the principal's office. Mr G Nakeni, headmaster of the Dutch Reformed Mission School, Meyer Street, Sophiatown, was waiting for me as I walked out of the classroom. I followed him to the fence next to the street.

'Was your father sick?' Mr Nakeni said.

'No, sir,' I said, thinking it was a rather pointless question, not worth interrupting the history lesson.

'You better go home.'

'Now, sir?'

'Yes.'

I returned to the classroom, reported to the teacher and gathered my books; I walked home leisurely, playing with a tennis ball along the way. There was a crowd gathered outside the corrugated iron which fenced in our yard, I slithered through the crowd and standing next to the gate were two African police constables and between them was a manacled man. I walked through the gate and as soon as Dorothea, a neighbour, saw me she started crying; she told it to me as simply and as gently as she could, leading me to the spot.

She informed me, between sobs and sniffles, that the battered and grotesquely ballooned nightmare, hardly recognisable as a human being, was my father; the swollen mass of broken flesh and blood, which was his face, had no definition; there were no eyes nor mouth, nose, only a motionless ball, and the only sign of life was the heaving chest. Recognition was impossible, I felt only revulsion and pity for the faceless man; he could have been anybody and the horror would have been the same, I shuddered at the brutality of the assault. I looked at the man back at the gate, who could have had the heart to do such a thing; he looked like other people, there was nothing visible which could set him apart from others, and I did not feel anything towards him.

The story was that there had been a quarrel with this man, that both parties had stormed away from each other in anger and later my father went into the extension of our yard in the hope that both of them had cooled down, but the man surprised him with a blow on the face which knocked him down; the man then proceeded to pound him with a brick until my father lost consciousness, from which he never recovered.

I returned to the blood-splashed spot where lay my father, and gazed at the distention, hoping to find something familiar in that mass, anything to bring the man closer to me, some mark of recognition, some sign of identification; and I could not cry, I wanted to break out and collapse at his side, but suddenly I could not remember his face and there was nothing to remind me; all through the interminable wait for the ambulance I did not, or could not bring myself to cry, I have never cried since that day when I was fourteen.

Death is never familiar and each death has its own special pain, each pain kills a little something in us, and I have looked upon death masks so often there is nothing left in me to be hurt by it. The pain of death has slithered into my mind, I use it as a weapon of vicarious vengeance, as a gesture of mercy, and at times, to punish myself, I arrange gory accidents for those I love; when I am annihilated by a sense of shame, arising directly out of my action or from the force and impact of events by which a friend suffered a moment's pain, I run away because of shame and rather than face them I kill them off in ugly accidents; then the horror and the pain of death would focus on the nightmarish sight of my father, and I fall into a state of anxiety and develop an itch all over my body, scratching until my skin bleeds; the pain becomes a reprimand, the physical moment of punishment.

Ma-Willie had been informed of the accident and returned home by way of the hospital, a widow.

'We are cast-off in the wilderness,' Ma-Willie said, in Sesutho. 'We are orphans, our shield is gone.'

'I hear you, mama.'

'O serithi sa rona from today,' she said, 'we are your children, to live from today in your shade.'

'Ee, 'me.'

'You must tell all our relatives, all our friends, send telegrams,' she said. 'Arrange for the children to be sent to Alex, it is you who must make the funeral arrangements, report to the Burial Insurance Society and they will do the rest.'

'You're the man now,' Uncle Lekoba said.

From that day I became a fourteen-year-old man responsible for a family of four; with some help I moved out the furniture from the bedroom and set it up for the ceremony of the wake; I changed into my only pair of trousers, bought the candles and the provisions for the all-night mourners, prepared and served supper to the children and Ma-Willie, who had officially assumed the traditional mourning dress.

She was joined later by all her sisters and brothers, their grown-up children, friends, neighbours and acquaintances, and the commemorational rites to death began over the body of the man who had passed on into – to nourish – cosmic life; they sat round the room in a circle, night and day, and sang through the requiem hymnals, the sad songs of the tebello, the wake, which most of the mourners knew off by heart. None of the people seemed to be horrified by the death, it only made them sad and full of pity. I received the sympathisers, acknowledging their condolences.

'It's a sad thing,' a sympathiser said, 'he was a good man; he was not rough, he didn't deserve the death he died.'

'To die like that,' another said, 'it's a shame; to die like an animal, like a tsotsi. God will see that man.'

'We all die our own death,' a man said, 'but this is not the death for this man, this is not the death he has made for himself; life has cheated him.' ...

William 'Bloke' Modisane was born in Sophiatown, the racially-mixed suburb of Johannesburg, in 1923. He became part of the famous group of black writers working for *Drum* magazine, working alongside such luminaries as Henry Nxumalo, Can Themba, Es'kia (Ezekiel) Mphahlele, and Lewis Nkosi. After Sophiatown was destroyed in 1958, Modisane moved to England, where he worked as an actor and writer; his only novel, *Blame me on history*, being published in 1963. He died in Dortmund, Germany in 1986.
Book Extracted: *Blame me on History* (AD Donker, Johannesburg, 1963)

Kalamazoo! The Life and Times of a Soccer Player
Stephen Mokone

I was born on March 23, 1932, in Doornfontein, a small Coloured suburb of Johannesburg, South Africa. Johannesburg is known as the 'Golden City' because of the many gold mines in the vicinity and the piles of white sand, glistening with a golden hue under the hot African sun.

In 1932, the United States was in the midst of a grinding depression, but for us in Doornfontein the depression abroad was meaningless. We were all too familiar with poverty, unemployment and undernourishment.

If you were white, this renowned mining region held the enormous promise of incredible riches. But for those of us born black, it offered little hope of ever rising in the world.

Somehow, though, my father, Paul Mokone, had risen above mean poverty. He owned a fleet of taxis which ran from Park Station and he also dabbled in real estate. A man with a delicate, open face, he had completed high school and had studied to become a Methodist minister. He refused, however, to be ordained, he told me, after he had found irregularities in church funds and was warned to keep silent about this fact.

Emily, my mother, was a dark-skinned woman with long, jet-black hair. She was very close to my father and, like most African women, she was family oriented.

Father played cricket, and I can remember him asking my mother to come and watch him play.

But Mother scolded him, 'You're just like a child – always wanting to play! Don't you have anything better to do?'

My father's smiling response was, 'Life is not all work...'

Among my fondest memories is my father lifting me above his head and acclaiming aloud to anyone who might be listening, 'I want Stephen to become a great cricket player!'

'Oh no,' Mother would protest, 'I hope he takes after me and plays tennis!' Mother was a very good tennis player; she loved the game and wished only to improve.

I was the second child in the family. I had an older sister, Georgina. We called her 'George'. Since she was twelve years my elder, we were never close in our early years. I also had a younger sister called Pauline 'Ouma'. I was stuck in the middle, so to speak.

Before I was six, we moved to what was then Sophiatown, a Black suburb west of Johannesburg. Why we moved I don't know, but I do recall my father arguing with his younger brother about rent money from properties which his brother was responsible for collecting.

At first I didn't like Sophiatown. It seemed filthy to me. Yet, everybody played soccer there – an obsession with the young boys. It didn't take me long to forget the squalor of Sophiatown when I joined the boys in a street team.

On Good Street, where we lived, we challenged kids from other streets; the losers had to pay a sixpence penalty. My team from Good Street won so often that soon I accumulated fifteen shillings. My father then added some of his own money to my winnings and purchased us a football of our very own.

Mother came often to watch me play in the street games. I got a thrill out of having her watch me, and I always tried my hardest to play well for her. It was a joy to see her get excited when I scored a goal. In her I had the best possible audience any boy could wish for.

We were not long in Sophiatown. Soon we moved to Pretoria, the capital city of South Africa, about fifty kilometres from Johannesburg.

Pretoria is beautiful, especially in summer when the jacaranda trees display their lavender blooms. Unlike Johannesburg, Pretoria is racist vis-à-vis Blacks in its viewpoint beyond telling.

We settled in Kilnerton, a little village outside Pretoria. Here we located Kilnerton Practising School and Kilnerton Institution, an all-Black school and college.

We had a house that was big and beautiful with many large rooms. I had my own room and an expansive window to view the world around me. I liked that window in the daytime, but not at night. Its size seemed to invite in the night-world and I would dwell on things that could happen to me without my parents knowing it.

My father, an extremely amiable and interesting man of great intelligence and wit and with sharp powers of observation, appeared to be an accomplished man in our Black world. Though he had travelled little, he was urbane. But now, paradoxically, he began sinking into wayward unsociability.

I couldn't understand what was making him so bitter, nor the reason for his spiteful mockery and irritability. Periods of passion or unhappiness over mistakes and losses had previously been completely absent from his life. It was as if he had written them all off.

Since then I have wondered whether he bore with him to his grave the memory of some incident, racial or otherwise, which he had confided to no-one – not even my mother. Or was he simply and finally overwhelmed by the combination of those diametrically opposed elements: the twentieth century and the life of a Black South African? For in South Africa, Black men exposed to the influence of the mighty winds of change from the West did not become historical figures. They became eccentric.

Vexation consumed him, especially when he spoke of politics and White arrogance in South Africa.

'I'm a foreigner in my own country!' he would shout. He made no effort to disguise his contempt for White people. Still, he had taken great pains to try to understand and analyse the White man and his ways, only to conclude at last that, 'Every man is capable of an evil act, but South African Whites are so inclined more than others!'

He resented, perhaps most of all, the manner in which White foreigners came to Africa, only to treat him as a stranger in his own land, while they acted as masters of all they surveyed.

Meanwhile, he despised the hypocrisy of the White churchmen. Bitter about not being ordained, he reviled the unethical behaviour of church officials. He would charge, 'They distribute favours to those they like and withhold the same favours from those they can't manipulate.

'The missionaries came only to destroy our beliefs and to teach our children to recite fine-sounding words they themselves did not believe, words like "brotherhood" and we already believe in that! They came here to save us from sin and when they found we had no sin, taught us sin so they could save us!'

He became most passionate and almost violent on these subjects, and he loved to argue with two Black ministers of his acquaintance, asking endlessly, 'How can you preach brotherhood in churches and yet practise segregation? How can you defend Whites who say they brought us civilisation and Christianity, yet hold Bishop Reeves and Father Trevor Huddleston in contempt for preaching the brotherhood of all men?'

I don't know what answers these ministers gave my father, but no-one who visited my father seemed to agree with his political thinking.

'Discriminate against me!' he said with his usual passion for the subject. 'Go ahead. Discriminate against me! I might not like it. But don't lie to me!'

Then he moved on to the concept of monogamy. He didn't understand the White man's teachings of only one wife.

'Our people have many wives and are faithful to them and take care of their children. Yet, the White man can't be faithful to one wife. Then, he's so irresponsible he doesn't take care of his illegitimate children and the State has to take care of them!'

I hadn't heard of Zsa Zsa Gabor or Elizabeth Taylor, but my father knew about them. 'Why is it they can marry a different man every few years and become heroines, while an African man with more than one wife is considered a pagan, uncivilised and un-Christian?' he demanded.

In fascination I would sit and listen to my father argue with his friends. Although I couldn't always follow the arguments, it appeared to me that he had the better arguments, and I was proud of him in this sense.

My mother never argued. Despite my father, she remained a devout Christian without questioning the inconsistencies in what the church preached and what those in power – the missionaries – practised.

Many of my father's political arguments were with his physician, Dr A Xuma. Dr Xuma had studied in the United States and he was deeply involved in South African politics. He was an *integrationist*, but I didn't understand the meaning of the word then.

Dr Xuma, though, was not a proponent of violence. 'I believe,' he said on occasion, 'that there are Whites of goodwill who can be trusted and see the Black man as a human being.'

'Talking won't help,' my father would interject with a scoffing sneer. 'Violence is the only way. Since the White man doesn't consider you his equal, how can you sit down with him to negotiate your freedom?'

Dr Xuma didn't have an answer for him.

I remember a day when my father came home boiling with anger. Taxi licence fees were going up. 'I have no vote,' he said bitterly. 'I am taxed without my consent…'

'Why not just pay it,' Mother said in her usual patient way, 'and get it over with?'

'It's not the money,' Father shouted. 'It's the principle!' I was truly baffled. I couldn't understand what the 'school principal' had to do with taxi licences!

Almost every Monday morning my father bailed his brother-in-law out of jail. My father never blamed his brother-in-law for his pass law infractions; he saw it as just another form of harassment by the White man. 'A man should not need a pass to walk the ground of his own country!' he would exclaim.

In 1947, while I was a student at Healdtown, King George VI visited Lovedale. The school turned out to see him, of course. When I told my parents about the king's visit, my father asked, 'Did you sing "*God Save the King*?"'

'Yes, we had to,' I responded.

'Ludicrous,' he shouted. 'Black children should not ask God to save a White king who oppresses them. The quicker he dies the better!'

I did not understand then why my father was always raging against

Whites. In the end, however, my father's views of the White man's court alone were to prove ominous to me. 'There is no justice,' he lectured me.

'Not in the White man's court. He is more interested in procedures and formalities than in justice. To think otherwise is to be a fool!'

Throughout my childhood the arguments continued relentlessly. Sometimes they were carried on at Dr Xuma's office on Hoek Street in Johannesburg; at other times at our house in Sophiatown, then in Kilnerton, and later in Lady Selborne in Pretoria, to where we moved in 1953.

The shadow of the future was to touch me in an otherwise meaningless event in my childhood. At Kilnerton we attended a church around the corner from our house. A visiting minister was scheduled for services and afterwards he was to eat dinner at our home.

We rose early and dressed in our best. In the kitchen, many of Mother's friends were assisting her in preparing the feast.

After church two ministers drove up to our house in a brand-new gleaming Ford. One of the ministers, a Reverend Maaga, had baptized me years earlier and in London, years later, I was to marry his beautiful daughter, Joyce Maaga!

In Kilnerton, as in Sophiatown, most of the kids played soccer with a vengeance. And they excelled at it. Frankly, most of them were better than I was!

When we moved from Sophiatown, I'd left the ball my father helped to buy, so we had no real ball to play with in Kilnerton. We made do with tennis balls. We played with them during every free moment, even in the school lavatories. When we didn't have a tennis ball, we played with a bundle of old rags tied together with string. A rubber ball was a luxury hardly accessible to us.

Our playing fields were marked by pavements, cans, stones, shoes and empty cigarette packs. We often used our shirts for markers. But play we did, and from dawn to dusk the noisy, hard-fought games filled the street. For me, though, it didn't end there.

At home I practised 'heading' against my bedroom wall, despite my mother's constant complaining about what the ball did to the walls. Then I lined up my shoes in my bedroom and practised dribbling around them. Soon the 'ball' became an extension of my being. In time it was me; soccer was me.

On Saturday afternoons my friends and I walked to the Kilnerton Institute to watch the older boys play against opposing schools. Admission was free and the games pitted the country's young, up-coming stars against one another. I could never sleep on Friday nights, so eager was I for Saturday to arrive.

We all had our heroes. Mine was Prince Mabila. He could have played for any great team overseas. He was a marvellous player with the best ball control I had seen. I worked to model my own playing after his style.

Meanwhile, my sister George had a friend, Gideon, who played for one of the top teams in Pretoria, the Methodist Football Club. Gideon took a liking to me. Wherever he and George went, they let me come along. Since this was usually to the soccer grounds, it suited me fine. In between, Gideon spent many hours coaching me in the intricacies of the game.

I practised and practised. I knew I was not as good as the others. Since I was so skinny, no one believed I could become a great – or even a good – player. This encouraged me to try hard, and to spend more hours with the ball.

Finally, I introduced myself to my hero, Prince. He took a liking to me, teasing me, saying, 'You'll never be a great player. No, never!'

So I trained for hours on end, kept after it, wanting to succeed in the worst way to prove to everyone, including my idol Prince, that I could become a good player. When I was twelve years old, people began saying, 'He's a pretty good player for his age,' and I sensed I might be on my way to the stars, though the confidence was lacking!

In the fourth standard at Kilnerton Practising School, the principal called me into his office. 'You've been selected as the official reserve player for the school,' he told me.

Bursting from his office with the news, I went crazy. I ran up and down telling anyone who would listen to me: 'I'm the official reserve player! I'm the official reserve player!' What elation!

But my nightly prayers changed greatly from that night on. 'Dear God, please let one of the regular players be injured so I can be called in!'

Of course, I didn't really want anything bad to happen to the players – just enough so that another player would be sitting out while I went in to play my heart out.

Soon afterwards a Kilnerton player was hurt in a game against Riverside Practising School. I entered the game as the substitute, expectations high. I scored two goals! Never again was I off to the side.

One day 'Starkie' – he had his hour of glory later, playing for the South African Black National Team – came to our house with Gideon.

Starkie said, 'How would you like to play with the Methodist Football Club youth team?' I thought my ears were deceiving me.

'Sure,' I stuttered, not quite believing this wonderful piece of luck. But it was my chance and I knew it.

I began training with the youth teams. I must have impressed some people, because almost immediately I was moved up to the second team.

A skinny kid with frail thighs, I lacked stamina and pace. But I excelled in dribbling, shooting and quick starts. Gideon continued to coach me, showing me different techniques and tricks which would stand me in good stead in the years ahead.

After playing only a few games on the Methodist second team, I was promoted to the first team. Wonderful! And it was all so easy!

We were playing the Celtics at Bantu Sports Ground in Johannesburg. A player went down with an injury. I was sent in to replace him. I scored two goals in the game and I was a member of the first team.

Dan Twala, a radio announcer and a big-time impresario, was so taken with my playing that he devoted five minutes of his Saturday morning sports programme to reviewing my style of play. Yes, I was on my way.

Upon completing sixth grade at Kilnerton, my father applied for my admission to Healdtown School in the Cape. I was accepted, and off I went.

The school was big – too big for me, though there were many pretty women interested in making me their son, never mind. It was too far from home. I didn't have friends. Worst of all, the school was very weak in soccer. Within a month I became ill and returned home where I announced, 'I'm not going back there ever again.'

Since I was the only son, I knew I could manipulate my parents easily. They gave in, of course, and so did the Methodist Club officials who were glad to have me back.

Since I was already an established player in the Methodist Football Club, miracles were expected of me. I became what can only be termed 'an overnight sensation'.

Back in school in Kilnerton I did not realise it, but my future wife was a student there. In those days though, the love of my life was Betty, a pretty, soft-spoken, shy girl. Betty was very popular with all the young men.

Betty and I had been close friends for almost ten years. But I had never considered marriage. Now Betty was ready for marriage, and I wasn't. Soccer was my only life as my late teens passed. In fact, soccer was the 'woman' I was 'married' to.

Soccer continued to be more important to me than anything else throughout my stay at Kilnerton. Then, three years later, my parents began to feel that soccer-playing was distracting me from my schoolwork. Again I was sent away, this time to Durban to attend Ohlange Institute.

It was my father's hope that I would become a lawyer, so I studied Latin. Since I had never met a Black lawyer and had no role model, I couldn't sustain the image of myself as a Black lawyer and said as much. My father sent along his friend, Dr William ('Willie') Nkomo. Nkomo discussed medical school with me and for a time I entertained the thought, but only briefly.

Like most African men, Dr Nkomo was a great aficionado of soccer. He ended up coming to watch me play. And it was Dr Nkomo who, along with several friends, would drive all the way from Pretoria to Durban to see me in competition when I was first selected for the South African Black National Eleven.

I shall never forget that trip. In his excitement after the game, Dr Nkomo urged me to celebrate with a drink of brandy. Since I never imbibed, it took only a couple of tumblers to get me drunk. Dr Nkomo enjoyed it all mightily, and never forgot the first time I got intoxicated!

I was still at Ohlange when I was selected to represent the South African Blacks. At the age of sixteen, I was the youngest player to ever represent South Africa.

The years 1951 and 1952 were good to me. I was like a poker player with a very hot hand. The Bush Bucks Football Club was the best in South Africa. I was honoured by their invitation to play for them.

Four other players were regular South African representatives. They were Seven Days, Tom Zulu and two of the best I've ever played with, Ace Moeketsi and Stadig Vusie. Ace and Stadig (meaning 'slow') were inside forwards. Since I was also an inside forward, the Bucks converted me to a centre forward.

Except for the Orlando Pirates and Moroko Swallows in Johannesburg and the Dinareng Football Club from Lesotho, we had virtually no opposition. In 1951, the Bucks won both the league and the title cup in Durban. Although I had joined the Bucks after the season started, I ended up as top scorer in the league goals, a feat made easier by the generous help of Ace and Stadig...

Stephen Mokone was South Africa's first soccer superstar. Born in Doornfontein in 1932, Mokone became an international soccer player at the age of sixteen, before becoming the first black South African to play professional football in Europe when he joined English club Coventry City in 1955. He went on to play for Dutch side Heracles, Spain's Barcelona, and Torino in Italy. By 1959 he

was rated as one of the best players in Europe. After his soccer career, Mokone obtained a doctorate in psychology, and was appointed assistant professor of psychology at the University of Rochester. Unfortunately, he was arrested in 1977 and jailed for nine years for assaulting his wife. In 1996 he founded the Kalamazoo South African Foundation, of which he is currently chairman.
Book Extracted: *Kalamazoo! The Life and Times of a Soccer Player* (De Jager-Haum, 1988)

Down Second Avenue
Es'kia Mphahlele

For all that it mattered, the depression of the early thirties did not seem on the surface to add an ounce of pressure more to the poverty of the Black man.

We still had one tarred street for the police to patrol and for the white superintendent of the location to drive his sleek shining car along. There were still a few electric lights dotted about street corners and none in the houses; the smell from the sewerage centre in the plantation below us still came in a suffocating wave. Of course fewer of us went to the Dougall Hall bioscope because the market and the golf links were scantier and the white people didn't want to pay as much as they used to. They brought the price down from ninepence to sixpence for carrying vegetables five miles to Sunnyside suburb...

There was much less to eat at home, and boys and girls of our age group raided Indian hawkers' backyards for discarded fruits, bread and vegetables in garbage bins. But then we had always done that after school. We planned our strategy of entering through the back gate. Some of the hawkers were vicious with the sjambok, especially Cassim Hassim. Some of the women connived at our acts; others poured rice crust and water on us from the balconies, just to have a laugh. Often we looked up to the balconies and laughed with them while we shook down rice grains from out of our shirts. We returned to rummage again. Little Links and Danie, the noisiest boy down Second Avenue, whom we could seldom trust to 'pull off a job' with a sense of duty becoming a Fox, raided one yard. Ratau and China went to Moosa's wholesale establishment for 'tin-my-Moosa'. This meant that they would ask Moosa to off-load vats of bananas from a truck and get a tin of black-skinned overripe bananas for it. Ratau was the quietest and steadiest of us and said little; China came of parents who always dressed smartly and were reputed to be well off. For Ratau this was a 'decent' assignment, and for China – a kind of sport. Moloi and Isaac, the round-faced boy who came from Bantule, another location two miles away, and I, struck elsewhere. Isaac attended school with us and preferred to play with the Foxes. And so we fanned out over the Asiatic Bazaar.

At the end of the raid we met at the river, just below the police station, with a good haul of oranges, spanspeks, carrots, tomatoes, bananas and other items: all rotten in parts. We went to the tap at the corner of the police tennis court and washed off as much rot as we could. After the meal we got dry sticks and ran them the whole length of the corrugated-iron wall of Fung Prak the Chinaman's yard. He made malt and sold it to the local shops for illicit home beer-brewing in the locations. Our little game annoyed his vicious bulldog inside and it followed the rat-tat-tat, barking ineffectually all the time. There were days when we divided the booty and took it home.

Twice a week we took sacks and made a long journey home to the municipal ash dump in the last suburb west of town. There we scratched and scrounged for coke for use in our home braziers. We came back all white with ash. And when we washed our cracked scaly feet, we felt like dancing a jig from the stinging pain when the feet dried.

It was during those years that I began to regard the Indian as someone who was also privileged to have more money than us or the Coloured people. He traded among us, and yet he kept aloof from our sufferings, unmoved by them. He appeared to me, in those years, as somebody who could never suffer; who didn't die; who couldn't cry or care. We laughed and joked with him in his shop; we called each other pet names; but it seemed that we could never project ourselves into each other's lives and share certain things. But then we didn't care to. The Chinaman, on the other hand, was a surly, disgruntled creature who just dragged his feet about and moved with a sinister stoop. How could we not believe our parents when they told us never to venture beyond the counter of a Chinaman's shop because he ate human flesh? Fung Prak's tiny wife would stand on her veranda until customers came in. She stood there, her arms folded, laughing at the heavy-booted African policemen marching past, their buttocks stretching the slit at the back of the coat. She hardly had any buttocks. There she was, her lower teeth receding as her upper row was advancing; and as she turned to walk into the shop the hem of her dress clung to the woollen stockings, on one leg and then on the other.

I couldn't consciously probe into the attitudes of the Asiatics; I simply felt a barrier beyond a certain point of contact.

There were other and deeper changes at work in Marabastad, in Bantule to the west of us, in Lady Selbourne, six miles farther, in Cape Location next to the Asiatic Bazaar, and in the peri-urban locations east of town. Boys of our age were getting rough and knife-happy. Scores of them left school and joined the won't-works and some of those who had lost their jobs. They stood about on shop verandas, made rude jokes and guffawed with broken voices, chewed bubble-gum impudently and smoked insolently. Boeta Lem (Brother Blade) from down our street easily collected a nice bunch of hangers-on about him. They hero-worshipped him as an ex-convict. They brought him food and money from their homes. They spoke a lot about the wonderful performance of their counterparts 'on the Rand'. Somewhere in the Golden City, we felt, big evil things were going on. And our parents blamed it all on this mystical bond.

'If I see you again listening to what that Boeta Lem says, I'll chop your neck into pieces, pieces, pieces with an axe!' grandmother warned us. 'He's a heathen, his mouth smells like a drain. His father can't do a thing with him any more, and heathen too, if you want to know. All he does is sit there in his house, kill lice between his nails just because his son would rather go about sweeping God's streets with his tattered trousers and go about rooting in garbage cans instead of working. He doesn't even know which way the church door's facing, by Titus who lies in his grave. Both of them will soon be eating rats and dogs.' Titus was my grandpa, her late husband.

Marabastad seemed to be turning inside out, showing all her dirty underwear. 'The world is coming to an end,' grandmother said with a sigh, 'as sure as Titus sleeps in his grave. What we see today is a sign of God's anger. When I was young there wasn't so much hate; boys and girls didn't insult their elders like this; and we helped one another during famine. The world is nearing an end.' She frightened me that way.

'Nonsense, Hibila,' Old Rametse from the lower end of the street said, 'this is the beginning of a new world. I worked for a white farmer, Van Wyk his name was. "Petros," he used to say, "listen here, Outa, if ever your children go to the city, know it's the end of them. My son Koos is long gone, and now Grieta's going, and I know they're lost. But thank God in the heavens they come of an upright and God-fearing house. If they throw away their Bible teaching, God forgive them. I've written to Dominee Brink at the Groote Kerk to look after them."' Old Rametse chuckled. 'Ah, Hibila, that Van Wyk was a kind man but still a big Baas. I've been here now – let me see – ten plus five years – how many? – fifteen, and only last year I saw young Koos in town with a girl hanging on his arm. They were both drunk but not so bad. He's a fellow with a big shadow now, and you think he'd know me? Ha-ha, I stopped him and I said, Greetings, Kleinbaas, remember Petros from the farm? I saw in those eyes that he remembered me, but he said, "Get out of my way, Kaffir!" and he passed on. Now I ask you, Hibila, if the white man goes on like this and he has everything, farms, money, good clothes, clean face, what were you and I – we who live on borrowed things? Give me that mug of coffee, my boy.' It was a special privilege he enjoyed, to be given coffee in our home. When I wasn't feeling so good, as often happened when he was around, he reminded me.

'Borrowed things, borrowed things,' Aunt Dora said after he had left. 'He thinks we were born yesterday. Everybody knows he has a lot of money hidden somewhere. And yet such a miser too. Look at the khaki he wears – a man with so much money.'

No one really knew how rich old Rametse was, if that was true. But people spoke of it as a fact. A few days later he came to our house waving his arms madly. 'You've never seen such a thing. That *skelm* has done it again. It's me this time. Son of a rat, son of a pig, son of a heathen, son of a baboon, son of a crocodile without a name, son of a runaway mother!'

'Who's that?' grandmother asked.

'That piece of filth called Boeta Lem. Stole all my money from under my mattress. My woman saw him, saw him run out of the house, saw him with her eyes. I've worked for years for my money, long before his mother carried that lump of sin in the womb. His hands are getting mouldy in his pockets because instead of doing honest work he wants to ruin other people. Little Shepherd, he has taken my life away with the money!'

'Go to the police station,' Aunt Dora suggested.

'Where do you think I'm going?'

Aunt Dora laughed secretly. He made his way out toward the police station, talking aloud and gesticulating. 'Modisana!' he kept saying.

The police did not or could not prosecute, although the Blade was taken to the station. 'God's no fool. He'll stumble and fall one day. You'll see.' That was grandmother's ruling. Ma-Lebona, Ma-Janeware, and even the cross-eye woman next door, said grandmother couldn't have been more right. 'God will deal with him.' Old Rametse's story of how much had been stolen changed much. He said it was five pounds, then twenty, then ten. And still people didn't know how rich or poor he was.

It seems God did catch up with the Blade. One Saturday night he assaulted a teen-aged girl in a dark field near the Dougall Hall. He had forced the girl, at the point of a knife, from the door of the cinema to the field. The girl ran home to report, and the police got on Boeta Lem's tracks. He was picked up at the Columbia. ...

The next week, on a Sunday, Second Avenue residents swarmed at the gate of the Blade's home, where he lived with his father and stepmother. The people were angry. He had been bailed out, and they didn't like it. Aunt Dora went, not grandmother, who said she was sorry her leg was sore, otherwise she'd go and tell 'the heathen Blade a thing or two, roll him in the dust a few times and lower his price on the market'.

'Let him come out!'

'Let us see him!'

'We don't want animals here!'

'What, he gets a lawyer to speak for a criminal!'
'And it's his father, he knows his son's a criminal!'
'He's giving his son more pluck to do bigger crimes!'
'That lad will kill another man yet God's my witness!'
'What is it you want to do with the lad?' Old Rametse asked a knot of people at one end.
'Are *you* going to ask that, you whose money he stole?'
'I know, but I also want to know why I should be here.'
'We want to take him back to the police station. They must keep the dog chained until it goes to court.'

Old Rametse nodded understandingly.

'Speak to his father,' said the Blade's stepmother, panting and waving her apron this way and that as if to disown the Blade.

At last the father came out of his hovel, his son's hand in the grip of his, sinewy and trembling.

'Speak to them, speak to them,' the stepmother babbled, her fat hands fidgeting with the hem of the apron. 'I've long been talking about this boy of yours. I'm weary of it, Jehovah knows in the heavens. Speak to them.'

'God's people!' the man began. The noise gradually subsided.

I always remember how dignified the Blade's father looked on that day, even in the state of agitation.

'God's people!' he repeated, 'what do you want of me?'

'We want your son, he must go back to the police cells,' a woman said.

'That's right,' another echoed. 'You've no right to keep a criminal in your house.'

'And even hire a lawyer for him.'

'If he'd raped a white girl he'd have been kept locked up until he should hang.'

'You must deliver him.'

For a few minutes Boeta Lem's father seemed lost for words. Then, 'God's people, hear me. You men and women here have children. You're lucky some of them are not like this lad here. You're lucky some of them haven't raped and stolen. It hurts me when a boy of my own blood makes life miserable for other people. For every stab he gives a victim I get a hundred in my heart, not so easy to heal. You say if I'm willing to pay a lawyer to try to set him free, it means I like the dirty crime he has committed, and others before that.'

He paused, and I could see he was weeping. His son stood there beside him, with a dirty sleeved vest for a shirt, and a wide flannel bag for trousers, out of which his long bare toes peeped. He looked both frightened and defiant.

'Whoever thinks that is a cruel person. Why do I hire a lawyer then? I don't know, I can't tell you.'

'What about my money?' Old Rametse said, his Adam's apple pushing sharply, and the sinews and veins in his neck telling a story of pain.

'That is a matter for the police, Son of Rametse,' the Blade's father said. 'I've brought him outside with me so that he should know what people think of his wickedness.'

A wave of mumbling swept through the crowd, and they dispersed, threatening doom, predicting chaos, invoking God's instruments of punishment. 'We leave you to chain your own dog then,' one said, throwing up his arms.

Boeta Lem subsequently appeared in court. He was sentenced to twelve months' hard labour.

'Let a black man do anything to a white girl, they put him into jail for many years, but because this time it is a Black girl, what is one year in jail?'

Columbia Hall cuddled in the centre of a row of Indian houses in the Asiatic Bazaar, just wedged between Marabastad and the Cape Coloured Reserve. It was an old building, with sooty walls that were painted and repainted time after time to give the deception of attractiveness. On either side of the low platform that was meant to be a stage, was a door leading to a lounge room that covered the breadth of the hall in the length and was partitioned into cubicles, each fitted with a couch. The lights of the Columbia were never bright.

... Talking pictures had just arrived in Pretoria. A new Indian-owned bioscope hall, the Star Picture Palace, opened for the first time in the Asiatic Bazaar with a showing of *The Singing Fool*, featuring Al Jolson. Excited crowds flocked at the cinema to see the new wonder in the history of the film.

We were permitted to go – my little uncle and I, escorted by an older uncle and Aunt Dora. Every night there was something on at the Columbia. What better night could there be for going there? But then I doted on the movies, and it would break my heart to hear the other boys recall among themselves what they had seen at the Picture Palace. I had a little money I had made at the market, and I could afford the admission fee of a shilling at the Columbia. So, once I had been given my ticket, I lost myself in the crowd and dashed to the Columbia just round the block. There would be an introductory programme of shots and a silent film before Al Jolson.

I was let into the Columbia. I came face to face with the U-NO-MES dance band, whose music had before only floated to our ears as we passed the hall; violently, noisily, but vigorously. Thinking back on it now I remember the sad note of depravity, self-abandon, sweet, sensuous dissipation 'Marabi' jazz sounded. The small jazz combos like U-NO-MES and the Merry-makers beat out a new two-to-the-bar jazz, the second note in which was accentuated by a bang on the drum. The name 'Marabi' came from *Marabastad*. From there it went to the Reef. Handbills in pink or green or white could be seen on electric poles and rusted corrugated-iron walls which read:

THINGS ARE UPSIDE-DOWN! AND WHY? 'CAUSE THERE'S GALORE SENSATIONAL, FANTASTICAL, SCINTILALATING, REVERBERATING JAZZ EXTRAVAGANZA BRING YOUR GAL, SPIN YOUR GAL FOR THE PALPITATING MARABI RHYTHM OF U-NO-MES AT A DAYBREAK DANCE AT COLUMBIA EVERY NIGHT

I stood against the wall in that misty hall of dim lights. Couples clung to each other very tightly, swayed sideways and backwards and forwards at the hips. Their faces were wet with perspiration. Occasionally a man or girl wiped it off with the back of the hand. They swayed to the monotonous tune, seeming to hear or see nothing, lost in the savagery of the band's music. They might even be blissfully unaware of the fact that just round the block, Al Jolson was bringing the magic of the age – the sound film. I continued to stand there, drinking in all the dust that rose from the concrete floor, the dim lights, the smell of perspiration and tobacco smoke. That was the Columbia, the name that spelled horror and damnation to those who concerned themselves with human conduct ...

... I enjoyed Al Jolson all the same. A few weeks later we saw Charlie Chaplin's *City Lights*. TALKING, SINGING, DANCING became familiar labels on cinema hoardings. At first, I was a little uneasy at the prospect of going out of business. The boys wouldn't need my services any more as a reader of the titles on the screen. They'd have to listen to the dialogue. But soon I drowned my little fears in the novelty and expediency of it all.

That was the Marabastad of the depression years. In spite of poverty, the people found other outlets for the urge for recreation, besides the Columbia. More jazz troupes sprang up. On public holidays a horse-drawn cart might come down Barber Street with an old piano on it and about four other instrumentalists, playing Marabi just for the love of it and a troupe would be singing *Happy Days are Here Again, Tip-toe to the Window*. It was grand to dream of unknown tulips, roses, lazy lagoons, mandolins in Santa Lucia, beautiful ladies in blue, old Father Thames, the unknown sunny side of the street. The same thing happened on New Year's Day. Picnic groups were formed, and the fun started only when they were arriving back home. Each company had its own band

and uniform. There were the Sunbeams, Sonny-Boys (which included girls), Callies, Red-White-And-Dizzy (*dizzy* meant *green*). These names corresponded with the football teams the parties were attached to. When they arrived in lorries and toured the location and displayed their colours, their plumage wasn't that of depression-stricken birds at all.

Preachers in church spoke vehemently against immorality. They denounced places like the Columbia and foretold eternal punishment. And they collected the endless dues from the people: money for the monthly ticket; for the quarterly ticket; money for the half-yearly ticket; money for Holy Communion; money for the minister's journey to a conference; money to build a church in some outlandish area or another; money for the minister's bicycle. 'We're poor, we have no money any more,' people said. But they brought something and laid it on the table. And regularly the white superintendents came to preach sermons. Every church except the A.M.E. had a white minister as overseer. And when they did come, the congregations turned up in full force to listen to the white preacher. The stewards and the church councillors were more correct and officious than usual on such days, keeping up a tight-jawed look of responsibility. Stout prayer women looked immaculate with their dazzling red blouses and white starched hats. But the dazzle of these colours was toned down by the sleek, shining black shawls they had on. How very much of birds the women reminded me!

There was a surge of revival services in the various churches. Grandmother herded us and left my brother, sister and me in the Methodist church hall, as our mother was Methodist because my father was nominally one. Then grandmother, Aunt Dora and the rest of the family went to the Lutheran Church, because my grandfather had been Lutheran. The night of the eve of Good Friday, Lutheran women sang from street to street, waking up their church members, singing all the time. The music jolted us out of our sleep and we rubbed our eyes and sat up until the last chords of that grave music could be heard faintly in the distance, and we slumped back into sleep.

But church attendance generally dropped those days. And the preachers blamed loose morals for it. The depression was God's punishment they said. Women, old men and children of our age kept up their attendance. The young men and women stayed away. The old men slept most of the time. Most of the time we looked at the women, at the preacher and then at the sleeping old men.

There was more beer drinking. More boys and girls left school and had children. And the preacher pointed a large finger at us who remained, mute, helpless, tethered to some family custom and honour. In spite of Boeta Lem's absence, 'bright boys', as they called themselves, didn't go slow. Instead, they broke up into rival gangs: XY Ranch; Jumbo Ranch; Texas Ranch; Express Ranch; Uppercut Ranch. They stopped men in the street and undressed them completely at the point of a knife and left them naked. The clothes were sold ...

At this time, I acquired the passion to roam from one church to another on different Sundays. I just loved change; it was so refreshing, and I could listen to a sermon painlessly coming from different preachers. I loved the music of the Lutherans. It didn't have the monotonous pattern of many of the Methodist A.M.E. hymns. I loved the incense and regalia in the Anglican church; I found fun in listening to the A.M.E. pastor who liked to mix English and Sotho in a sermon. 'That man is mad,' grandmother said. 'The day his gods descend upon him and ask him where he has thrown his mother tongue, he'll scream.' I just thought he was funny. And then I was constantly amused by the way in which he wound bits of string round his ears to hold his eye-glasses because they were old and broken.

There was a tiny iron enclosure housing a small congregation calling themselves the Gaza Church. I couldn't summon enough courage to go to it. During those years of the depression a number of people went about claiming to be prophets and faith healers. Nzama, the pastor of Gaza, was such a 'prophet'. On Good Friday each year he entered a deep hole in the plantation below his church, at the lowest end of our location. He stayed there and 'rose' on the third day – Easter. Some said he went through the period without food; some that his wife sent him blankets and food when no one was looking. But Nzama and his congregation claimed that he actually died and rose because he had the powers of Christ.

Another time a woman took her paralysed son to Nzama for faith healing. Nzama went through his ritual, and when the patient didn't respond, he set about cutting the stiff and contracting sinews of the ankles and the knees. The child died and Nzama was arrested and jailed. I shuddered at the thought of venturing into Gaza. I didn't.

I told grandmother about my wanderings. She said I'd end up by attending no church at all. 'Heathen like your useless father.' The accent she always put on the word 'heathen' didn't have the same ugly forebodings it used to. 'I suppose you'll soon be wanting to go to that tent church up the avenue. I'd cut off your head for you. I'd cut you into pieces, pieces, pieces.'

The tent church up the street was an institution of the depression years. Pastor M'Kondo came with his sickly wife from Alexandra Township in Johannesburg. They had broken away from the Methodist Church of South Africa. He was said to be a branch of what was commonly known as the Donkey Church. Its emblem was a picture of Christ entering Jerusalem on a donkey. Bishop Ramusha of the new church was noised about as a powerful preacher. His mother church had raised one of the several categories of dues from 2s. to 2s. 6d. He had protested to the white authorities, but they were adamant. He left and took with him thousands of members.

Soon the local Anglican priest, Pitso, pulled out of his church with a large following. This was after a quarrel with the Bishop of Pretoria. He formed his church called the African Catholic Church. But he later felt so bad about it that he took the people back to the Anglican Church. He was sent away to some distant place to do penance, and was never again seen in Pretoria.

Hundreds of young men and women were drifting into Pretoria from the northern Transvaal. Occasionally I met some of the men who were big boys when we were at school together in Pietersburg. These men worked as domestic servants in the suburbs.

On Sundays they came down from the suburbs as far away as seven miles from Marabastad, to Bantule on the other side. They had their playground there. A bare grassy patch where they boxed bare-fisted. On such days we went out of our houses to look at them in rival batches, march up Barber Street. They had on shorts, tennis caps, tennis shoes, and handkerchiefs dangled from their pockets. They crouched, shook their fists in the air so that their plastic bangles round the wrists clanged. They moved with long strides like a black army, and their legs glistened with petroleum jelly or soap grease which they smeared carefully after washing. It was a common saying that when they sprang and shouted and crouched like that, their 'blood was boiling', and they were in vicious mood. Every Sunday white mounted police escorted them to Bantule.

At the playground they formed a ring and rivals went in in couples for a gruelling, bloody and savage bout. Anyone could go in and challenge someone from an opposition stable. That was the kind of boxing we liked to do on the white sands of Leshoana river in the topical moonlight, when I lived in the north.

These people came to be known as *malaita* – Sotho for *ruffians*. When they dispersed, the police got close on their heels and beat them on their backs with sjamboks. This seemed to make the *malaita* mad. For they scattered and took different roads to town. Some went through Marabastad, some through the Indian and Coloured Reserves. The police were supposed to prevent their entering these locations, but they were so brutal in the use of the sjamboks that it had the opposite effect ...

Es'kia Mphahlele, another member of the famous team of *Drum* magazine writers, was born in Pretoria in 1919. In 1945 he became a teacher at Orlando High School, but was dismissed in 1952 as he objected to 'Bantu education'. He then joined the team at *Drum* magazine, obtained a master's degree from the University of South Africa, and, in 1957, went into exile. While in exile, Mphahlele taught at universities in Africa and America, and served as director of the Congress for Cultural Freedom in Paris. He returned from exile in 1977, and was professor of Comparative and African Literature at Wits from 1978 until he retired in 1987.
Book Extracted: *Down Second Avenue* (Picador Africa, 2004)

Boy from Bethulie
Patrick Mynhardt

The name Bethulie is derived from the Hebrew biblical word Bethula, apparently meaning virgin, or virgin soil. There were four suburbs, *Rooidorp*, *Hongerbult*, *Noodvoor* and *Max'mo*. There was no Catholic Church in Bethulie, but Mass was said at intervals by a travelling German priest, father Schultz, who always wore a cassock and a pith helmet and looked quite a sight sitting on top of the enormous wool bales in the open railway lorry that brought its load from Smithfield to Bethulie station. On other occasions he would arrive in a small, grey German Ford, with a mattress on the roof in case no one offered him a bed for the night.

Mass was celebrated in the 'sample room' of the Royal Hotel, which was run by Mr and Mrs Flink, who were Jewish. The sample room was the room where the commercial travellers displayed their wares to the local shopkeepers. If this room was unavailable, father Schultz would say Mass in one of the few Catholic families' spare bedrooms, where a washstand or dressing table would serve as an altar. It was in front of one of these that the first three of the four Mynhardt children were baptised. The first, a girl, christened Katherine Joan Theresa (always known as Kathleen), was followed by Daniel Petrus Johannes, and then Michael Rudolph.

Since the nearest large, well equipped hospital was in Bloemfontein, 120 miles away, my father had his own small hospital built on land backing onto our property. This was known as The Nursing Home, and here many lives were saved, many brought into the world, and some were lost. The hospital had a permanent white nursing staff of two – nurse Haasbroek, and the ill tempered and formidable, flush-faced, sister Botha. I particularly remember her for her veil, her red cross and her bedpan. She was forever *woer-woering* around with her bedpan as if the entire district had diarrhoea.

After twelve years of successful practice, my father decided to specialise, so the Mynhardts set sail from Cape Town, nurse Haasbroek accompanying them, in one of the Union Castle mail ships, the Athlone Castle. First to Guys Hospital in London, my father having forgiven the British for the Boer War, then to Edinburgh and the Royal College of Surgeons. The final stop was Dublin and the Rotunda Gynaecology and Obstetrics Hospital. Next came a tour of Europe, and study spells in Vienna, Budapest and Berlin, the children having been left in the care of the able nurse Haasbroek at the grandparents' home in Dublin, directly across the road from a Catholic church. On their return, my mother asked nurse Haasbroek what she thought of Ireland and the Irish. 'Mrs Mynhardt I have *never* seen such polite men in my life – whenever I'm in the front garden with the children, every single man who walks past raises his hat to greet me.' Now anyone who has ever been to Ireland knows that even the most paralytically drunk Irishman will never pass a church or a chapel without crossing himself or raising his hat ...

... The Mynhardts returned to Bethulie and, on 12 June 1932, I was born. Perhaps because our father was the mayor, the district surgeon and the railway doctor as well as the village doctor, I seemed to have been involved with life and death from a very early age. Death held a morbid fascination for me. I never missed a funeral in Bethulie. I'd be sitting in front of our house, my feet dangling in the water furrow, and if I saw a funeral procession proceeding uphill towards the cemetery I'd rush for my bicycle and pedal hell for leather, arriving just as they were lowering the coffin into the grave. I would join in the hymns and psalms and the tears, never knowing who was in the coffin.

The graveyard fascinated me and I loved wandering around examining the tombstones and inscriptions. One derelict little grave particularly haunted me. It consisted of a white marble cross, a small curly-haired boy leaning over it. The inscription read 'In Loving Memory of Erskine Kruger, Died, Aged Only Four.' I was demented, as I was three and a half! When my mother explained that the little boy's mommy and daddy had gone to live in Bloemfontein and were too far away to put flowers on his grave, I decided to make a weekly pilgrimage and do so myself. I would go to Ma's display cabinet, select an exquisite little Delft or Dresden vase, fill it with *vygies* or *veldblommetjies* and put it on the grave. A week or two later the hailstones would smash it to smithereens, and off I'd have to go for another, this time Rosenthal or Royal Doulton, filling it with *aandblommetjies*, *viooltjies* or *leeubekkies*. This would inevitably be pinched by some poor white or *kaalvoetklonkie* (barefoot boy) and I'd have to replace it yet again.

The vases were disappearing at an alarming rate from the display cabinet and the servants were constantly getting it in the neck for stealing or breaking the madam's flower pots! One drizzly day my father attended a funeral, the grave virtually next to that of the little Kruger boy's. He happened to recognise a cut glass vase he had recently bought my mother. 'That's our blasted *blompot* (flowerpot), and it's going back home!' Hiding it under his raincoat he took it back to the display cabinet and I took it back to the graveyard, and my mother fetched it back to the living room and I took it back to the grave. Many a *blompot* and vase *woer-woered* from the Mynhardt house to the graveyard!

Because he was the district surgeon, our father had to visit patients on the outlying farms and for me it was a joy to accompany him on these journeys and to open the numerous gates along the rough, dusty, corrugated roads. The nearest neighbouring town was Springfontein, twenty-five miles away, and between Bethulie and Springfontein there were twenty-five gates for me to open. On these journeys, my father, a very romantic man, would recite 'The Green Eye Of The Little Yellow God' (Kipling, I think), Shakespearean love sonnets and *'Wilgerboomboogies'* by Totius. As the farmhouse came into view he would burst into nostalgic song with *'O Boereplaas'*, the tears rolling down his cheeks.

We would arrive at the farmhouse and, while my father attended to the patient, I'd wait on the veranda, sipping strong, sweet, milky coffee, dunking my *boerebeskuit* (rusk), and begging for another story. I would be told tales of the Boer War, the English and the Boers, the awful concentration camps, the *rinderpest* and the *groot droogtes* (great droughts).

During my long career English people have asked me why I bother to act in that awful vile guttural kitchen Dutch Afrikaans language. I very quickly inform them that Afrikaans is the youngest language on earth, only officially recognised as such in 1925, and originally one of the two official languages of this country, prior to which English was the only official one; and that Afrikaans is one of the most poetic, virile, expressive and inventive of languages. I illustrate this with words like *bromponie* for scooter; *klomp pomp, groep woep* or *tamaai naai* for gangbang; *katelknapie* and *pompjoggie* for toy boy; *vroetelpappie* for sugar daddy; *woefkardoes* (*woeffiekardoesie*) and *brakkie sakkie* for doggy bag; *skilfer tertjies* for pastries. I then recite Macbeth's 'Tomorrow and tomorrow and tomorrow' speech in Afrikaans and, while they are recovering from the beauty and power of it, I add that we Afrikaners have a sweetie that we call *suurklontjies*. And what do the English call them? Sour balls!

Our father was the mayor of Bethulie for about twelve consecutive years, and each time he was re-elected he would appear in a beautiful cream suit, silk shirt, matching silk tie and pocket hankie from Austen Reeds, Regent Street, London, stand on the steps of the little Bethulie town hall, and deliver a wonderful thank you speech in English and Afrikaans. He was theatrical, quite an orator, and rather a showman, and perhaps some of this rubbed off onto me at a very early age. And then there was my Irish mother, with her gift of the gab and the blarney, and maybe I inherited some of that, too, as well as the mysticism – the Latin, the chanting and the incense – of the Catholic Mass, which we four *Roomse Gevaartjies* attended every Sunday with our devout mother.

Our father rarely managed to attend his own Dutch Reformed Church, because of pressure of work, but whenever there was a severe drought he would, in his capacity as mayor, be forced to attend. On these occasions we would be dragged along to go and pray for rain. The Dutch Reformed preachers of those days really excelled in the hellfire and brimstone style of preaching, and I am sure that some of this rubbed off on me too, because everyone says that before I was four I was the biggest drama queen Bethulie had ever seen. At the slightest provocation I would preach, deliver sermons, or conduct funeral services. If my rock rabbit died or a *sprinkaan* had a *miskraam* (locust had a miscarriage) I'd gather everyone around me for the equivalent of a state funeral, and the tears would flow while I held forth in typical Dutch Reformed fashion.

When our parents entertained the cream or the hoi polloi of the village at a cocktail party I'd climb onto one of the low windowsills and hide behind the drawn curtains. Then, at the height of the party, the guests sitting there with an asparagus or an olive in one hand, champagne, sherry or cocktail in the other, I'd fling the curtains aside and deliver one hell of a sermon. '*Broeders en susters julle gaan in die HELLLL beland met al jul drank*', and of course the olives and the asparagus and the sherry, champagne and cocktails would fly. I would then bless them with '*Dominus Vobiscum, Et cum spiritu tuo*'.

Our house was a constant coming and going of events, people, dramas, suicides and births, deaths, crises, meetings and *vergaderings*. When the village got something new, like an abattoir or its own electricity supply, or a new sanitary flush lavatory system, replacing the old bucket system, and old Paultjie, the night cart driver (purveyor of *poeffies*) was pensioned off, we'd be honoured with a visit from Prime Minister General Hertzog; or General Smuts; or the Minister of Finance, Mr Klasie Havenga; or Mr Jan Hofmeyer; or the Administrator of the Free State, Dr Hans van Rensburg, the founder of the *Ossewabrandwag* – a violently anti-English and pro-German organisation. Another visitor was Dr J S Moroka, a distinguished African doctor from Thaba Nchu and ANC President from 1949-1952.

I vividly recall Dr van Rensburg and his lovely wife, who was reputed to look like the famous Hollywood Chinese film star Anna May Wong, coming to Bethulie for one of these 'events' and I, as the Mayor's son, dressed to kill in a silk pageboy suit, had to present Mrs van Rensburg with a basket of flowers. She had a fringe and short, shiny, close-cropped, pitch black liquorice-like hair, which mesmerised me into wanting to lick and take a bite out of it, and after curtsying, my eyes glued to her head, I tripped over her feet and fell right into her lap, flowers and water all over her.

During these 'State Visits' the events and festivities went on all day long and eventually climaxed in a 'Mayoral Ball' in the town hall across the road from our house. On these occasions we children were not allowed to be heard or seen and would hide on the back veranda and peep at the VIPs. Once the guests had trooped over to the town hall, we were permitted to finish off the leftover savouries and snacks. All I ever wanted was the leftovers in the little glasses and, of course, I'd be paralytically drunk for two days, sleeping it off, with everyone saying, 'Shame, have you heard, Doctor Mynhardt's little boy Patty has been bitten by a Tsetse Fly'. I loved the taste and effect of alcohol, and I am sure it all started during a trip to the Kruger National Park in 1936 when I was four.

During a lengthy breakdown I apparently began screaming the place down for water, and we had run out. Eventually a Portuguese truck driver arrived and sold my mother a bottle of cheap sherry and I was dosed with this until I fell asleep. During another breakdown, father and brothers and my wonderful nanny, Mama Kittywe, had to sleep out in the open while sister Kathleen, Ma and I slept in the car, but at the roar of a lion or the snapping of a twig the 'men' would come leaping in on top of us. Kathleen and Michael, sitting in the back of the Willy's Knight, had one of their frequent tiffs and she flung a steam iron at him, missing him but smashing the small rear window. For the rest of the journey poor Mama Kittywe had to sit next to that window holding up a tray against it 'to keep out the lions' while the culprits sat tightly huddled together at the other end.

Whenever we had visitors for sundowners I'd forever be pestering them for a sip of theirs, and they'd try and put me off by saying it was *medisyne*, but I'd have none of it, insisting 'Give me medicine, I'm sick.' My love for the stuff was shared by our coloured gardener, old *Windvoël*, and my parents had a terrible time hiding the alcohol from the two of us. One afternoon Ma went golfing as usual in her swanky, streamlined new 1937 straight eight engine Buick, with its ivory-look steering wheel, spare wheels on the running boards and its very distinctive 'brrromm', which could be heard a long way off. I woke up from my afternoon nap and couldn't find my dummy anywhere. Apparently, I sucked dummies until I was about six, but was forever losing them. Come four in the afternoon I'd start to panic at the prospect of no dummy at bedtime, and would have to run to Mr Kristal's shop with the little red order book, select a new dummy, and have him enter the purchase. If I didn't like his range I would dash to Turner's chemist shop, choose a posher one and have it entered in the little blue book. We had different coloured order books for different accounts.

When the family eventually moved to East London, they found thirty or more dummies all over the place ...

... On this occasion I decided 'to hell with the dummy, I'd *steek 'n dop of twee* (have a swig or two)'. Now began the search for the booze, but it had been hidden very well, more because of *Windvoël*, than because of me, as my drink problem hadn't quite reached the proportions of his. At some earlier point my parents had bought a barrel of wine, which, because *Windvoël* had been caught at it a few times, they'd hidden behind the wardrobe in their bedroom. Then, for no rhyme or reason, *Windvoël*, went missing. He was eventually found a few days later, passed out on his back behind the wardrobe, his mouth directly beneath the tap of the barrel and the barrel empty.

On the day of the missing dummy, at the bottom of the same wardrobe I found a beautiful, exotic, curvaceous looking bottle still wrapped in cellophane. I was ecstatic as I thought I had found my favourite peppermint liqueur, Crème de Menthe. At that moment I heard the Buick firing up at the golf course, so, in a panic, I began to tear off the cellophane, trying at the same time to remove the gold covered cork. By now the Buick was tearing hell for leather down the main street and when I heard Ma pull up in the driveway, I put the bottle to my mouth and in panic gulped down as much as I could. All I can remember is bubbles *borreling* out of every orifice. Ma found me looking like Betty Grable in a bubble bath. I had drunk shampoo! I had my first stomach pump before I was six.

Shortly after this, the magistrate's wife, Mrs Chowles, came to the house for sundowners and, when I told her how much I loved cocktails, she invited me to fetch a bottle from her the next day. I thought the bottle was just for me and not for the whole family, so my pal Johannes Becker and I went straight after school to fetch the cocktail. Iris Chowles was a strange, very beautiful crippled lady with a heavy walking stick, and we were all in awe of her. When she made it very clear that she wanted the bottle back, and under no circumstances was I to forget this, I assumed she meant she wanted it back right away. We ran home, fetched two little empty Redro fish paste glasses from the pantry, and climbed onto the roof of our garage to share the bottle. After three glasses Johannes was violently ill, vomited all over the place and fled home, leaving me alone on the roof with no choice but to polish off the nearly full bottle and return it to Mrs Chowles, as I didn't want to keep her waiting. The task completed, I had to get off the roof and down the tree next to the garage, but every time I tried to put my foot on a branch, I actually put it between the two I was seeing! I do not know how I got down, but I slept for hours, only to wake up dementedly worried about what had happened to Mrs Chowles's bottle. After days of agonising it transpired that in my drunken stupor I'd given it to one of the maids to return ...

Patrick Mynhardt was born in the small Free State town of Bethulie in 1932, and is one of South Africa's most accomplished actors. He moved to London in the early 1950s, obtaining roles in two West End plays, before returning to South Africa in 1960. Throughout his fifty-year career as an actor, Mynhardt has been in over 150 stage plays and 100 local and international films.
Book Extracted: *Boy from Bethulie – An Autobiography* (Wits University Press, 2003)

The Children of Soweto
Mbulelo Vizikhungo Mzamane

We buried him on Sunday. There were several other funerals being held all over the township that Sunday, funerals of others who had died in the shootings earlier that week.

His death had come as a great shock to me. Life was difficult to imagine without him. In class he had always sat next to me. We lived in the same street. We had grown up playing marbles, spinning tops and flying kites together. Our street team had dominated the other street teams we played against in our football challenge matches, in the dusty township streets, where treacherous holes were worse than the most hard-tackling defender. He and I had formed such a deadly combination as strikers that we had been nicknamed 'the terrible twins'. We had been inseparables. I remember as though it were only yesterday how hurt I felt the day he took out his first girlfriend, Violet, to Harlem Cinema; and how on our way back he had asked me to travel home, alone, while he saw Violet to her home. We had fought rival street gangs with *bog-draads*, made up of wires intertwined to make them thicker, scout belts, bicycle chains, slings and stones as members of the same gang. We had gone together to caddy at the golf course or to carry at the market. We had attended the same schools right from our days at the lower primary school, and many were the days we had played truant together in order to explore the complex network of tunnels which connect the township's water and sewerage pipes. We had suffered harassment and intimidation in the hands of the Hazel gang side by side. We had risen together to positions of prominence in the S.R.C. and none could claim to have been more dedicated and committed to our cause than we were. His death came as a great shock to me because I could not remember a time when he had not been by my side.

It was a chilly Wednesday morning in the middle of June.

Looking back in time we can usually tell to the very minute when it all started; the day Dingane's forces were routed at Blood River, the day of Bulhoek, Sharpeville and so on. Some of the manifestations, we later discover, had been in evidence for days, months, generations previously. The whole of the preceding summer had evinced all the symptoms and been full of omens, but we never noticed until after the event. With the wisdom of hindsight there are some people who can tell us they saw it all coming; who remember feeling inexplicably depressed the whole of that preceding week; whose very dreams, interpreted retrospectively, had been ominous visions of the future. Looking back in time, we can usually find the exact moment when a new epoch began, whereas when it happened it was simply just another day indistinguishably linked to others. Such was that fateful morning in the middle of June.

We were marching along the main road, some three streets away from ours, when we encountered them. They stood across the road, blocking our way. We had been marching resolutely through the townships, with children from other schools, gathering yet more others as we proceeded. Boys and girls aged between ten and twenty. Students from Orlando High, Musi High, Naledi, Sekano-Ntoane, Morris Isaacson, Orlando West, Zola, Madibane, Eiseleen, Jabulani Junior Secondary, Tladi Junior Secondary, Molapo, and Thesele. Along with them thousands of primary school children. The march had been organised to demonstrate our opposition to the imposition of Afrikaans as a medium of instruction in our schools.

Addressing us first in Afrikaans and then in broken Zulu, they tried to order us to disperse. But we had grievances which could no longer wait. We surged forward, aiming to sweep them out of our path if they would not give way. By now our frenzied numbers had swelled and swelled. We shouted *'Amandla!'* (Power), *'Inkululeko ngoku!'* (Freedom in our lifetime) and 'One Azania, One Nation', as we marched on, our clenched fists held high. The air resounded with menace. We sang. Our song drowned the remonstrative voice issuing from the loudspeaker. We shouted our defiance in song:

Asikhathali noma bes'bopha
We don't give a damn, even if
    imprisoned
Sizimisel'inkululeko.
For freedom's our ultimate goal.

He and I and student leaders from other schools, carrying denunciatory placards against the System, were marching in front.

Suddenly from just ahead of us there was a great rumbling noise. Several times the thunderous explosion came, as if the very roof of heaven was collapsing over our heads.

Pandemonium broke loose as we scampered for protection from the nearby houses, he and I and a handful of others hurling stones as we retreated.

He stumbled and fell, with an anguished cry which pierced through my heart as surely as if it had been the Roman soldier's sword.

'They've hit me,' he cried and collapsed to the ground like an empty sack of potatoes.

Khotso Duiker and I tore ourselves from the retreating crowd and crept on all fours to where he lay.

Khotso was our Treasurer in the S.R.C., which was made up of student representatives from all the townships' secondary and high schools. He was dedicated, level-headed and tough. He often spoke of an Italian novelist he had read called Giovanni Guareschi, by whose code of conduct he tried to live. 'Even if they kill me,' he'd say, 'I will not die.' In the days preceding our big Wednesday demonstration, when the SBs had tried all sorts of intimidating tactics to compel our S.R.C. to disband, he had been in and out of police detention, ostensibly for routine questioning, countless times. It didn't seem as if anything could ever dampen his enthusiasm or undermine his commitment.

'Hold him on the other side,' I said to Khotso. We struggled on, with him between us, to the safety of the nearest yard.

The shooting had lasted for seconds perhaps, but it had seemed like ages. To be sure, I had expected to be blown to pieces at any moment. But nothing as dramatic happened.

We handed him across the fence to some students who had preceded us to Ma Vy's yard and jumped in after them.

'Bring him over here,' I said.

Khotso rolled his school blazer on the ground close to the wall. We lowered him to the ground with his back to the wall.

'Where does it hurt?' I asked. Only then did I notice the streams of blood oozing through his fingers as he held his hands clasped to his tummy.

'Khotso, keep an eye on him,' I said. 'I won't be long.'

'All right, folks, some of you go from house to house to see what help we can get,' I heard Khotso saying to the others as I darted away.

I leapt across the fence to the next yard, across the next street, through another yard to the next one and then into the street, until I reached his home. His elder sister, Sindiswa, was cleaning the sitting-room floor when I burst in through the front door. Their parents were at work. She and her brother were their only children. Upon my entrance she quickly sprang to her feet.

'What a fright you've given me!' she said with both hands clasped to her heart. 'With all that nasty shooting going on outside I'm scared to even step out of this door. It's as if something terrible is going to happen any time. What on earth is the matter?'

'Sis Sindi, we've got no time to waste,' I said. 'Please come with me.'

'But why, what's wrong?'

'I'm afraid something frightful has happened to your brother.'
'Oh! No, he's not been killed, has he?'
'No, no, no, not that.'
'Where's he then?'
'Come, you'll see.'

I led the way out. Sindiswa followed close behind, her knees red with floor polish.

She tried to pump out more information from me, but I was somewhat too dazed to give any coherent explanation as we trotted back, through side alleys and backyards, to where I'd left the others in Ma Vy's yard.

Ma Vy herself, who ran a spot (which is our euphemism for a drinking joint) at her house, was already there.

Ma Vy was a buxom lady in her fifties. She was called Ma Vy after her eldest daughter, Violet, who had been my friend's sweetheart when we were still much younger, before they parted. The story of Ma Vy's family was public knowledge. Violet had been forced to leave school after Standard Six to work in order to supplement their family income. He and Violet began to drift apart the moment she left school. I was not at all sorry to see them break up because, among other things, she had taken up with the Hazels, a knife-happy gang of merciless thugs who reigned over our township with an iron hand. They terrorised school kids by taking all the money we brought to school for lunch or waylaying us when we were sent to the shops by our parents. The Hazels had bluntly told him that if carried on with Violet, they'd cut him to pieces. I convinced him, though he was adamant at first, to drop the affair. I'm not sorry that I did, for there are moments in the townships when it is folly to play brave. The ego has no actual physical proportions.

Ma Vy had not known anything about Violet's affairs. She was too busy figuring out how to feed her husband and their six children. Her husband, whom everybody simply called Ma Vy's husband, had been out of work for more than three years. Before then he had been a factory hand at Vulcan's in Croesus. His right hand had been caught in a machine and chopped off. Vulcan's paid him R500 in compensation money. They also paid for his treatment and the cost of fitting him with an artificial hand. After leaving the hospital he set out to blow his money like it was made of soap bubbles, so that very soon there wasn't a cent left. That made him go back to work. But Vulcan's was laying off several factory hands made redundant by the introduction of new machines. Moreover, the operation of the new machines required higher skills than blacks were allowed in law to possess. Ma Vy's husband began to besiege the Unemployment Bureau until he thought he'd never see the day when he didn't have to rise before five every weekday and take a train to town to go and line up outside the offices of the Bureau, with multitudes of other job-seekers, for a job which never came. He soon abandoned these fruitless efforts and took to drink the way a cat takes to milk. As far as his family responsibilities were concerned, he simply drifted into blissful oblivion and euphoric apathy.

That was when Violet left school and abandoned herself to shebeen-crawling and the orgy of weekend-long parties with the Hazels, on the money they had forcibly extorted from kids or by mugging people returning from work on Friday evenings with their pay-packets bulging. She always brought her own earnings home intact. On that score her mother had nothing to complain about. If on most Friday and Saturday nights Violet didn't sleep at home, it was more than her mother could have been reasonably expected to know. She was now running a shebeen, which did a thriving all-night business, particularly at weekends. As her own business expanded, she left her job as a domestic servant in Parktown. On the Wednesday of the shootings she had witnessed the shootings from her window, which overlooked the main road. She had seen us flock into her yard and when the shooting stopped came out to attend to the injured.

When we arrived, Sindiswa threw herself into the small crowd of students who had gathered round her brother. One look at him, propped against the wall, his face ghastly pale and contorted with pain, and she burst into a most heart-rending wail.

'*Wu! Umntana' sekhaya,*' she cried, 'they've killed him, they've killed him!' She threw her hands into the sky and held them clasped on her head.

When his eyes lighted upon hers, he affected a smile but said nothing.

'My child, we must rush him to the hospital immediately,' Ma Vy said. She was kneeling beside him. 'In the meantime let us move him into the house.'

Sindiswa then did a most unpredictable thing. Like a woman possessed, she picked him up and carried him in her arms, as if he were a baby. She staggered a little but moved resolutely towards the gate facing the main road, which was deserted except for the police and some newspaper reporters.

A piebald township mongrel, lethargically scratching fleas, stood watch beside the gate. It looked up momentarily at Sindiswa and immediately lost interest.

She walked out of the yard, with tears streaming down her cheeks.

'*Yeyeni bo!*' Ma Vy exclaimed. 'Where's she taking him to?'

'I think she's going to get a taxi, auntie,' I replied softly.

'But we can't allow her to go alone.'

Khotso and I trooped after Sindiswa at a discreet distance, while Ma Vy and the others watched us apprehensively. We walked on with a great sense of foreboding. We expected the police to unleash a thunderbolt at us at any moment.

A few policemen detached themselves from the rest and came towards us. Many reporters, their cameras flashing, rushed forward despite efforts by the police to hold them back. I saw two policemen grab a black photographer like so much dirty washing, rip out the film from his camera and crush it under their heavy boots into near-pulp. But some of those photos, with Sindiswa carrying her dying brother in her arms, like a pilgrim bearing some sacrificial offering, found their way into the world's leading newspapers, as we were to find out later when we went into exile.

With our ugly presentiments still undiminished, Khotso and I closed ranks behind her.

The mongrel, still lounging unperturbed at the gate, did not so much as raise its head in our direction.

'Sis', Sindi, let's put him down while we wait for transport.'

I sat on the pavement and invited her to rest him on my lap, which she did, with Khotso's help.

He was breathing with increasing difficulty. A faint smile played on his lips, but furrows of pain showed on his forehead and in his eyes. His wound was no longer bleeding freely. Ma Vy had tied a piece of cloth torn from one of her sheets round his tummy.

'*Wat makeer met hom*?' A white policeman asked when they reached us.

'*Uthi umlungu kwenzenjani?*' a black police sergeant called Hlubi translated.

Hlubi was the most dreaded policeman in Soweto. His name spelt blind terror. He was rumoured to be fearless and ruthless to the point of recklessness and sadism. Stories about him were legend. One story had it that enemy bullets turned to water before him and gun barrels puffed harmless smoke. Some said he could also turn into a black cat and stalk unwary criminals like a cat after mice. And once in their midst he would again assume human form. They said that during his annual leave he always went home to Soshangane to be strengthened by the most powerful doctors of that land of illustrious *inyangas*. In Alexandra township in the days of gang warfare between the Msomi gang and the Spoilers, when Hlubi was still a young private on the rise, they say he once came between the rival gangs, who were taking snipe-shots at each other across opposite ends of the street. The gangs switched targets and aimed at him. He stood there while bullets sailed harmlessly past until, their ammunition exhausted, the gangs fled. At the Back of the Moon, where the gangs used to drink during their momentary periods of truce, which could be as short-lived as each gang leader's state of sobriety, they used to post sentries all round the joint and around the police station to spy on the movements of the police. Despite such precautions Hlubi would suddenly appear, as if from nowhere, and blow his whistle to summon the other police, waiting in their squad cars and black marias a few streets away, to come and collect their haul. And not a single one of his victims ever managed to escape. In this way he came to be attributed with the distinction of having broken the Msomi gang and the Spoilers almost single-handed.

When the era of vicious gang warfare subsided in Alexandra, he was transferred to Newlands to help smash the criminal squads which had begun to rear their ugly heads in Western Native Township, Newclare and Sophiatown. With the help of the *knobkierrie*-wielding Zulus he smashed most of the gangs there, too, and unleashed a spate of atrocities such as the townships had never seen before and probably the whole of black Africa since the *lifaqane* wars. He used to accord special favours to Zulus coming to seek work in Johannesburg by arranging for them to obtain work-seeking and residence permits without difficulties (they then had no problem in finding a room, mainly in the newly opened hostel in Mzimhlophe), in exchange for their help in clubbing down any youth they met in the streets. The Zulus composed a new battle cry which sent cold chills down every young man's spine. They used to shout *'Ngashay' ikepisi kwaphum' utsotsi'*, meaning there's a *tsotsi* lurking beneath every cap so hit every man wearing a cap, you can't go wrong. Ayres and Smith experienced a sudden slump in their sales figures. As the township's youth wouldn't take all of this sitting down, a running battle developed between the Zulus and themselves, which called for more effective organisation from all sides.

Various mobile stores soon emerged all over the townships and did a roaring business in three-star knives, baby browns, knuckle-dusters and, for the very poor, socks loaded with sand, broken bicycle chains and *bogdraads*, very cheap but effective. The 'Russians', a gang of blanket-clad Basotho mainly from Newclare, who always moved about with their long sticks hidden under their blankets, brought them out in the open and fell upon both groups indiscriminately. Every other group hitherto uninvolved began to put out their battle regalia within easy reach. The Pedis, famous for their prowess with bare fisticuffs, went on a preventive rampage. This also put the Mpondos on a war footing, who drew out their *ntshumentshus*, made of thin but strong wires the size of bicycle spokes, which killed without drawing blood or causing any superficial injuries. Their more peaceful cousins, the Bacas, who had made the gumboot dance famous and were employed by the City Council as nightsoil men, began to wreak havoc upon the townships with their *sjamboks* and buckets. There are many who have ascribed this outbreak of violence to Hlubi's squad. Hardened criminals who have survived their jail sentences bow their heads and lower their voices whenever they describe their treatment by Hlubi.

'What's the matter with him?' Hlubi repeated the white policeman's question.

Sindiswa simply blew, so unexpectedly the policemen were left gaping. Looking back, I believe her outburst then had something to do with the manner in which she was later hounded and harassed by the police, so that when she could no longer take it, she skipped the country, although to the best of my knowledge she had remained largely apolitical, unless joining in the singing of a few freedom songs at her brother's funeral and raising her fist in the black power salute, along with thousands of other mourners, can be construed as engaging in politics. Anyway, it cost Sindiswa dearly, including a broken nose.

'You have a bloody nerve!' she said. 'First you kill my brother, then you ask what's the matter with him!'

'Sis' Sindi, please calm down,' I said.

'You're nothing but common murderers!'

She spat venomously on the ground and paused for a while, as if savouring her unspoken poisonous thoughts.

'You!' She pointed to Hlubi and other black members of the police force, her eyes wet, her voice tear-stained and her expression virulent. 'You would shoot your own children for a miserly thirty pieces of silver. I could peel you like peaches and God himself would call it justice. You're incomplete; the human parts of you are missing. *Sies!*'

I was beginning to think that a taxi would never come or that if it did it would come too late to be of any use.

Up and down the street police were diverting traffic off the main road, I noticed with added despondency.

His breath was beginning to fail him. Despite the chilly weather sweat showed on his forehead.

Just then, to infinite relief, Bra P. arrived in his BMW.

The police had allowed him through.

Bra P. was in many ways so enigmatic he might have been a character straight out of Cannery Row. He was held in awe and respect by both the old and the young of Soweto, although precisely on what his reputation rested nobody could say. But in their infinite wisdom, born of the most gruesome and excruciating experiences, township folk have grown to trust the rumoured word more than the printed one. The evidence of their own instincts, sharpened and refined by the demands for survival, carries more weight than the most thoroughly researched and carefully prepared programmes of the S.A.B.C. which claim to deal dispassionately in facts. Only a few facts were known about Bra P. and the rest was pure conjecture. However, the people knew, as if by intuition, that no legend, no matter how bloated in its subsequent editions, ever grew out of nothing. Bra P.'s life-style seemed to give a lot of credence to some of the things that were said about him. His wife had died many years ago, when we were still children chasing around tennis balls in the streets. She had left him no children and he had never remarried. He was decidedly one of the most well-to-do people in Soweto, with a passion for expensive German cars. Indeed, this could be said to have been his only form of indulgence for he neither drank nor smoked, nor was he known to ever chase after women. He owned the latest BMW model and a Mercedes 280 SL.

Bra P. was what the legal *gurus* usually describe as 'a native of no fixed occupation', although as far as anybody could tell he had never been pulled in for vagrancy or charged under the Influx Control regulations. He had a clean police record and exhibited remarkable smoothness in his operations and with his tongue, which in normal times would have enabled him to choose between the most popular pulpit in any parish and a seat in parliament, rising in either case to become a prince of the church or to the highest executive position in the land.

He had been born in the early days of old 'Kofifi', when African politicians, priests and pick-pockets lived cheek-by-jowl with Indian pacifists and Chinese philosophers. His relationships and contacts with people of other races and in every profession dated to those days in old Sophiatown. Bishops of certain churches anxious to avert looming schisms within their churches, politicians wanting to heal imminent rifts within their parties, government officials desiring to quash serious scandals implicating them in corruption, gangsters seeking the most effective methods of eliminating opposition – all had been known to seek advice from Bra P. Neither the restrictions imposed on others by the Group Areas Act nor the Job Reservation laws circumscribed his freedom of movement or association. But in other directions he had been hemmed in by all kinds of legislative constraints for so long that he had come to consider them as a kind of protective hedge. His association with crimes of every description was accepted as normal and admirable by township residents. From his early youth he had led the kind of gangsters you read about in Dugmore Boetie's Sophiatown sagas of which the Hazels of our time are but a poor apology and imitation. Everything he touched invariably turned out to be against the law as surely as if he'd had the Midas touch.

Bra P.'s prosperity was somehow connected to the fact that he had rejected the theories of honest labour and private ownership of removable property almost from infancy. He was master of every criminal technique in existence connected with larceny, fraud, robbery, safe-cracking, house-breaking and theft. He was reputed to be engaged in certain nefarious dealings with every big crime syndicate from Springs to Randfontein. His influence, which was rumoured to be quite considerable, was said to stretch as far as the diamond city of Kimberley and the *dagga*-growing districts of Pondoland and the Maluti mountains. In this regard it was also noted that he had once beaten the daylights out of a certain prominent but presumptuous journalist who'd had the effrontery to publish an exposé of organised crime on the Rand in which Bra P. was said to be implicated and to feature prominently. The same journalist had previously been showered with accolades for his daring revelation of the abuses of prison labour, of Africans convicted of petty offences under the pass laws, by white farmers in the potato-growing district of the Eastern Transvaal. But success, like the *skokiaan* many drank in those days – and the reporter in question was known to drink like a fish – can sometimes go to the head. As many people pointed out, not without fear of the wrath which such recklessness in the name of enterprising journalism could unleash on the heads of many innocents, it is one thing to expose the true and proven enemies of the people and another to turn in one who is black and struggling like yourself. And that is how the people tended to view a certain category of criminals who were known to behave sometimes like wilful children thwarted from achieving their fixed purposes, but who otherwise never terrorised the townships unless somewhat frustrated in their dealings when their blind rage, like a tornado, could strike everybody.

Bra P. had never been known to react violently in public; people who knew him preferred to keep it that way. But not so the journalist concerned. He filed a case of assault with the police and let it be known that he'd die defending the freedom of the press. It didn't matter that people told him that, after all, it was a white press. The reporter in question died a few weeks later, coming from a drinks party, of multiple stab wounds, and the murder was never solved. So that his case against Bra P. had to be thrown out of court for lack of evidence. A second more spectacular and devastating part of the article promised for the next issue of *Drum* never saw publication. But such rumours as the reporter had floated clung to Bra P., like the halo from an artist's impression of the archangel Michael.

Others said that no policeman dared to lay his fingers on him.

Bra P. was also a keen sportsman, had played centre-half for Sophiatown Rovers, and was now honorary President of the National Professional Soccer League, by virtue of having been one of its first major sponsors when it was formed, before white industrialists caught on to the bandwagon. He was behind the first soccer match between a white professional team and a black side, when Germiston Callies played Orlando Pirates in Maseru, and those in the know ascribe many of the advances made in multiracial sports in the country to his untiring efforts, especially behind the scenes. This alone made him a very important figure in the life of the township, where sport rivals politics in importance and is only rivalled by shebeens in vying for the undivided attention of township residents. Generally he was considered to be a greater celebrity and exercised more influence in our lives than either the Minister for Plural Relations, Sports and Culture or Soweto's Mayor, Mr Rathebe.

Bra P. had been directed to us by a group of students sent by Khotso to seek help. They had dashed about pleading with everybody they knew who owned a car to rush our injured friend to hospital. Many people with cars had gone to work, but the few who could be found at home were unwilling to meddle in a case which appeared to involve the police. Next to death itself what township people dread most are the police. You can never get anyone to lend you a hand in a case which shows all the likelihood of involving the police, no matter how remotely; just as you can never get anyone in their right senses to help you with those other minstrels of death known in the township parlance as *tsotsis*, who kill as easily as it takes to say '*Voetsek*'. Between the police and the *tsotsis* it is difficult to decide exactly who rules the township – very often both have very well-defined spheres of influence and a kind of no-man's zone where they strike terror into the stoutest hearts; both are backed by a massive state machinery which would definitely recoil upon itself if it were to know the truth about the extent of its own involvement. Only one kind of being can be said to tower above the police and the *tsotsis* and is the spiritual mentor and the physical sustainer of both these groups. He is not the State President either, but is the man who consorts with both groups, from whom they derive their real powers. He can bring down the highest placed officers in the land at the drop of a hat and can break the most vicious gang of *tsotsis* as if they were made of so many twigs. Bra P. was just such a man.

He was strolling towards the main road to see what all the *rockshin'*, as he called it, was about, when he met the students who had been sent to organise transport, and without the slightest hesitation offered to help. They told him were to find us, so he sent them back and went for his car.

He stopped a few yards from us, came out of his car and walked towards us. He recognised Sindiswa immediately. She was still 'damnalising' the police, as township folk would say. Bra P. knew almost everybody in our township by name. As for us, we had grown up right before his very eyes, as they say.

'Sindi, get into the car, *asseblief tu*,' he said.

'Bra P., they've killed my brother, they've killed my brother, they've ki...lled him!'

'All right, all right, Sindi. Just come with me. Let's get the lad to the hospital. He's not going to die.'

He put his right arm around her shoulders and gently but firmly led her away. He opened the front door for her to get in.

She obeyed but continued to shout – '*Lezinja*, they've killed my brother, they've ki...lled him.'

Bra P. came back to help me and Khotso carry our friend into the car.

'How is he, boys?' he asked.

He stopped to take a closer look at him and asked – '*Kunjani*, Muntu?'

'*Yesslik*!' he moaned softly to himself.

He looked up at the police. His eyes narrowed, just a little, and his mouth twisted, ever so slightly.

We carried our friend to the back seat of the car and there laid him to rest.

'I'll need your help, boys.'

We needed no urging. Khotso and I got on either side of him in the back seat.

Muntu died on the way to hospital ...

Mbulelo Vizikhungo Mzamane was born in Brakpan in 1948, and grew up in townships on the Witwatersrand. He was taught by *Drum* magazine writer Can Themba while in secondary school in Swaziland, before obtaining a degree from the University of Botswana, Lesotho, and Swaziland. In 1979 he went to Sheffield, UK for his doctoral studies, and then to the United States of America where he taught at various universities. On his return to South Africa he was appointed vice chancellor of the University of Fort Hare in the Eastern Cape.
Book Extracted: *The Children of Soweto, a trilogy* (Longman, 1982)

Towards the Mountain
Alan Paton

When I was six I went to school at Berg Street Girls' School, which took small boys in the early classes. I went there with fear and apprehension, though of course that is a common experience of small boys and girls. But I think my fear was extreme. I was in fact a sissy.

I did not go there unlettered. My mother had taught me to read and write and count. She was a good teacher and I was a willing pupil. Like most beginners I was put into Class 1, and after a day or two I was put into Standard I, thus virtually dispensing with what might be called infant education. This happened to me on yet one more occasion, and it meant that I went into high school about three years younger than the average.

This however cannot be compared with the school career of South Africa's wonder child, Jan Hendrik Hofmeyr. He went to school when he was eight, and was put into Standard I in January 1902. In March he was in Standard II. In January 1903 he was in Standard III, in March he was in Standard IV, in August in Standard V. In 1904 he did Standard VI and Form A, and in 1905 Form B and Form C. In 1906 he went into the final class, Form D, and for the first time spent a full year in a class. He went to university in short trousers, a boy amongst men. Whatever else this spectacular career did for him, it made him – in the deepest sense – forever solitary.

I was certainly solitary at Berg Street Girls' School. Whatever my home may have lacked, it was my shelter, the place where I was warm and safe. And when I got into the classroom, I was warm and safe again. The misery of my life was getting from one shelter to the other. The streets and the playground were places of peril. In the playground I stood against the brick walls in the sun, watching the other children play. I would have played if they had asked me to, but no one did.

I did not wish to attract attention, but I did. I wore a pair of shoes that did not lace up, but had a strap that went over the instep and was fastened by a button. These shoes were pronounced by one of the older boys to be girls' shoes, but I denied it, I am sure not hotly and angrily, but no doubt quietly and gently. I had no idea that such a small matter could attract such great attention, but soon there was a crowd of boys around me, and there was general agreement that I was wearing girls' shoes.

After a while they left me, and there I was standing alone, thinking to myself, these shoes look like girls' shoes. I lifted one foot and put it on the other but this of course hid only one of the shoes. So I walked to the big school verandah, and sat down on one of the benches, for there I could put both of my feet under the bench and so hide the shoes. But I had not been sitting there long when a teacher came to me and said, 'Sitting, sitting, go and play in the sun.' She said, 'Aren't you well?' But I had no great experience of lying, so I told her I was well, and she said, 'Then go into the sun, it's against the rules to sit here now.'

My fear of bigger boys was extreme. It was cowardice that led me into my first offence. We were walking home after school, and a girl of about my age was walking ahead of me. Some of the bigger boys ordered me to push her off the pavement, and I obeyed. I did not think further about it, either to feel shame or regret. It was an act of expediency, designed to save me from further attention. When the shame and regret came later, they had no element of nobility. Next day when I got to school I was ordered to report at the headmistress's office, and there stood the little girl. The headmistress asked if I had pushed a girl off the pavement, and I again, with no experience of lying, said yes. She then lectured me on the contemptibility of such conduct. She looked at the trembling six-year-old boy and passed sentence upon him. He was to eat his lunch on the girls' verandah. I have now lived for seventy years since that punishment, and never again have I pushed a girl off the pavement.

My strongest memory of Berg Street Girls' School is a strange one. I wrote it down more than forty years after it had all happened, because it seemed foolish to feel pain and shame about it any longer. It was a cold day at school and a bitter wind was blowing. We had eaten our sandwich lunches, and were in the playground. It was with dismay that I saw coming up the street towards the gate of the school the black boy who worked as a servant in our house. It was not the sight of him that dismayed me, but the fact that he was carrying a basket, and over the top of the basket was a clean white cloth. I knew at once that it was food, no doubt hot food, that my mother had sent her son because of the bitterness of the day.

I knew that this would attract more attention to me, so I went further along the wall so as not to be seen by the boy. I had not been standing there long when some of the schoolboys came to me and said, your boy's here with a basket. But I, though inexperienced in lying, denied that such a boy could be there. So they brought the boy, and of course it was our boy, and he smiled at me uncertainly because of the strangeness of the place, and I denied all knowledge of him. But he told them he was certainly our boy, and that I was the son of the house, and that my mother had sent me something warm to eat and drink. I denied him the second time.

Then one of the schoolboys took the white cloth off the basket, and there was a jug with a cup in the mouth of it, and another white cloth in which something was wrapped up. He took the cup out of the mouth of the jug and said, cocoa, hot cocoa. He opened the second white cloth and there were the scones that my mother had baked. And I knew that while they were hot she had opened them, not with a knife but with her hands, and had dropped butter into them, to melt and sink yellow and sweet, into their hearts. But I denied her.

One of the schoolboys said to me, 'What are you going to do with it?' 'It's not mine,' I said. He asked, 'Can I have it?' 'It's not mine,' I said. He was so persistent that in the end, although the food was not mine, I said he could have it. So they shared it out. What the black boy thought of it all I don't know. When they had finished he put the jug and the cup back in the basket and covered them with the white cloths. Then he saluted me and went out of the gate, but I did not acknowledge his salute, for why should I salute an unknown boy?

When I wrote this story forty years later, I called it 'The Gift', and I ended it with these lines:

> As I remember, my mother asked me when I returned if this strange story was true, and I did not lie to her as I had done to the boys at school. I do not remember that she spoke any further. I do not remember that she patted my head or smiled in any special way at me. I do not remember that she ever told the story to my father, but that does not mean that she did not. I do not think she told it to my brother, because he would have plagued me with it. I have no doubt she kept it in her heart.
>
> And so would any mother keep it in her heart. For this is one for whom she fears, going forward and retreating, now confident, now afraid, making his way from her womb into the world.

I finished my Standard I by pleasing my parents, and I am sure myself, by coming top of the class and winning a first prize. It is my big regret that I did not keep any of the books given as prizes. Now that I am old I would like to be able to take them in my hands, and I am sure that if I could read them now, they too would strike resounding chords. It is strange that at twenty a man can destroy a book treasured at six, and at seventy wish that he had not. It may be that at twenty he puts away childish things, but that at seventy he wants to have them back.*

In 1909 the Natal Education Department built a new school called

---

*My sister Eunice questions this account. She says that the books were stored in a trunk and were destroyed by rats, and that I was desolate. I think her account is the correct one.

Havelock Road Boys. The school was not far from our house in Pine Street, and its first headmaster was Mr Harward. Again I went to a new school with fear. The school went to Standard VI so that I now had to deal with big boys, many of whom were decidedly rough. Here I committed my second offence. I wrote the word 'fuck' on the wall of the school lavatory.

For this I was taken by one of the older boys to the headmaster. Mr Harward's sentence was that I should go home and report my offence to my parents, who would deal with it in their own way. I made my way home with much apprehension and told my mother of my wickedness. Then we sat down to wait for my father to return from work. When she told him he called me into one of the rooms and shut the door. He then chastised me, how grievously I cannot remember. That was the last time save one that I wrote on a lavatory wall. Of the meaning of the word I wrote on this first occasion, I had no inkling whatsoever, though I knew well that it was not the kind of word that one would use in front of one's elders and betters.

I must not give the impression that I was totally lacking any spark of individuality. It so happened that I was one day returning home from some errand or another; I was walking up Church Street towards Pine Street, where I would turn right and walk down the hill to our home. I must have been nine or ten years old, or at the most eleven. As I walked up Church Street a soldier from the regiment at Fort Napier was walking down. He had probably had a few drinks, for as I passed he snatched my hat from my head and threw it into the drain that ran at the side of the pavement. In the early days of Pietermaritzburg these drains, in Afrikaans *sluite*, in Natal English *sloots* carried water from the hills into the town, and citizens drew water from them for their houses and gardens. But I think that at the time of this incident this was no longer done, and the drain water must have been foul.

I rescued my hat and was filled with a burning sense of affront and injustice. Could I let this insult go unpunished? I decided that I could not. Clutching my hat firmly in my hand I went after the soldier. I now exhibited the courage that is born of anger. I launched myself at the soldier and delivered a kick at his back. Whether I reached his bottom is doubtful. But I certainly kicked him in the back of his thigh. With angry curses he turned to grapple with his assailant, but the boy was winging his way home, with unChristian joy in his heart.

A visit to Durban was a tremendous excitement. The first visit that I remember was to the beach at night, and the sea terrified me. Then there were the ships in the harbour and the zoo at Mitchell Park, and the subtropical richness of the trees and shrubs. There was Musgrave Road, which even at that age I recognised as a residential street of wealth and beauty, of big rich houses in tremendous gardens, many of which ran down unfenced to the road; of these houses hardly one remains today. But for me the great excitement was the tramcars. In Pietermaritzburg there were only two routes, one from the Botanic Gardens to Retief Street, and the other from Howick Road to Scottsville. They intersected at right angles at the Town Hall, and the tramcars met there on the stroke of every quarter. But here in Durban they arrived at the post office every minute, from Toll Gate and Marriott Road, from Stamford Hill and Umgeni, from the Beach and the Point, from Congella and Umbilo. One of our holiday treats was to take the circular route from the post office up Berea Road, then along the whole length of Musgrave Road, and down Florida Road back to the Post Office. It took forty minutes and cost I think threepence for a child. It was like the Sunday piece of cheese, not to be devoured in one or two bites, but to be savoured piece by piece.

These childhood years, which were characterised by an intense response to nature, now witnessed an intense response to words and books, to *Tom Sawyer* and *Huckleberry Finn*, *Alice in Wonderland* and *Through the Looking-Glass*, *Water Babies* with some very difficult passages, *Kidnapped* and *Treasure Island*, *Robinson Crusoe* and *The Swiss Family Robinson*. The word 'fell' in *Water Babies* captured my heart.

My father subscribed to *Chums* for us. It came once a week, and its arrival was an event and a weapon to be used by my father. After some time he changed to the *Boys' Own Paper*. Comics were strictly forbidden, so we read them at school; the comics of those days were full of misadventures of amiable simpletons, who walked innocent-eyed into the most diabolical traps. They did not deal with war, sex, violence, and death; why they were thought to be harmful I do not know.

My father was devoted to the novels of Sir Walter Scott, but I do not remember whether I read them then or in my high school days. But I believe I read them all, and I am sure I read them before I started on Charles Dickens, when I was about thirteen. I would not find Scott easy reading today, but I had no difficulty then. Nor did I find the long and descriptive passages tedious. It has been suggested that reading habits have changed drastically with the increased tempo of life and I think this is true. My own have changed considerably. I believe that if you write in chapters they must be short. I find that even when I am reading a good writer it irks me when the chapter goes on too long. If the writer does not use chapters, but divides the work into sections, then I want each section to be separated from the next by a space, and this space should be as much as would be required for three or four lines.

Just what kind of child I appeared to be to my parents I don't know.

Perhaps they were glad to have produced one so safe and studious. But I was not prepared to leave the writing of books to Scott and R L Stevenson. I cut the few empty pages that I could find in old exercise books into four equal pieces, and made small volumes out of them. My mother stitched the pages together. I then wrote in them, in a style resembling print, stories and other pieces, modelled no doubt on *Chums* and the *Boys' Own Paper*. These, plus some real books, formed the stock of a bookstore of which I was both manager and salesman.

My brother Atholl was on the whole not interested in literature, and certainly not in the childish game of making it and selling it. He was born on 31 January 1904, just a year after me, and was named after the earls and dukes of Atholl. Though he has been dead now for nearly forty years, I remember his birthday every year. But now I had acquired two sisters who were more willing to join in my games. My sister Eunice, named after her mother, was born on 4 December 1907, and my sister Ailsa, named after the famous island rock in the Firth of Clyde, on 6 July 1910. My own names were Alan Stewart, the first with no special significance except that it was Scottish, the second the name of the royal house. My father's love for all things Scottish was very deep, and he imparted it to at least one of his children.

I introduced my sisters to the world of commerce, and we had a little shop which sold jams, meal, salt, and diminutive loaves of bread which my mother made for us. I then entered the building trade, and made bricks; the material came from 17 Pine Street, a vacant plot next to us, and the bricks were made red by having geranium petals stuck to them while they were wet. Atholl was inclined to ridicule these activities, and he corrupted my sisters, who adopted an ambivalent attitude to my work, cooperating at one moment and poking fun at the next.

I can only suppose that it was a happy childhood except for one thing, and that was the authoritarian and often arbitrary rule of my father, which my mother tempered when she was able. But for three things I am grateful – the opportunity to walk the hills of Pietermaritzburg, to know the stories and noble passages of the Bible, and to enter the world of words and books.

When I turned ten I reached the top class at Havelock Road Boys, and was eligible for the Natal Bursary Examination. If I were successful I would win a bursary that would pay for my fees and books at Maritzburg College. If I failed I could try again at eleven, and again at twelve. I was successful and went to Maritzburg College in February 1914, having just turned eleven. I suppose it does not matter now, but I would not wish any of my grandsons to enter a high school at that age.

Alan Paton, author of *Cry, the Beloved Country*, was born in Pietermaritzburg in 1903. After studying at the University of Natal, Paton worked as a teacher, before being appointed principal of the Diepkloof Reformatory in 1935. His thirteen years there helped shape his political consciousness, and, in 1953, Paton founded the Liberal Party, which opposed apartheid and proposed a non-racial government. The party was banned in 1968 after the government instituted its Prohibition of Political Interference bill. Paton died in Natal in 1988.
Book Extracted: *Towards the Mountain* (David Philip, Cape Town, 1980)

The South African Autobiography
William Plomer

When my father had returned to South Africa in 1914 he was commissioned with the rank of captain in the South African forces, and put on to help with the enrolment and transport of large numbers of African drivers and carriers for the campaign against the Germans in East Africa. He attached great importance to the status and welfare of every individual, and chose to keep full records of the enlisted men. This was not done in East Africa, where the men were no doubt regarded as expendable. Many were lost there, and never heard of again. Many others, returning to Durban in the last stages of dysentery and fever, died at sea, into which not only their bodies but their identity discs were dropped. My father tried to make some amends to these obscure victims of the war by seeking out evidence of their deaths, so that their next-of-kin might be notified and payment made allowances of money owing to them. This solicitude, this trouble taken over not merely expendable but expended black nobodies, confirmed the official view of my father as a conscientious civil servant, but a cranky and tiresome negrophilist.

In the middle of the war my father, who had been refused active service either in South-West or East Africa, made another attempt to be sent to France. The War Office in Whitehall had asked the South African Government to recruit and equip a labour corps of Africans for service as stevedores at ports and rail-heads in France. He had much to do with the raising of this corps and managed to obtain permission to go with it to Europe, but was told at the last moment that it was essential, because of his experience, to remain in South Africa as its records officer. Possibly it was thought that if he went to France with the corps he might over-stimulate the self-esteem of its members. He established his office near Cape Town, and was kept busy there until the end of the war, when he awaited the return of his wife and children.

To an observant boy the voyage out, after the drabnesses of England in wartime, was as good as a play. The ship was crowded, mainly with people who had been waiting for the end of the war to return to their homes, families, or vested interests in South Africa. As happens in ships and in prisons, they quickly revealed mutual attractions, antipathies, or indifference. It was a society constituted by chance and existing briefly in isolation and idleness, and individuals were brought into clear focus, like moths under a magnifying-glass.

Usually seated together on deck were two semi-millionaires from the Rand. Slightly too well dressed, they stuck together, talking, one supposed, much about money and a little about politics. 'The knights,' said somebody, 'are so exclusive' – an observation which might have annoyed one of them: he was a baronet of very recent creation.

Two of the female passengers, if one chose to compare them, afforded a striking contrast and symbolised two different kinds of society. One was Lady Buxton, the Governor-General's wife, whose quiet dignity, easy simplicity of manner, and good humour tinged with sadness were not merely charming but fitting to one who presides but does not struggle. One felt she had taken on, without fuss or a grain of self-importance, what may sometimes have been the uncongenial share of her husband's fraction of authority in a still vast and powerful empire – a perfect embodiment of what is meant, in the best sense, by a ruling class, its best sense being that of responsibility.

The other was a Johannesburg Jewess, who was travelling with her husband.

'Almost the only woman on this boat,' said my mother, 'who dresses with any style, but it's a style too splendid for the boat.'

The lady was in her forties, tallish, quite handsome, with a shapely body skilfully corseted and a collection of smart new clothes which she meant to try out long before rejoining her circle in Johannesburg. In an evening dress of Venetian-red lace, with stockings and high-heeled satin shoes to match, she would appear on deck alone after dinner, her big eyes gleaming under heavily darkened lids. Then, with a too carefully manicured hand weighted with two or three conspicuous diamonds, she would raise a more than ordinarily long cigarette-holder to a mouth made up to match her dress.

Everybody stared at her and made remarks about her, but hardly anybody seemed to talk to her, and her husband, obese and taciturn, was generally in the smoking-room with a cigar. There was something distressing in her decorated solitude. Her restless glances made it seem that her clothes and jewels had not given her confidence. Her very vitality seemed to make her ill at ease, as if she didn't quite know what to do with it. She seemed worldly, but for the moment at least, without a world of her own. It was as if she enjoyed what are called the good things of life but was waiting for the best things. By over-stressing her appearance she became a figure of drama, and in her mobile eyes the torments, past and future, of her race seemed to be glinting darkly.

My mother did not like people to feel uncomfortable, and wanted to talk to her, all the more because we have always been a pro-Semite family; but she would have hated to appear to be taking any initiative out of anything like idle curiosity or a sentiment akin to pity, and she kept waiting for a suitable opportunity to fall casually into conversation, and kept being thwarted by circumstances until quite late in the voyage.

The usual shipboard pairings-off occurred, quickening as we neared the Equator, and mostly tending to cool as we drew nearer to the ties and separations waiting just beyond the horizon. All this was vivid to a schoolboy escaping from murky wartime winters in England: so were our ports of call.

One day Ascension Island sprang from the sea like an old coloured print with its rufous rocky foreground, a few white buildings, on one of which a magenta bougainvillaea had spread like a stain, and the Green Mountain towering in the background. I had been sharing a cabin with a landowner from St Helena. When we got there he was met by his own carriage and invited us to drive with him on a conducted tour of the interior, so off we drove through Jamestown, in the wake of Lady Buxton and the local Governor. St Helena was not at all the horrid rock which history books had led one to imagine. There were flowers and pretty people everywhere. Wisps of tropical mist ran past like long scarves of grey chiffon in mysterious levitation. The sun came out on groups of peasants working without haste and without rest in a steeply sloping field of sisal. On the winding upland roads donkeys trotted past with loads of melons or brushwood on their backs, and by the roadside young girls offered for sale necklaces of dyed Job's-tears. At Longwood the tepid Atlantic breeze blew through Napoleon's empty rooms with their austere remains of decorations in the Empire style, like faint echoes of Malmaison, and through the windows one could see rows of blue agapanthus lilies wagging and nodding like the heads of people in a crowd. A smell of wood-smoke from a hut in a ravine, flowering creepers, flying mists, and steamy fragrance – a lovely place of exile, but not for a self-made militarist emperor. The whole ambience was still of the early nineteenth century.

When the ship docked at Cape Town, in the enormous warmth and radiance of a perfect afternoon, we looked down and saw my father standing alone on the quay to meet us. He looked slender and sunburnt in an elegant lightweight uniform of bleached khaki. I suppose I ought to have felt some lively emotion, but he seemed almost a stranger. I had seen little of him in my life, and the last four and a half years in war-darkened England were something he had neither lived through nor was capable of imagining. I had very few memories, thoughts, or jokes to share with him, and the rare remembered happy moments of companionship with him were eclipsed by memories of his senseless angers, grievances, and prejudices. I knew he 'meant well' towards me, but the sight of him gave me no sense of homecoming. He was a man with a craving for the affection he had missed in childhood, but not, apparently, for the affection of his sons.

There is an understanding poem by Cowper against the sending of boys away to boarding schools. To a father he says it is no good complaining of 'filial frankness lost':

Thou well deserv'st an alienated son ...
Add too, that thus estranged, thou canst obtain
By no kind arts his confidence again.

But my father had never really had my confidence.

In London I had been very ill with the Spanish influenza, but he was more interested in telling us how he had not had it himself, and of its ravages in Cape Town. At its height, he said, the main street, Adderley Street, had been empty at noon, except for a wagon laden with uncoffined corpses. The coloured people had died in thousands and many had been buried in common graves. I don't think he ever asked a single question about my life in England, or my feelings.

He had been living for some time at the International Hotel, and we joined him there. It was a long, low building on an elevated site and had a long, wide, shady verandah behind scarlet-flowering hibiscus hedges. The food was better and more abundant than we had seen for a long time, and I found the physical pleasure of being at the Cape intense. Drunk with warmth, like a bee in spring, I wandered the streets or in the resinous stony pinewoods on the slopes of Table Mountain, or under the heavy-shadowed oaks planted in the seventeenth century by Simon van der Stel, or into the gallery of minor Dutch masters – clean, cool pictures of a domesticated civilisation.

Sociable, my father had a taste for good living, old furniture, fine china and gardens, but none for literature or painting. If he did nothing, at this or any time, to encourage my preferences, it was because they didn't interest him. And there was soon a head-on collision over a triviality. One day at lunch there were some magnificent grapes for dessert. I took some, and noticing that they looked a little dusty washed them in a finger-bowl before eating them. My father surprised me by making a scene. He was white with rage, and, as always when he was emotionally tense, one could see the whites of his eyes showing demonically all round the iris. I think the objection was that my niceness was out of place in one who had his way to make in the world. After all, I wasn't on my way to join the long-disbanded Cape Mounted Rifles, where such finicky behaviour might have been not at all 'The Thing'. I replied, with what must have been a maddening air of condescension, that I wasn't going to eat dirty grapes to please him or anybody else. I then took a few more, which I also washed, with what must have been infuriating deliberateness, before eating them. By nature too docile, I had always had a core of independence, which was now very gradually, too gradually, beginning to harden.

We visited or entertained some of his hospitable friends – the cultivated woman with a collection of eighteenth-century fans, and a bishop, to lunch, the rich couple with a house in the old Dutch colonial style, the English colonel with a fruit farm. Presently we moved out to the remembered salty air and white sands (as Kipling observed) of Muizenberg, and then, before returning up-country, to the delicious town of Ceres. Lost on an inland plateau at the end of a branch railway, it was famous for its variety of heaths and proteas.

To arrive in Johannesburg, in the thin bright air of the highveld, five thousand feet above sea level, was exhilarating. It was especially so in 1919, if one was young: the world was supposed to have been changed for the better by the war, and bright hopes floated about like cheap balloons. Peace had not yet freed my father: though now out of uniform, he was to be occupied for many months more in tidying up the affairs of the African labourers who had returned or failed to return from France. After so many nomadic years he would have liked a settled home among cherished possessions, but my mother was not physically strong enough to run a house. We therefore went to live in a comfortable and well-run boarding house in the well-to-do residential quarter called Parktown.

It was thought that I must go back to school. I was only just fifteen, and my father superstitiously believed that unless one passed examinations and gained degrees or certificates one would have no future. I went back to St Johns, as a day-boy. Although I had been happy there before, I had been so conditioned by my years in England that I returned almost as a stranger.

'Look who's here,' I heard one boy say to another on the very first day, 'the Emperor of China.'

I hid my hands in opposite sleeves and made a grave and courtly bow, as if to confirm my identity.

Not only the trees but the buildings had grown. There was a handsome new chapel, a swimming bath, and two sides of a new quadrangle, with cloisters: the place had quite lost the pioneering, Early Christian air which had formerly given it such a character of its own. Father A. was now the headmaster; before long he was to startle everybody by forsaking the celibate Community of the Resurrection for the connubial bed. Father B. had returned from France, where he had been a chaplain to the forces, with a wound and a decoration, and looked more like an eagle than ever. Father C. had become a bishop. Father D. had vanished. And Father E., with his skimpy, reddish, Apostolic beard, was still shambling about in cassock and biretta, a football in one hand and a bunch of keys in the other, still smiling and nodding gently and resignedly at me because I wouldn't play games.

Pink and white cosmos still waved below the terrace; on windy days red dust-devils still raced across the grassless playing-fields; a play of Shakespeare's was still produced every year – but somehow the spell was broken. Houses were being built on the Kopje, so why climb it? I felt no incentive to work, I was not in harmony with my surroundings, there was nobody to direct my mind, the future was indistinct. I fooled about, idled and dreamed, head and heart were hungry, I was driven in upon myself.

In the holidays I pursued culture by choice and society under parental pressure. Society meant mostly tennis and dancing, though I was not predestined to be either a tennis-player or a dancing man. For the first time I got used to the company of girls and young women – the dumb *ingénue*, the jolly tomboy, the clinging goose, the sinewy sports-girl, the prim prig, the maternally inspired social climber fresh from a Swiss finishing school, the calculating teaser, the nubile monkey. One's attention was directed, as an awful warning, to a nymphomaniac. She was in her thirties and married to a most respectable husband. Women told each other that no man was safe alone with her, 'even for a moment'. Men confirmed this, and made jokes about it. To me she looked predatory. Lean and supple as a cat, she dressed very well but very plainly, often in well-cut tweeds, as it were *en chasseuse*. Her dark hair, done in a modest and even severe style, set off an always colourless face, and in its 'interesting pallor' her restless dark eyes, not large, glittered observantly. It was the mouth that chiefly caught one's attention, the thin, unappeasable lips of a monomaniac. And were there no nice, ordinary girls? Oh, yes. Aren't there always? And there was an intellectual, a finely bred Jewess with a delicate profile like an ancient Egyptian queen and a quiet voice and manner.

I did not take much to most of those whom I partnered on the tennis court or steered round the dance floor – nor they, I dare say, to me. 'William is so critical,' somebody said to my mother. I was. A displaced adolescent in a state of physical and emotional excitement, I found the consumer society in which I moved wanting in charm; it seemed mostly boring and second-rate. Nobody was making anything except money or plans to make more money. Most people climbed and pushed in pursuit of illusory gains or prestige. And for many of the women their chief happiness, or ambition, was to receive invitations to entertainments given by the Governor-General, at this time royal, Prince Arthur of Connaught.

Imagine him standing, dutiful but surely bored, to receive his guests at a dance. His consort stands at his side. Her golden hair is bobbed, and this is thought almost outrageously modern and daring. Her face is unmarked by thought. And a great many very large diamonds scintillate, with every movement, on her head, in her ears, round her neck, on her corsage, wrists, and fingers. Some of them no doubt came out of the African earth above which they now give out an incessant display of coloured prismatic sparks. Royal liveries of scarlet flit or linger in the background, and among the dressed-up guests approaching to be announced and received an anxious debate can be heard on the theme, 'does one or does one not remove one's gloves before shaking the proffered hand of Royalty?' This scene is the crowning ornament of a materialistic city, beneath which at this very moment white men and black are incessantly grubbing for gold ...

William Plomer was born in Pietersburg in 1903, and was an industrious writer who was the author of many biographies, autobiographies, works of poetry, and prose fiction and non-fiction. His education mainly took place in the United Kingdom, and, upon returning to South Africa in the mid-1920s, he began work on his most famous novel, *Turbott Wolfe*. In 1926, Plomer became co-editor of the journal *Voorslag*, which promoted a racially equal South Africa. After leaving as co-editor after just three issues, Plomer went to teach in Japan, and then returned to England where he worked for the publishing firm Jonathan Cape. William Plomer died in 1973.
Book Extracted: *The South African Autobiography* (David Philip, 1984)

Across Boundaries – The Journey of a South African Woman Leader
Mamphela Ramphele

… My memory of my childhood goes back to a rainy day at the beginning of 1953 when we were moving house from one end of Kranspoort to another. We used a mule-drawn cart to transport the household furniture and personal effects. It was a confusing day for me as a little girl who could contribute nothing to the process, though I was made to understand very clearly that I had to keep out of the way of the busy adults. It was strange to sleep in a new house which was to become my home for the next twelve years.

The notion of home as more than the physical structure one inhabits took on a special meaning for me as a little girl. Our new home was a mud-brick house with a mud floor which had to be smeared with cow dung at least once a fortnight by my mother. The floor itself had to be strengthened and smoothed over with specially prepared mud mixed with dung (*go dila le go ritela*) at least once a year. The house had three bedrooms, a kitchen, a pantry, and a living-room, which served both as a dining and a relaxation area. Children were explicitly discouraged from using the living-room. It was reserved for adult use, and had to be kept in good shape for the entertainment of visitors who dropped by quite often. There was a front stoep (veranda) and an enclosed mud-floored space (*lapa*) at the back of the house, which was used most frequently by the family, particularly in the afternoons when the sun hid its hot rays behind the Soutpansberg. We often sat on floor mats made of goatskin and straw. The few chairs which we had were mainly used by visitors, and women and children deferred to men in this respect.

The house had a large garden with flowers in the front, and vegetables and fruit trees on the rest of the property. A pig-sty and fowl-run stood at the farthest end of our backyard next to the pit latrine. I can still remember the characteristic smells around our house – a mixture of fresh flowers, dry earth and a whiff of tobacco from my father's pipe.

The village in which we lived was well planned with three main streets: Bloed, Mahomed and Church streets as well as two semi-developed ones on the outskirts. Each street had an irrigation furrow which was used by residents to water their gardens in turn. There was one tap for the hundred or so households. Refuse removal was the responsibility of individual householders, as was the cleanliness of streets. Most households used the open veld on the other side of the gravel main road as a public toilet. This patch of veld *(phomoshene,* derived from the word 'permission') was polluted beyond description by human excreta, but it was strategically hidden away by thornbush.

Kranspoort was a tidy village. Villagers were proud owners of flower and vegetable gardens and numerous fruit trees. Great effort went into maintaining their houses. There were only two families other than the dominee's with cement houses. One belonged to a well-to-do builder and the other to a teacher who headed a school in the Soekmekaar area. The teacher's wife, Mrs Pauline Moshakga, was my mother's great friend.

The laundry was done at the river every week. Huge bundles of laundry were carried on women's heads to the river. Washing clothes provided an occasion for village women to meet and share the latest news and concerns. I picked up a lot from the unrestrained talk of the women, who treated us children as part of the open environment and spoke their minds quite frankly on many issues including troubled marriages, family feuds and general village politics.

I had hoped to be able to start school in 1953, having just turned five in December 1952. I found staying at home very boring. But I was given no choice by my parents, as I had to look after my younger brother, Phoshiwa, then seven months old, because my great-grandmother was getting on in years and could not cope alone with a baby. I cried bitterly on the day school opened, but had to come to terms with the finality of the decision adults had made. I subsequently spent many happy days playing with my two baby brothers, Sethiba and Phoshiwa, in our house and yard, particularly amongst the fruit trees. I learnt to climb the orange trees which were closest to the house, but was discouraged from this activity by my great-grandmother, who feared for my safety. She also said that it was inappropriate for a girl to be climbing trees. I was later to pay the price of an injury to the back of my right thigh, which has left a permanent linear scar.

Our household in Kranspoort was organised for maximum efficiency by my mother, who had to juggle her roles as wife, mother to seven children and schoolteacher without the benefit of domestic help. She was a tough marshal and expected every one of us to make a contribution to the smooth running of the house. We woke up at set times and had specific tasks allocated to each of us which had to be done before and after school. There was a division of labour between the boys and the girls, but it was not rigid. My brothers had to fetch water from the village tap just as we did, but they had the benefit of using a wheelbarrow, which could carry two twenty-litre containers. They also shared in the making of endless cups of tea for my mother and her occasional guests.

They made their own beds, and later when both my sister and I were at boarding school or working, the younger ones learned to cook, bake, iron and so on. My mother was a pragmatist. Traditional gender roles were cast aside to make room for survival.

My father was a great provider for his family. We were the best-fed children in the area. He often came home unexpectedly with a goat or sheep for slaughter. If none of my brothers were home at the time, he would encourage me to help him slaughter the beast. Those were the most tender of our moments together. He never referred to me by name, except in class where he was my teacher. He always called me *Mommy*, because I was named after his mother-in-law. We had great fun skinning the beast and opening it up, and finally eating the liver roasted on the coals as a reward.

My father was also a generous man. He believed in sharing scarce resources with those less fortunate than us. We always had children from needy families in the district living with us, so that they could attend school. Such decisions he would make on the spur of the moment whenever he identified a needy child, much to my mother's frustration. We were not wealthy, but by local standards we were well off. We slept on floor-beds until the 1960s when we began to share beds in the children's rooms. To make our floor-beds we spread either straw mats or goatskins on the mud floor with a blanket placed on top. My mother made soft feather pillows (from carefully selected and preserved chicken feathers) for each of us, and we had enough warm blankets to cover ourselves even during the cold winter months.

My mother was a strict disciplinarian. She was intolerant of any naughtiness on our part, and also ruthless in punishing any misdeed. I received many beatings for breaking things, which made me even more nervous and thus led to further losses. I remember an occasion in 1959 when she had gone to a Mothers' Union church conference in Meadowlands Township in Soweto, and we had been left in the care of my father. It was dusk, and I was wiping the glass cover of our paraffin lamp, from which we derived reflected prestige, when it fell from my hands. What a disaster! I put the pieces together and knelt down and prayed: 'God, nothing is impossible for you. Please put together what has been broken and save me from the inevitable.' Disappointment awaited me when I opened my eyes. I hid the lamp away and lit a candle. My father, who was at the time lying on his bed and reading, did not comment on the candle when he came out to have his supper, but after two days, he called me. I burst out crying, expecting the worst. He embraced me, wiped my tears and sent me off to the shop to buy another one. I could not believe his response. I still cherish that touch of softness.

We were nonetheless deeply appreciative of my mother's domestic competence. We enjoyed treats which many children in the village had no idea about: freshly baked bread, dumplings, soup on cold days, pancakes, canned fruit, jam, cakes and puddings. Our greatest regret was that we could never have enough of the treats, particularly pancakes, which were my father's favourite and of which he was given the lion's share. I learnt to cook and bake quite early in life, because I enjoyed being near my mother and watching what she was doing. I promised myself that when I was old enough I would make myself a plateful of pancakes and eat them to my heart's content – a promise I kept years later, in 1974, when I was expecting my first child.

My father kept aloof from many family concerns. He kept to his room in his favourite position – horizontal – with a book in his hand. We longed to get to know him better, but were not rewarded much. We would delight in taking tea in for him, and in doing whatever would give an opportunity for direct contact. When occasionally he came into the kitchen, where most of the family spent their time, it would be like Christmas! We would giggle at each one of his few jokes and hang on to whatever he had to say. But these were brief and rare occasions.

When my father became angry or grumpy, we would be quite scared. He would fly into a rage over a mistake one of us had made some days before, which we would have even forgotten about by then. Perhaps one of my brothers had been careless with tools or livestock, or had not performed his domestic chores properly. On other occasions it would be complaints about the way my mother and we girls ran the household, which did not meet his high standards. Those were painful days, and unless *Koko* Tsheola intervened timeously, we would end up being beaten. I can only surmise that he bore grudges, and that he was inhibited by his shyness from expressing his feelings. Alcohol released him from these inhibitions.

His role as both father and teacher to his children was also not uncomplicated. So too his relationship with his wife, who had to negotiate the tensions of collegiality at work and a marriage partnership. He was always punctual and could not tolerate anything less from others. This was infuriating for my mother, who had to attend to his domestic needs and still be on time at school. He was a wonderful teacher who enthused his pupils with the joy of learning. Although he was supposed to teach us through the medium of North Sotho, as was required by Bantu Education at the time, he quietly insisted on teaching us in English during the course of the year, and would only drill us in North Sotho for examination purposes. I still remember some of the ridiculous words such as *okosijeni* (oxygen) which we had to learn in science. He also departed from the official syllabus, which had a heavy ideological content, though he would caution us to produce what was required for the external examination at the end of Standard 6.

I was a naughty pupil, because I got easily bored in class. I was rarely challenged intellectually. My father tried to keep me disciplined by seating me next to boys, in the vain hope that I would be shy and quieten down. I soon found a way of amusing myself, in most cases at the expense of the boy I was sitting next to. One such boy used to be so frightened when asked questions in class that he would wet himself as soon as his name was called out. I would draw the attention of the whole class to this poor boy's pants by turning around to gaze at his wet patch.

I had problems reconciling my father's role as my teacher and parent. He would appear to treat me so indifferently in class that I was saddened. Although I was his best student, few if any words of praise would come my way. He expected me to do well, and would show disappointment if I got anything wrong. He also seemed to be much stricter on me than on other children. Any mistake would unleash severe punishment. I had to be perfect.

My father had a sizeable library to feed his love for books. I had access to the full range of Shakespeare's plays, the *Encyclopaedia Britannica* and many English novels and books of general interest to my father's generation, which I read through as soon as I could. I remember many conversations between adults in my presence, to which I was not supposed to be privy, but which I perfectly understood in my own way.

My childhood social world was complex in its own way. Our neighbours across the street were the family of a widowed woman who worked as a domestic in Louis Trichardt, fifty kilometres away, leaving her children in the care of her kindly mother-in-law, *Koko* Sanie Seko. The second oldest girl, Rebecca, was a very aggressive person, a street fighter known for her toughness. On the few occasions we played with them, we ended up with a disagreement or even a fight. We thus tended to play on our own and avoid the street.

These neighbours resented our position of relative comfort. My mother's generosity in sharing left-over food with those less fortunate did not placate them. Their mother also became sulky and moody towards my mother on the few occasions she was home over weekends or on leave. It became so bad that we stopped having anything to do with them. The last straw was when one of my mother's large black pigs, fattened for the next winter slaughter, was found dead. A postmortem revealed that someone had pierced it with a piece of wire, which was left *in situ* – a more agonising death the poor pig could not have experienced. The carcass, which had signs of sepsis, was not fit for human consumption and was used to make soap for the household. Rumours abounded about who could have been responsible, but we never got to know the truth.

There were neighbours who were part of my childhood world. *Koko* Mma-Abinere Tau (Mother of Abner) was a large woman whose property adjoined the back of ours. She liked sitting on the veranda of her house and surveying all passers-by. She got the latest news from casual conversations with those who cared to stop for a chat across the fence. Her house was dark, poorly ventilated and untidy. She also liked eating meat that was off, which she claimed was tastier than fresh meat. Her house had an unpleasant odour. She came in handy whenever my mother needed to dispose of unwanted meat which had gone off. She was a stingy woman, known as the Jew, because people in this village perceived Jews as particularly stingy people. A story was often told of her putting a steaming hot teapot between her legs to conceal it from passers-by who she feared would have been tempted to drop by for a cup of tea – a not unfounded fear, given the practice of the time. She demanded being greeted by children passing by and would clear her throat audibly to attract attention; if that failed, she would resort to scolding those she labelled as disrespectful.

Showing respect for adults was an important attribute sought and nurtured in children. I remember being reduced to tears by a cruel comment from a woman, known as Setlotlo, who lived in our street. I had greeted her and her guests in the customary way, *Realotsha!* (Greetings!), but she was engaged in a conversation with other adults on her veranda and did not hear me. Those who heard me responded in a loving way, but she turned and scolded me fiercely for being disrespectful and not greeting. I was rescued from this verbal abuse by the others, but even then she did not apologise. Children's feelings were frequently hurt in this manner.

Koko Mma-Abinere had redeeming features too. She had a beautiful soprano voice, which she put to good use as a church choir member and Sunday school teacher. She also had a good sense of humour and an ability to laugh at herself. Her husband had deserted her and was rumoured to be having an affair with Setlotlo, who had at one stage burned her severely by pouring boiling water with caustic soda over her back. She spent many months at Elim Hospital. She often joked about the fact that her beauty transcended the scars occasioned by that traumatic experience.

Kranspoort had a friendly village atmosphere where personal safety was not at risk. We grew up with a deep sense of physical security.

There were tight social networks in this closely knit community. The residents felt bound together by the common identity of being believers (Christians) in contrast to 'the heathens' (non-believers), also referred to as *ba gaLosta* (lost ones), who lived on surrounding farms and who were regarded as inferior. The term 'heathen' was used quite unconsciously in conversations about 'the other', and was also a rebuke for those residents failing to behave 'properly'. It was partly this 'insider' versus 'outsider' approach which led to the break-up of the mission station in 1956 over a dispute to bury an 'outsider', who was mother of one of the residents ...

Social networks revolved around kith and kin. Many households had extended family members living in different parts of the village and, because of its small size, most kept in almost daily contact with one another. There were also close friendships which involved parents and children from particular households. These friendships evolved into close reciprocal relationships which approximated kinships. It was the custom in this village to address others respectfully using the same terms normally reserved for relatives, such as 'uncle', 'aunt', 'sister', 'brother', 'granny' and so on. It was thus sometimes difficult to distinguish between kinships and friendships, unless one knew the family histories of those involved.

Support flowed along the contours of social networks. Those well connected were protected from the harsh realities of poverty and the disruptive effects of migrant labour, which were a common experience of most households. Households shared and borrowed necessities from one another as part of life. Food was the most common item of such exchanges, though the natural fertility of the area and the bountiful fruit and vegetables also ensured that few people ever went hungry.

Emotional and other forms of social support were also an important aspect of village life. Many women had to raise their children alone because their men were migrant workers. Most of the affected households functioned reasonably well, aided by regular remittances and annual visits from the migrants. That the experience of absent husbands was common reduced the pain of separation. Similarly affected women rallied together for mutual support.

There were also a few women migrants, such as our neighbour whom I have referred to, who were single parents or widows and had to leave their children in the care of others to seek employment to support their households. Some children ended up living at home without any adult present, but relying on neighbours for adult support in times of need.

I developed some understanding of the remittance patterns of several households because my father handled the village mail as one of his responsibilities as school principal. The mail arrived twice a week on the railway bus, which passed through Kranspoort on its way to and from Alldays, farther west along the foot of the Soutpansberg. The mailbag had to be fetched at about 10.30 a.m. by one of the schoolboys and brought to the school for sorting. The post was then distributed at the end of the school assembly when names of recipients of letters were called out, and their children or neighbours' children collected and delivered them. Registered letters were treated differently. Once notified, children were asked to alert their parents or neighbours, who had to come personally and sign for their registered items. The same applied to parcels. It was clearly a system based on trust, but sensibly tempered with safeguards.

We often had people come to our home after school to collect their registered mail which my father kept for them. Some came to enquire about possible parcels even if they had not received notification. These were the desperate women whose men were not regular remitters. My mother often gave them food on the quiet as they left our house.

Households who lived on the margins of supportive networks experienced abject poverty. These households tended to be on the outskirts of the village, and were in most cases relatively new arrivals. Their properties were also not as well endowed with fruit trees and were less fertile, providing little opportunity for growing vegetables. The irrigation water which flowed along the street furrows reached them last, and often when it was too late and too dark to water properly.

Pain and joy were shared by residents. People supported one another in times of illness or loss through death. Funerals were communal responsibilities: at these times every member of the community played a supportive role. News of death was spread by word of mouth and people rallied to the bereaved household. A few old women would immediately move into the household to provide support, and remain there until some days after the funeral. Younger women helped with the practicalities of keeping the household clean, fed and comfortable.

Women were also responsible for preparing a meal for all those attending the funeral. A beast, commonly an ox for a grown-up man or a cow for a woman, was often slaughtered the night before the funeral. It was in some cases an expensive affair, but fellow villagers brought food and other goods as well as monetary contributions to help the affected family.

Children were not allowed to go to funerals, except those of close relatives, but we often watched processions as they passed by, and clandestinely listened to the conversations of adults around these issues. Death remained a mystery to us. Our curiosity was not seen as legitimate by adults, so we could not ask direct questions. There was an uneasy silence around death.

My closest encounter with death in my childhood was in 1955 when my mother gave birth to a baby boy on a Saturday afternoon (although I remember the day vividly, I don't remember the date). It was a home birth assisted by the local midwife, Sister Nteta. We were shown the child after it was bathed, and were excited. Birth was another mystery – an area of silence which children had no right to explore. My paternal grandmother had come a few weeks before the birth to help support my mother during this period. Early on the Sunday morning my grandmother called my sister, elder brother and me, and told us that the baby was no more. The child had died during the course of its first night. I did not understand how this was possible, but from my sister's reaction, I understood that its death was a reality. Her tears were infectious. We were later asked to go to the Sebatis, my mother's relatives, for the day.

I still remember seeing my father outside the kitchen window, just before we left, digging what must have been the baby's grave, in an enclosure (*lapa*) on the side of the house. He was assisted by one or two other men. We came home that afternoon to find a freshly smeared mud patch which my great-grandmother, *Koko* Tsheola, looked after and to which she repeatedly applied a mixture of cow dung and soil for the next few months until it faded into the rest of the *lapa*. It was customary for newborn babies and stillborns to be buried within the homestead – they were not regarded as fully developed, independent persons to be interred in the public graveyard. We were not given the opportunity to share this loss with my mother, whom we hardly saw for the next days, as she was confined to bed. This silence was very confusing to me as a child.

Sharing festivities was also part of life in Kranspoort. The residents knew how to celebrate in style. Weddings were elaborate, as were Christmas and New Year celebrations, which were particularly valued as times for family reunions and sharing of treats brought home by the *makarapa* (returning migrants). Almost all children were bought new clothes, and, for the fortunate few, new shoes were included. Homes were decorated with fresh colourful, mud and cow-dung applications, as well as decorative paper ribbons and balloons for those who could afford such luxuries. Most people strung strips of colourful left-over material, and hung them on doorways. There were no Christmas trees, nor did anyone expect Father Christmas to come with presents or a stocking full of goodies down non-existent chimneys. People shared food and drink and the joy of life in song and dance.

On Christmas day children walked in groups from house to house asking for 'Christmas', rather like the 'trick-or-treat' which American children indulge in on Halloween. Towards late afternoon, groups of children from different street choirs assembled in strategic places for friendly singing competitions. Good dancers displayed their talents. My most embarrassing moments came when I was pressured by my friends to join in the dancing. I was a typical wall-flower. I was shy and tended to hide behind others, or bolted when I sensed that the net was closing in. Nonetheless I enjoyed the carnival atmosphere with all the streets brightened with colour, laughter and song.

I was never really a sociable child outside the family setting. I preferred my mother's company to that of children my age. So I took on myself the role of a human pram and made myself useful by carrying my brothers on my back, thus relieving my over-worked mother from the task. I also went around visiting with her on Sunday afternoons – the only time off she enjoyed. My presence enabled her to socialise with her friends in the secure knowledge that my baby brothers were in good hands ...

Mamphela Ramphele was born in the Bochum district of the former Northern Transvaal in 1947. She qualified as a medical doctor at the University of Natal in 1972, and worked closely with black consciousness leader Steve Biko. She also holds a PhD in social anthropology from the University of Cape Town, and a BCom degree in Administration from the University of South Africa. In 1996 she was appointed vice chancellor of the University of Cape Town, becoming the first black woman to hold such a position at a South African university. In 2000, she became one of four managing directors of the World Bank.
Book Extracted: *Across Boundaries: The Journey of a South African Woman Leader* (Feminist Press, New York, 1996)

Beside Myself – An Autobiography
Antony Sher

... I remember us all sitting on boxes and cases in the hallway that first evening – sunset and sea visible through the open door – eating sandwiches and drinking pop, surrounded by the smell of fresh paint and new carpets. I remember Mom commenting *yet again* on the lucky coincidence of this house's name – she was born and brought up in Montagu, a pretty spa town 120 miles north-east of Cape Town – it was surely a sign that we were meant to live here, and live happily. I remember feeling very safe. I was in a strange place, yes, but Mom and Dad were here too, and my siblings, Randall (sixteen), Verne (thirteen), and Joel (four), and our trusty cook, Katie, and our current maid, Elizabeth. I would be looked after. My meals would be provided, my cases would be unpacked, my bed would be made, I didn't have to do anything, make any decisions, explore this unfamiliar territory on my own. I wasn't to know it then, but the next time I would change addresses, going into the army after school, and to England after that, the experiences would be so alarming that I'd be left with a permanent fear of moving. Now all journeys unsettle me, even small ones like between the homes that Greg and I keep in London and Stratford. 'Is it the Wandering Jew in me?' I ask Greg solemnly.

'Maybe,' he answers. 'Or just your way of getting me to do all the packing.'

On that beautiful evening in 1959 I suppose it would've been our servants, Katie and Elizabeth, who hauled the cases upstairs and emptied the contents into drawers and cupboards. Supervised by Mom. Dad would've done nothing. He was probably pouring the second or third massive Scotch in the side room off the lounge, the room he was to claim as his den and bar. Maybe some of his drinking pals were round that night. These tended to be family, mostly uncles: Uncle Nicky and Uncle Arthur, Dad's brothers – both very gentle men, the first large and calm, the second short and nervy (shell-shock from the war) – or Uncle Jack, married to Mom's sister Rona: a charismatic man with large ears, big belly, a rolling walk, a twinkle in his eye.

At first I was in a big bedroom at the front of Montagu House, sharing with Joel. I remember standing at the window one day, soon after we moved in. The view was of the Queen's Hotel, a marvellous colonial establishment, all rolling gardens and shaded verandas (later knocked down to build the President, where we're currently staying), but what actually caught my eye that day was the sight of Dad hurrying along Alexander Road, heading up towards the roundabout, and Marlborough Mansions. His mother lived in the ground-floor flat. A huge East European woman with a faint moustache and the musty smell of old age, suddenly flapping her hands to alleviate her rheumatism, she terrified me. Dad was always popping up the road to see her, but there was something different today, something about his walk, his face. He didn't look like Dad at all, but young and lost. That evening, Mom explained to us that his mother had died. I'm afraid I was rather relieved.

A few years later the big bedroom was split down the middle with a hardboard partition. I was delighted to get the half with the wall safe, which I prized. The division had been created to allow Joel and myself some privacy. Shortly afterwards I managed, I don't know how, to get our Coloured garden boy, William, to give me foot and even bum massages. He stopped this after a bit and tried to explain why: 'It's not healthy, Master Ant.' I felt disappointed. Still pre-pubescent, I was genuinely innocent of the fact that these pleasurable sensations were connected to something called sex. William was Cape Coloured and I've always found his people very attractive, with their long, lean muscles, the dance to their walk, their elastic-band accents stretching and snapping at words.

I was about fifteen when I started masturbating – in the bed in my partitioned room. I clearly remember the first smell of sperm (*vaguely like some stuff Katie uses in the backyard, a kind of soap, or is it bleach?*) and an overwhelming sense of relief; I'd been a late developer physically. Now I became very proud of the manly features appearing on my small body. One afternoon I brazenly changed out of my swimming trunks in front of a window which looked on to the upstairs *stoep*, while Margaret – our new current maid – was ironing there. She gave me a sly smile and touched her head, the tight black curls there, commenting on what was sprouting in my groin. I took this as a sign of encouragement and a few nights later went into her room – the 'maid's room' in the backyard – to show her my hard-on. Like William, she tried to find a way of explaining – '*Haai* no, this isn't OK, Master Ant!' I had made no clear plans for this particular hard-on – what I wanted her to do with it – and when she rejected me, I just assumed it was because she worked for us: she could get into trouble for initiating one of the young masters of the house. I knew nothing about the Immorality Act, forbidding sex across the race barrier.

I knew very little about the apartheid laws at all. I wasn't aware that blacks were forced to carry passes, and to live separately, in townships. (This didn't apply to Coloureds at first and when I was growing up their beloved District Six was still intact, in the middle of Cape Town.) Even though I was aged eleven in 1960, when the Sharpeville massacre occurred, I have no recollection of it. It wasn't just that the government was ferociously efficient at censorship; no, ours was the most apolitical of households. The whole family voted for the Nationalists, in an automatic, non-thinking, but quite affectionate way, calling them the Nats. Mishearing at first, I thought this was a real name, another uncle perhaps – Uncle Nat. Neither of my parents read books much. Dad liked his morning and evening newspapers, the *Cape Times* and the *Cape Argus*, and Mom favoured glossy magazines from abroad, about fashion or Hollywood. No word of criticism about apartheid ever made it into Montagu House and, as far as I could see, all of us – the masters and servants living there – were perfectly happy.

In time I would come to understand that apartheid had a damage effect on us, the whites, the fat cats, as well as its obvious victims, known then as 'non-whites'. You can't grow up in a crazy world – a world that judges people on the colour of their skin – without going a little crazy yourself and my family have an impressive record (not untypical among South African whites) of drink problems, drug abuse, eating disorders and other cases of friendly fire. But during the fifties and sixties we thought we were happy. No, that's putting it mildly – we thought we were in paradise. We'd made a pact with the devil for this paradise, but it was a tame one; it didn't call for any violence or cruelty on our part.

'This South African sunshine is nice and bright, hey?' Uncle Nat said to us. 'Just bask in it. Just close your eyes. Leave the rest to us.'

Whenever I talk about this, I hear myself sounding like the citizens of the towns of Dachau or Auschwitz – 'We didn't know, we didn't know!' In fact, I'm saying something worse – not that we didn't know, but that we didn't see. Robben Island was there, right there, clearly visible from the pretty white beaches of Sea Point, yet we didn't see it. We closed our eyes and basked. Prisoners were on that island because their skin was the wrong colour, and there we were, fooling around with our own, trying for darker and darker tones, in our pitch-black sunglasses, not *seeing*.

If I really think hard I can summon a vague sense that something was wrong, just on the corner of my vision. The drunkenness of the Coloureds, for example. A vicious, despairing kind of drunkenness, with women fighting and men urinating in the gutter – these sights glimpsed from our air-conditioned limousines as we cruised past District Six en route for the bioscopes and department stores in town. There wasn't a big black population in Cape Town, so their misery was even less apparent. But then one morning the *Cape Times* gave the inhabitants of Montagu House quite a fright, even the children. The paper felt duty bound to tell us about an evil plot, which had been uncovered and foiled by the police – just in time! Thousands of black people from the townships of Langa and Guguletu were planning to march on Cape Town and seize it. The newspaper published maps allegedly collected during the police raids, showing key points for the takeover of the city. One was at the top of our road, at the roundabout, just across from Marlborough Mansions: the Greek café on the corner, Tony's Café. This was to have been one of the headquarters of the black army.

I felt more puzzled than scared. For the first time I heard the grown-ups use the phrase 'They'll murder us in our beds', but I didn't understand it. Why should these non-whites feel so vengeful? And ungrateful. We treated them well, we the Sher family, we were good to our servants and to the staff at Cape Produce Export Company, Dad's firm which sold raw skins and hides overseas. Yes, the non-whites were an inferior form of life – Uncle Nat's State and Church taught us this – but why should this make them miserable? Were dogs and cats, horses and donkeys, all going around harbouring terrible grudges? All awaiting their chance to turn on us? (I read *Animal Farm* round about this time, and decided yes, they probably were.) Anyway, the *Cape Times* was very reassuring. It said that the wicked ringleaders of the plot, a few Commies, liberals and other low life *skollies*, had all been caught and imprisoned. Our heroic police force and our army were the mightiest in all Africa. Nothing of this kind could ever happen again.

The other major event that shook us in Montagu House during my youth has come to symbolise the surreal world of apartheid South Africa for me. Prime Minister Verwoerd's assassination in 1966. It was very dramatic. Shortly after 2 p.m. on Tuesday, 6 September, as the afternoon session got under way in the House of Assembly in Cape Town, one of the parliamentary messengers, Demitrios Tsafendas, crossed to Verwoerd, drew a long knife from under his jacket and stabbed him to death. (By now I'd read *Julius Caesar*, and again literature and life came crashing together.) I listened to Verwoerd's state funeral on the radio – Uncle Nat didn't permit TV till 1976, long after I'd gone – and was very taken with the eloquence and emotion of the broadcaster. This was historic. This was our Kennedy killing. Well ... with a crucial difference, South African style. Both were enigmatic murder mysteries. But while the plot behind *The Dallas Gun* was endlessly subjected to public investigation and debate, our version, *A Dagger In Parliament*, became an eerily closed book.

Years later, when I got to know Helen Suzman, she told me about being in parliament that day – she was the only Progressive Party MP, the *only* official opposition to apartheid. After the stabbing was over, a goggle-eyed, finger-wagging P.W. Botha, later to be State President himself, charged across to her and yelled, 'It's you who did this – you liberals – now we'll get you!' Though wildly wrong in his accusation, Botha wasn't alone in assuming this to be a political act. Verwoerd was known as the Architect of Apartheid and his assassin was of mixed blood. This *must* be political. But no, our papers quickly assured us, paradise was safe, there was no plot, no unrest, nothing political was going on. Demitrios Tsafendas was simply a lone madman – a madman who claimed that a giant tapeworm lived in his guts, urging him to do the deed. Next we heard there'd be no trial; the judge at the hearing said he couldn't judge Tsafendas 'any more than I can judge a dog' – our beloved Prime Minister had been killed by a madman with a devilish case of indigestion, nothing more to it. Yet there'd be no cushy asylum for this particular madman. Oh no, no, he'd be locked in prison and the key thrown away. And that was it; the matter was closed as securely as the door to Tsafendas's cell. No trial, no evidence, no public examination of the facts, just a bizarre sentence. It was Kafkaesque (even down to the presence of the giant insect), yet nobody I knew found it strange. Until recently I didn't find it strange myself. Then I read Henk van Woerden's excellent biography of Tsafendas, *A Mouthful of Glass*, and was amazed. Here's the story of a man born to a Greek father and a black mother in Mozambique, savagely rejected by his own family, humiliated at boarding school in the Transvaal, kicked from country to country like a piece of junk, now a sailor, touring the world on the weirdest of odysseys, searching, searching for home, the ultimate displaced person and all because he's a *baster*, a half-breed. This same man ends up killing the Architect of Apartheid. And the act isn't political? Naturally the government preferred this interpretation and had the perfect excuse. The man was mad. But are we born mad or do we have madness thrust upon us? What about national madness, state madness? These were not questions our betters wanted us to ask. Otherwise we might have scrutinised the two men fastened over that dagger – a victim of racism and its high priest – and said to ourselves 'Well there's clearly a lunatic here but which one is it?'

Sir Antony Sher was born in Cape Town in 1949, and, after a spell with the South African Defence Force, moved to the United Kingdom in 1968. He trained as an actor at the Webber-Douglas Academy of Dramatic Art, and then went on to join the Royal Shakespeare Company in 1982. Throughout his distinguished film and stage career, Sher has received many awards, including the Laurence Olivier Award for his performance as Richard III in the Royal Shakespeare Company production. He was knighted for services to the theatre in 2000.
Book Extracted: *Beside Myself An Autobiography* (Arrow Books, 2002)

Every Secret Thing
Gillian Slovo

Once again my memory fast forwards, this time to New Year's Eve, 1962. It had been so hot that night in Cape Town that I had drifted off to sleep with the melt of ice cubes dripping down my neck. And then, suddenly, it was the middle of the night and I was awake. Dazed I looked around, trying to figure out what it was that had wrenched me from sleep.

I saw a woman's figure framing the lighted doorway. She was speaking softly, in an angry whisper. 'Who would be so inconsiderate as to hide beneath a child's bed?' she hissed.

I blinked, adjusting my eyes to the gloom. The curtains were half-open and I could see moonlight slanting across my friend, Margaret's, unmade single bed. It was empty. I looked again towards the doorway. This time I noticed Margaret standing behind her mother, peering in.

I heard a noise, coming from the end of my bed. I sat up in time to see a policeman's peaked hat emerging from beneath the bed frame. Another sound, this time from the wardrobe: there were two of them in the room, searching desultorily.

When the second pushed his way out of a forest of girlish clothes, I saw that he'd been cloned from the same block as the first. He had the same stubbled brown hair moulded to the back of his head, the same stiffly creased trousers which ended in gleaming black shoes, the same brown jacket wide at the shoulders and tapering in to a waist pinched by the tight plastic black belt which served a double purpose of containing his holstered gun, and the same edgy defiance working overtime to toughen his callow face. Seeing me, he used his head to gesture his colleague towards the door. Within minutes, both men had gone.

I was ten years old and holidaying in our family's regular summer venue of Cape Town. That year, however, with my sisters elsewhere and my parents served with banning orders that stopped them leaving Johannesburg, I was in Cape Town on my own. It was the first time I remember being so completely separated from my family. I remember lazy days spent cooing over a clutch of month-old puppies or trudging the steep eighty-four steps from the high point of Cape Town's Kloof Road down to the white sands of Clifton's Fourth beach. Our expeditions were mostly unfettered by adult company since Margaret's parents, Sonya and Brian Bunting, long-time comrades of my parents, were both subject to another one of the government's growing pot-pourri of despotic laws – house arrest. Brian was on night-time curfew while Sonya was completely restricted, given permission only to leave the house for three hours out of every twenty-four in order to look for work.

Work: there was not much chance of that. The world had closed in on us: all our friends were similarly restricted and no stranger would have been prepared to take the risk of hiring a named communist. So Sonya would occasionally use her 'time off' to sneak out to the beach with us. That night, when I saw the policeman floundering around our children's room, I wondered guiltily whether Sonya's transgression – made, I was sure, for my benefit – was what had sent them in.

But of course even in South Africa the security establishment didn't have sufficient manpower to check on every dissident's hourly movements. Their visit was mere routine. Every year since I, and presumably the police, could remember, the Buntings had thrown a huge New Year's Eve bash. This year, because of their banning orders, a gathering of more than three people in their house would constitute a crime. Which is why the police had burst in at midnight, to check for reds hiding under the Buntings' beds.

The raid was one amongst the many all of us experienced in that year, part of our new normality. After the police left, that early dawn of 1963, Margaret and I didn't even bother chewing it over. She got into her bed and I lay down in mine and we drifted back to sleep.

Within days my holiday was over and I was flying back to Jo'burg. It was my first time in a plane and I was on my own. A ferocious storm, the like of which seemed to keep thundering through the whole of my 1963, jolted at the plane's metal body. I sat rigid, the seat-belt cutting into my stomach, trying to pretend that I didn't notice that after each rearing up of the plane, it appeared to fall by an even larger distance. I breathed in the collective queasy silence as streaks of jagged lightning lit up the sky.

The storm was too ferocious, we couldn't get through. The plane really was going lower. Within minutes it had reached ground level and we landed on a small airfield somewhere in the middle of rural South Africa. Holding tightly to the slippery rails, I followed a line of passengers down the steps and through the pelting rain to an airport building which looked more like an old warehouse than a terminal. There weren't enough chairs to go round: we huddled on the floor, the other passengers in their family groups, me on my own, waiting for the storm to blow itself out.

But the storm was stronger than us and eventually we were grounded for the night. With an air hostess as our guide, we were siphoned off into a coach which drove slowly out into the darkest night. I was a lone, unaccompanied child. When a couple sitting opposite, heard me give the air hostess my name, they exchanged a meaningful glance. Experience had taught me all the possible interpretations: I knew that what had passed between them wasn't the most extreme of the possible reactions – horror that they were sitting so close to a notorious Slovo – but rather the equally predictable and more liberal response that managed to imply sympathy for my parents' goals with distaste for their means.

In the three years since Sharpeville, the battle for South Africa had been irrevocably changed. If Sharpeville showed the world what apartheid really involved, it also heralded the end of legal protest within the country. By declaring an Emergency and banning the ANC, the government had demonstrated that peaceful protest would no longer be tolerated. Only one option faced the activists – give up or raise the stakes. How could they give up? It wasn't possible. They turned from passive to active resistance.

In his unfinished autobiography my father describes the decisions they took:

> The first phase of armed action in 1961 was a sabotage campaign directed against government installations. Instructions were issued to avoid attacks which would lead to injury or loss of life. No one believed that the new tactic of sabotage could, on its own, lead to the collapse of the racist state. It was the first phase of 'controlled violence' designed to serve a number of purposes. It would be a graphic pointer to the need for carefully planned action rather than spontaneous or terrorist acts of retaliation which were already in evidence...
>
> And it would demonstrate that the responsibility for the slide towards bloody civil war lay squarely with the regime.
>
> The point was strongly featured in the proclamation accompanying the first sabotage acts which expressed the hope that 'even at this late hour' the actions would awaken everyone to a sense of realisation of the disastrous situation to which the regime's policy was leading, and would bring the government to its senses before it was too late and before matters reached the desperate stage of civil war.*

A sober assessment this, written by my father, in hindsight of their early military plans. And yet I know that he believed more than that then, and that, caught up in the excitement of the shift to action and of the Boy's Own adventure on which they had all embarked, the end of injustice in

---

*Joe Slovo: The Unfinished Autobiography, Hodder and Stoughton, 1996: p152.

South Africa still seemed to be imminently within his grasp.

He was so central to what was going on. In 1961, he, along with Nelson Mandela, became the initial high command for the new army – Umkhonto we Sizwe – MK for short. A small group which included my mother's journalist friend, Joe Gqabi, were sent to China for training while internally a sabotage campaign, aimed at government installations, was launched. Amateur bomb-makers slipped chemical bombs into buildings that were the visible symbols of apartheid: Bantu Administration and pass offices. In the countryside railway lines, telephone wires and overhead electrical cables were blown into mangled pieces. The photos in the papers momentarily shook white South Africa out of its complacent daze.

The government responded with a mass of repressive legislation, cracking down so fiercely that it became apparent that there was no longer any turning back. Their Camelot was well and truly dead.

As the stakes got higher, secrecy drifted over every section of our lives. It reached such a pitch that my mother no longer made even the most innocent arrangements by telephone. If I wanted to go to a friend, she would write a special note which she made sure I delivered only once I was inside the school gates. We put on uniforms and went, scrubbed and polished to school, but it was getting harder to pretend our daily routine was following the same, uncomplicated path as all our nice white friends.

Many white people wholeheartedly backed their government. There were others who disliked apartheid, who would have wanted it all to be different. But the early sixties in South Africa was a time when it was no longer viable to sit on the fence. Conmitment carried penalties – sides had to be chosen. As the terror deepened, a gulf opened between 'them' and 'us'. That year, 1963, was the time I noticed it.

I was used to sidelong glances darted my way when people thought I wasn't looking. I was a well-trained child who'd learned the dangers of indiscretion. I sat in the airline coach, silently polite, enduring the journey down a country lane and into one of those orderly, methodically laid out, sterile *dorps* that dot the South African landscape. We were driven from one small hotel on to the next, unloading passengers at every step. I was a victim of a South African Airways Catch 22. As an unaccompanied child, I had to stay with the air hostess but since the air hostess couldn't go to bed until all the passengers were safely tucked in, neither could I.

It was gone four in the morning by the time we learned that every hotel room within a radius of twenty miles was full. There were only three of us left in the bus – the driver, the air hostess and me. We did a u-turn and drove back to the airport.

In a hangar we found a group of men – white airline crew and white airport engineers – lounging by a large wooden work bench, playing cards while two half-empty bottles of cheap brandy did the rounds. When we entered – me and my tippy, tappy uncommunicative, beehived companion – ribald jokes rose to greet us. I can still hear them, those gruff male voices echoing in the sawdust-encrusted space. Even then I couldn't make out their meaning – they were speaking in Afrikaans, a language that a childish intransigence had stopped me from learning. I was a waif, standing in the huge empty space, in enemy territory while manly suggestiveness was countered by womanly guile.

Eventually one of the engineers took pity on my exhaustion and suggested we stay at his house. But my ordeal wasn't over. There was only one bed available and so we had to share. I will never forget that night. I spent it lying stiffly beside an air hostess who was dressed in a light blue nylon shortie nightie, her teased blonde hair splayed out above her on the pillow. Between her world and mine was an immense and widening gulf. I hardly slept. I was so conscious of what she didn't know – that I was the child of parents who were working to bring the downfall of everything she held dear. Perhaps something I muttered in sleep might give me, and them, away. I lay the whole night terrified she might find me out.

Or at least that was how I saw it then. But now as I look back at my childish self so stiffened by proscription, I wonder whether it wasn't something else that had kept me awake: not moral rectitude but jealousy, not fear of discovery but a craving to be like her. That air hostess with her blonde hair was a living example of someone with a normal, carefree life. In my imagination the thing that caused her to worry was whether her lipstick matched her nail varnish not when the police would next come calling. Somewhere deep inside of me, I lusted for that kind of normality. I had built a wall of defiance around myself, placing my dazzling parents at its invulnerable centre. Only in the darkest night, alone, in the middle of South Africa could I allow myself a twinkling of desire for ordinary life.

I think of my mother then, of her French perfume and her carefully straightened hair and I wonder whether it was like that for her as well. She was, to a stranger's eye, a defiant communist, quirky enough to care about her appearance but willing to break every one of society's conventions. And yet when I look at her in the photos of those days, with her neat suits and her carefully constrained hair I see a woman whose secret ambition might have been to be Jackie Onassis.

From mother to daughter and down again. Tilly transformed herself from a Yiddish-speaking child into a fearless dowager whose English accent was crystal cut. My mother was utterly defiant and yet struggled almost her whole adult life to disown her unruly Jewish fizz. And I, her growing daughter, lay beside a sixties Barbie doll pretending to despise what my heart desired.

Back to Johannesburg to normal life. I was in my last year of primary school and the starting gun had just been fired on the competition for the end of year prize. In my own way I continued passing for white, pretending that my life and my school friends' lives were on par. It was easy to pretend. I knew how different were our realities but they did not. Their days were played out in an immutable childish paradise, insulated from harsh reality. The history they learned started in the seventeenth century with the arrival of Jan van Riebeeck and ended in a white victory over the savage hordes. The black people they met emptied their garbage, made their beds, mowed their lawns and cuddled them when they were sick, and all of this with a smile. The anger that was brewing in the country couldn't really touch them. They must have seen the occasional picture of a policeman peering at the remains of a blown–up phone box, but all this was so very far away. Big brother, their government, was watching: it would take care of them.

We three children of Joe and Ruth pretended, for as long as we possibly could, to be like them. We listened, as we always had, to radio plays and afterwards, we'd creep down the corridor to our bedrooms, keeping our backs to the wall because, for reasons we never analysed, we were scared someone might stab us from behind. The front door would go; it would be one or other of our parents returning from a mysterious outing which we all pretended hadn't really happened. The next day the lowered voices and the soft clicking of the front door, would disappear from our memories. In the brightness of each new morning we ate our breakfast and were driven to school. With Shawn already at secondary school, Robyn and I turned up brightly in our short-sleeved blue and white gingham dresses, surreptitiously donning our reviled white panama hats as we moved through the school gates, ill-matching brown shoes polished to a gleam by our Elsie at home.

I learned fractions that year, taught by Mrs Bowskill with her ring of pearls resting on her fluffy pink bosom, her thick black-rimmed glasses and her sheer white hair. She was a teacher who had the light of knowledge shining from within, instantly believable, especially when she spoke of God. That was the year that, for a few months at least, I turned to her God, a Christian one who would watch over everything we did and, we hoped, over our parents as well. In the bedroom we shared, I forced Robyn down on her knees beside me and I told her how to pray to Him for forgiveness. Mrs Bowskill's God was stern but fair. We were sure that He would understand why we could not tell our parents about our religious conversion. They had their secrets – well, now we had ours.

Gillian Slovo, daughter of former South African Communist Party leader Joe Slovo and murdered journalist Ruth First, was born in South Africa in 1952. She moved to England in 1964, and went on to work as a journalist, writer, and film producer. She has written many novels, the latest of which, *Ice Road* (2004), was shortlisted for the 2004 Orange Prize for Fiction.
Book Extracted: *Every Secret Thing My Family, My Country* (Little, Brown & Company, 1997)

The Reminiscences
Thomas Stubbs

I left school in 1820, and was at once taken on board ship, leaving England for what was then regarded as perhaps the most mysterious, as it was certainly the last known portion of the globe. It was on ship that I had my last dinner of à la mode beef. I went on board with my father, my brother, and a lad named Tom, who was bound to my father until he should become of age. The decks were covered with the varied luggage of the Settlers, and everything looked to me strange and incomprehensible. My father proposed that we boys should try and go up the rigging. Tom, the eldest of us, at once started up, but he had not gone far when one of the ship's boys (we afterwards called him Dean Swift, as he was the slowest boy in the ship) went after him with some rope yarn, intending to tie Tom fast to the rigging. The moment he made the attempt, however, Tom held on with one hand, and struck the Dean between the eyes with the other, and the latter returned to the deck in a great hurry. This was not the last of the affair though, for when Tom came on to the deck, the sailors ever ready to get up a fight, backed the Dean against Tom. It was a poor chance for the Dean, for Tom polished him off in about five minutes. Before we sailed one of the ship's boys fell down the mizen hatch, and another overboard, so that on the whole we cannot be said to have started under very auspicious circumstances. We now started down the river, but at Blackwell we lay to alongside an old hulk. From our vessel we could see the gibbets on the shore where some mutineers had been hanged. I remember while we were lying here that a heavy fall of snow occurred. Immediately the boys made a slide on the deck of the old hulk, but they had not been sliding long, when, to the astonishment of all, one of the boys went right through the port-hole overboard.

Soon after this incident we put out to sea. We were about three weeks out when one morning, just after the Settlers had brought up their bedding for an airing, an alarm of fire was given. It appeared that some pitch had caught fire near the cook's galley, and was running over the decks. The sailors made a rush for the blankets to smother the fire, while some of the Settlers, not knowing what the sailors wanted the blankets for, made frantic attempts to get them back. Many of the settlers were Irish, some hailed from Yorkshire, some from Berkshire, and some from London. An Irish woman, named Holland, made a fierce attack on a sailor, and at the same time bawled out to her son, 'Dennis, yer spalpeen, will ye be letting them take all our blankets to have them burned, and us and the childer starved to death with cold?' In the meanwhile the sailors had worked so well that the fire had been subdued and we proceeded calmly on our voyage.

One morning, just after the deck had been swabbed, the cook called out for the settlers to come for their allowance of Burgoo (ie bad meal boiled in a large copper). An Irishman, about six feet six inches in height (whom we nick named Polly Long-stocking) was leaving the kaboose with his wooden bowl of burgoo, when the ship gave a pitch, and threw the Irishman on his back, and the burgoo on the deck. Seeing what had occurred, the second mate, a little proud upstart fellow, who wore extravagantly large frills on his shirt front came up to our Irishman with the intention of kicking him. A stout-made settler seeing this, seized the mate by the frill of his shirt and shook him as a terrier would a rat. The mate ran aft to the captain calling out 'mutiny'. The captain immediately called a muster of the sailors, armed them with cutlasses, and placed them across the quarter-deck. All the Irish rushed to the fore-castle, some armed with pieces of wood, and some with pieces of iron hoop. In the midst of them Mrs Holland could be heard calling out, 'Dennis, I say Dennis, will yis be showing yourself a man this day: we're not to be bate like a lot of gilly goolies by them fellows with their big knives; so stand to it for the sake of ye's country.' And so the uproar continued for some time longer, but eventually, after much trouble, it was arranged that the settler who shook the mate should give himself up. He was kept a prisoner for a day, and then released, and all was quiet until we reached the line. But of this anon.

The Bay of Biscay
We were just in the Bay of Biscay, better known than liked, when about midnight a terrific storm came on. The vessel laboured heavily through the huge waves that opposed her progress. The masts creaked the timbers groaned, and the wind whistled through the rigging. In the midst of this another ship, called the Ocean, also laden with 'tiger hunters', as the sailors termed the settlers, crossed our stern and took away all our cabin windows. The settlers were about on the deck in their shirts, trying to recover their property – the women groaning, children crying, and sailors swearing, while the sea continued to break over the ship, and threaten her destruction, until daylight. Gradually the wind abated, the waves went down, and again we sailed freely over the water.

Crossing the Line
About 8 o'clock one evening we heard a gruff voice hailing the ship

and asking her name. The look-out man replied to the questions as to destination, cargo, etc, and then the voice gave notice that its owner would come on board at ten o'clock the next morning. At the same time a few shots were fired, and some tar barrels lighted and set afloat. The grand and imposing appearance of the tar barrels at night had the effect of frightening a good many old women on board – not only old women but some, who thought they wore t ... s, were quite as bad.

The next morning the 'tiger-hunters', as the sailors called us, were battened down, with the exception of heads of parties, who, with the cabin passengers, were accommodated with seats on the poop, having an awning over them. An old gentleman settler agreed to play the violin for Neptune and his wife, and at about ten o'clock a gun was fired, and it was reported below that Neptune was on board. The old sea god and his wife soon made their appearance, she riding on a gun carriage, covered with the Union Jack, drawn by some fellows in masks, and with the violin playing in front. Neptune, himself was on foot. Two of the followers bore a soap pot, ie a bucket full of tar, while two others, each carried a razor made out of hoop iron, the one being finer than the other. In this order they proceeded to the quarter deck, where, on the port side, was a small boat filled with water, in which to dip those who were shaved. On the capstan stood a large tub filled with six water grog. The musician struck up 'Rule Britannia', and immediately four of the masked men armed with cutlasses, drew on one side, and prepared to carry out any orders given them. Old Neptune then gave orders to bring up the first novice and introduce him to his majesty and Mrs Nep. A regular chaw-bacon was then brought up from below. He look the picture of misery, his face being elongated to a fearful extent. This poor fellow was blindfold, brought to the boat, and seated on the gunwale, a guard holding each arm. In the meantime one of the men had mixed the suds – tar and fat, and with this decoction the unwilling countryman's face was smeared. He was then asked where he came from, and on opening his mouth to speak, the tar brush was inserted in the aperture. The razor was then brought forward, and this took off part of the tar and part of the skin. After three duckings in the water he was taken to see old Neptune and his spouse, whose healths he had to drink.

The next person operated upon was the second mate, a perfect puppy, who was disliked by all on board. He offered anything to be set free, and after getting a gallon of grog out of him he was dipped, but not shaved. As soon as released he rushed to his cabin, and did not show up again for several days. The upshot was the whole of the crew got drunk, the man at the wheel fell asleep, and the next morning no one knew where the ship was.

What would be thought of such a state of affairs now – the lives of 300 families, beside the crew, risked for the sake of a drunken spree?

We lived at No 47 Kenton St Brunswick Square, London, before leaving England. The ship we sailed in was the Northampton Transport, a regular old tub.

The boy that fell down the hatch was my eldest brother John afterwards killed by Zulus at Natal.

The parties that came with us were –
Clarke's Party, settled at Collingham
Smith's Party, settled at Stoney Vale
Stubbs & Brown, settled at Clay Pits
Mahoney's, settled at Coombs
Maj Pigot, settled at Pigot Park
Daigairn's, settled at Blue Krantz
Polly Longstocking ie Ned Shearan
The stout settler was Tomlinson
The Captain's name was Charlton
The First Mate was Becky
The upstart 2nd Mate was Haise
The fiddler was my father

The rations consisted of hard salt beef the sailors said had been three voyages to India; rusty salt pork, hard mouldy biscuit, oatmeal for burgoo, a little sago, cocoa, and sugar. I and my brother used to exchange salt pork for sugar, mix it with vinegar and soak the biscuit. We called it vinegar scouse, we did not get fat on it.

The young emigrant
My father John Stubbs, came out in partnership with J. Brown, brought out ten families, who nearly all left shortly after we arrived on the location. Their names were Thomas Fancutt, who owned and drove his own cart and horses in Grahams Town; he did well – died in Grahams Town.

John Warner a sailor went to Port Elizabeth.

Dan Wood, butcher, married our ser[vant] girl Betsy in Port Elizabeth after leaving us; lived there many years and died. One of his sons served with me in the Kaffir War 1852.

G. Blakemore had a large family – lived many years in Grahams Town, died there very old.

Stephen Denham died in Grahams Town, his son was apprenticed to me to learn the saddling business in Grahams Town about 1840.

Robert Renolds, we called 'old Bobby'; wheelwright, remained with us until our family was broken up by the death of our father and mother; one of the most faithful men ever lived, he afterwards married a widow Godfrey, & died in Grahams Town.

[Thomas] Mainman, left us and married a Miss Wainwright – was lost on his voyage to England. He sailed out of the Cowie in 1824.

Tom Foss left us after my father's death and died in G. Town about 1850.

Tom West, ran away in 1821. I saw him once after about 1846, in Grahams Town. He lived with a Dutchman in Zwagers Hoek. I heard [that] while working in the garden he killed an old slave with a rake and had to work 7 years to pay for him; and then worked 7 years to pay for a young slave girl he took for his wife.

My mother had a cabin, she was ill all the voyage. I and my brother John were always among the sailors, so were allowed to be on deck the whole time.

I was too young to shave, so was only dipped in the boat, but had my tot of grog and was kissed by Mrs Neptune. She had a precious hard beard.

We had a great deal of sickness on board. I recollect one poor woman that died on a featherbed. She was sewn up in it and shot fastened to the foot end, but it was not heavy enough to sink her. We were then going about eight knots an hour. She floated as long as we could see her.

The armourer of the ship also died, and a sale was held of his goods and chattels on the quarter deck. Old Jimmy Bangs the cooper was auctioneer. The smallpox raged. A great many were thrown overboard among them our armourer.

It was a well known fact that there had been plenty of preserved meat and other nourishing food put on board for the sick, but it was also a well known fact they did not get [it]. There was an Agent for every two ships. Ours was on board the ship Ocean. We never had a chance of complaining to him, as we lost sight of her after she had run foul of us in the Bay of Biscay, and the Captain had nothing to do with the Settlers. The rations served out even to the sick were very bad.

The sailors had to fumigate the vessel every week between decks by placing buckets of vinegar in different parts and putting red-hot shot into them.

My mother had a small cabin to herself. She was ill nearly the whole voyage. My father and us boys, had berths just below the fore hatch, where the other part of our party, were stowed. We had a servant woman about eighteen years old. We called her, 'Black Bet', as she had dark rings round her eyes. She was rather a rum one. She occupied the berth under my father, they ran in tiers (that is two deep). One night, my father heard something like a man's voice below him, and on getting out, saw a man jump out of Bet's berth and run upon deck. He found a pair of shoes and on looking at them saw the name of Becky, our first mate. My father showed him the shoes the next morning, when he said, 'By Jove Mr Stubbs, where did you find them? Some one took them out of my cabin.' 'I have no doubt of it,' said my father, 'But I would advise you, to keep yourself and your shoes from my quarters.' Poor Bet was married to our butcher Dan Wood on board a man of war before we left Algoa Bay and I believe turned out an honest woman. I have said before, one of her sons served with me in Stubbs' Albany Rangers during the war of 1852. There were many other funny characters, among the Settlers – some young men on going to bed were continually turning into the wrong berths, but it invariably turned out, there was a woman in them. The consequences was there were some fights and lots of rows. At eight o'clock, all lights were ordered out. The word, 'Douse the glim' was called out down the hatch. I saw a settler's wife at needlework: when one night the word to douse the glim was given [I saw her] place the candle on the deck, and cover it with her clothes, standing over it until all was quiet then begin her sewing again.

We arrived in Table Bay in the night. Of course all hands were on deck early, glad to get a sight of the land after months at sea, but unfortunately we were placed under quarantine so could not land. There were some pigs and sheep brought on board. It was laughable to hear the remarks made by the Settlers and sailors about their tails. Our first mate, Becky, said they were all D--n old, for they all had lost their teeth in the upper jaw. One Settler remarked he could swear to them being old for they were quite grey in the face. Another said, he had heard the sheep had such large tails, that they had to be carried on a sort of small waggon made for the purpose, but he supposed the worst and smallest had been sent for us.

The landing at Algoa Bay and the waggon road to Stoney Vale
After sailing from Table Bay we were just a month arriving at Algoa Bay. It was a very dreary looking place: there was nothing but sand hills to be seen from the ship. The next day all hands were busy preparing to land. The road from the beach was round the sand hills by the mouth of the Baakens river. The tents were pitched in rows about where the market is now. I had agreed to remain on board and proceed with the ship to India, as the Captain promised my parents I should be taken care of, but on seeing my mother in the boat all ready to leave the ship, I just swung myself by a rope from the deck into the boat. They could not persuade me to return, and so we came ashore.

All the bedding was brought on shore and burnt because we had had the smallpox the greater part of the voyage. It was a strange sight the Canvas Camp, and the strange way some of the Settlers went about the cooking. After we had been on shore a day or two a lot of us boys took a walk, and on coming to the rocks, just where old Tee's stables stand, we saw a lot of Hottentots naked: they began to jabber and we began to run, and never stopped until we reached the tents. We thought it was all up with us.

Wagons were provided by government to take us up the country. We came up the old road through the Addo Bush – over Quagga Vlakte – passed Assegai Bush – Swart Hoogte, Mill River, Slaai Kraal, Cypher Fontein and out-spanned by the old wind mill which stood to the left as you go to Oatlands, Grahams Town.

My father, mother and us were invited to take tea with Alexander McDonald. He was Commissariat Store-Keeper and lived in a part of the building just opposite where Wood Brothers store now stands in High Street. 1874. We then proceeded up the hill past where the natives are located. It was covered with large thorn trees at that time. We passed the Governor's Kop (Collingham) and my father and family were loaded off at Stoney Vale, with Thackwray, Smith and others (in mistake) as the other part of our party with J. Brown, my father's partner, were taken on to the Clay Pits. It was here that Mrs Edkins let her child drop off her back into the camp kettle of soup – and where Mr Comfield shot at some wild pigeons through the top of his tent and his wife's high caul cap. We saw lots of game. I recollect C. Hobson shooting the first buck there. The wolves and jackals kept up a continual screeching every night.

There must have been very heavy rains before we arrived, for the whole country was running with water and the grass was knee high. Many a poor Settler nearly broke his neck by tumbling into ant-bear holes that were covered with grass: and many a Settler began a garden where he saw the water running out an ant-hole on the side of a hill, but which dried up before a month.

They then began as close to the rivers as possible, built houses, made gardens, and had every prospect of doing well until the flood came in '23 and cleared everything away. The distress was so great after the flood that the Government raised a Settlers' Fund for their relief, and those who were always looking out for the loaves and fishes, got the lion's share while the greater part of the poorer class got nothing.

Grahams Town in 1820
I must here describe Grahams Town as it appeared when we passed through it in 1820.

The road came down West Hill, through the river where the bridge now stands. There were no houses until you reached High Street. There lived a doctor where the Club House now stands; the next building on that side was the Tronk, afterwards used as a library, then Thompson's House, occupied by a Mr Dietz; the back part of Woods, occupied by Mr Wathall, the parsonage, a small house with the gable to the street where J. Ayton's store stands; a Guard House where the Cathedral now stands, with a flag staff where Fletcher's bakers shop stands. Farther down were one or two small houses, and at the back of Shepperson's Store a thatched building called the Somerset Arms. Where Mandy's house stands, was a battery, and across the street at the back of the Church stood the artillery barracks. That was the one side. On the other was a house at the top of High Street occupied by Mr P. Retief, who was afterwards murdered by Dingaan [in] Natal; next him the Commissariat Stores; a few small houses further down. On Settlers Hill were some huts; the barracks at Fort England; a battery on Market Square and one on the side of a hill going to Oatlands as also a black hole, the windmill, and small cottages. A large thorn tree stood in the middle of High Street just opposite W. Haw's store. It stood there in remembrance of Colonel Graham off-saddling under it when he first came to form a Town. I think it fell down about 1844 or 5. J. Loxton perhaps could tell for he had a barber's shop just opposite. Old Bertram had a store and had over his door 'Negotie Winkel' – the settlers thought it was his name, and always called him 'Old Nigerty Winkle'. There was also an old fellow, called Johnny Cromhout. He was sexton, saddler, harness maker, upholsterer, auctioneer etc. When he had a sale, he would go about the town, with a piece of copper plate and a stick, beating it and calling out to warn people of such a fact. He generally commenced his sale with 'This sale is held on account of Peter Retief: no credit for the settlers.'

I must not forget a disgusting sight that stood just above where the Albany Brethren's Lodge now stands, close to Dundas Bridge. It was a gallows, and on each side was a pole with a pulley at the top, and two cross bars lower down. They were used for the purpose of strangling, which was done by tying the arms, and pulling them up by the neck with a jerk to the block above. They were also used for flogging. I recollect a man named Jones, he had been discharged from the Royal Africans. My father gave him a piece of land to build a house and to cultivate. He was a married man and she was a remarkable good, honest, industrious woman. He was a hard-working fellow, but he was also a hard drinking fellow. After he had built the house and made a garden, he took a trip to Grahams Town and found two horses feeding near the town. It then struck him that a trip to Uitenhage would benefit his health, so caught them, and started off. But unfortunately for him, on his arrival at Uitenhage, the very man who had had charge of the horses, (for his master who was a store keeper there had started for Grahams Town a few days before) met Mr Jones who offered to sell him the two horses and stated he had bought them in Grahams Town. The man said 'All right. Come with me,' and handed him over to the jailor. Poor Jones was marched to Grahams Town; tried, and sentenced to be scourged under the gallows and hard labour for five years. The scourging was performed in this way. A pole [was] fastened across the gallows – the hands fastened in such a way as to bring the body against the pole and cause the back to slope forward. The executioner then commenced to scourge with a bunch of quince cuttings that had [been] drawn through the fire and mixed with a lot of split cane. A bunch in each hand, he stood behind the prisoner, and did not flog across the back as with the cats, but along the strait down the back, and cut the flesh off in strips. Then a quantity of coarse salt [was] rubbed in – that was what they called scourging under the gallows.

After the Settlers arrived on their locations, they were not allowed to go to town without a pass – except the heads of parties: and when they did go they had great difficulty to get accommodation, I have heard some say they had to apply to the Commandant (Col. Somerset) to get an order to be allowed to sleep in the tronk. No one could ever leave his district, without a colonial pass: he had a chance of being brought back by the Field Cornet.

There was a tax called opgaaf which had to be paid every year. The country being overrun with wild beasts, the government offered a certain price for the heads of various animals: for a tiger, Rixdollars 25 – wolf – Rds 5, and so on. When the heads were brought to the office, the ears were cut off, and you got a receipt for them but no money: these receipts were tokens as payment for the opgaaf ...

Thomas Stubbs was a young 1820 Settler who left school in England in 1820 and immediately set sail for South Africa. He travelled with his mother, father, brother and Tom, a young man in his father's care, as well as a servant named Bet. The family had lived in Brunswick Square, London and sailed aboard 'a regular old tub' called the Northampton Transport. The Stubbs were one of ten families on board the ship and Thomas was probably about thirteen or fourteen when he arrived in what he called the 'l(e)ast known portion of the world'. After a gruelling voyage, the Stubbs made for Grahamstown. Stubbs' autobiographical account of the journey and of his experiences in South Africa in the 1820s is a remarkable, unusual, and often witty set of tales that are rich in history.
Book Extracted: *The Reminiscences of Thomas Stubbs including Men I Have Known* (edited by W A Maxwell and R T McGeogh, Rhodes University Press, Grahamstown, 1978)

Shirley, Goodness & Mercy
Chris van Wyk

When ma comes home from work, always at about five in the early evening, she puts on her slippers and starts cooking. For me this is the best part of the day. I stand in the back door watching her and I glance from time to time at the setting sun dropping in slow motion behind the mine dumps on the eastern side of Riverlea.

I watch my mother peel potatoes, one continuous peel on each potato, which swirls round and round until it plops on top of the piles of other peels. Or she dices an onion into hundreds of equally shaped, sparkling little diamonds. Or I marvel at her hands, damp and clean and clamped together as if in prayer as she turns mince into frikkadels.

'That's a waste of time,' I tell her.

'What is?'

'Making the frikkadels.'

'Why?' She's amused that I dare say such a thing.

'OK, look, this mince was once a whole piece of meat, right?'

'Mhm.'

'And then the man in the butcher shop put it into that machine and it came out broken up in little bits like this, right?'

Ma says, 'Right,' but by now she can see where I'm going with this and she begins to laugh.

'So now you're trying to put it back together again.'

Ma says, 'Oh get away,' but she laughs out loud and nods.

She gives me easy, pleasant little chores.

'Go and throw this in the dustbin for Ma,' she says, handing me vegetable peels wrapped in newspaper, like a neat parcel. Or she throws a few pieces of garlic, ginger and a chilli into the little brass pot and asks me to find a block of wood outside and stamp away. 'Just don't get the chilli in your eyes.'

While she cooks we talk about lots of things. Mostly I ask her questions. I always say:

'Ma, can I ask you something?'

'Ja.'

'My name is Christopher Clinton, right?'

'Right.'

'So why the "Clinton"?'

'I liked that name as a middle name for you.'

'No, that's not what I mean.'
'What do you mean?'
'Why do we need middle names?'
'Uhm.' She puts some water in a pot to stop the onions from burning. 'Because one day you might forget your first name and then you can use your second name.'
'Really, Ma!'
'Oh yes.'
I'm ready to believe her, but then I see her trying to keep the smile from spreading and I know I've been tricked.
'Ma!'
Now she bursts out laughing and she says, 'We just all have middle names, I don't know why. Some people have three or four names. Just so they can have their mother's name, grandmother's name ...'
'I think it's just a waste of time.'
'Why?'
'Because nobody uses those names. Nobody says, "Christopher Clinton please come here a minute" you know what I mean?'
'I know what you mean.'
Ma asks me questions too. She always says, 'How was school today?'
'Nice.'
'Nice! That tells me nothing. Tell me something your teacher said. Something the principal said.'
One day I have some good news.
'I know Psalm 23.'
'The whole psalm?'
'The whole psalm,' I nod proudly.
'Well, what are you waiting for? Let's hear it.'
I stand facing her, hands clasped together in front of me, classroom style, and recite:

> 'Psalm 23 – a psalm of David
> The Lord is my shepherd
> I shall not want
> He maketh me to lie down
> In green pastures
> He leadeth me beside the still waters
> He restoreth my soul ...'

I watch Ma listening to me and see her own soul being restoreth. She puts down her knife and her dishcloth, and stands watching me, a smile of pure pride lighting up her face. Then suddenly, as I reach the last two lines, Ma bursts into excited laughter.

I had expected some kind of approval, but nothing quite like this. David, Mrs Abrahams had told us, sang these psalms to God to the accompaniment of a harp. Well here I am doing a rendition without music and Ma is bowled over.

So bowled over in fact that when my father comes home from work, she makes me recite it all over again for him. I duly deliver, with much the same gusto as before – with the same effect. Ma smiles and bursts into laughter. Dad laughs too in the end and tells me that I am one 'helluva clever *laaitie*'.

My reputation as a reciter of Psalm 23 grows with every delivery. To quote another psalm from the good David, I 'make a joyful noise' – or at least cause one – whenever an uncle, aunt or neighbour comes visiting.

Then, one day, I discover the reason why I am causing so much laughter. My delivery is word-perfect – except when I come to the end where, instead of: 'surely goodness and mercy shall follow me all the days of my life' I am going for: 'Shirley, Goodness and Mercy ...'

Despite this malapropism, I know that Ma and Dad are both proud of me. I think about David and Abraham, who was willing to sacrifice his son, and Daniel in the Lion's Den. I think about all these people and I say, 'These people really liked God and Jesus, hey Ma?'

Ma says, 'Actually Jews don't believe in Jesus.'

What crazy information is this! 'They don't believe in Jesus?'

Ma shakes her head. 'They don't.'

Jews, I tell myself, are taking one helluva chance. Everybody knows that you can't go to heaven unless you believe in Jesus. My teacher told us this, the preacher tells us this every Sunday in the Ebenezer Church. I think you can open the Bible on any page and it's right there in black and white. And now my mother tells me this – and goes on peeling potatoes as if she has just declared that it might rain tomorrow.

Well, I decide, if they want to go directly to hell, that's their problem.

'And the Muslims too,' Ma says.

'The Muslims too?'

'Oh yes.'

This is getting out of hand. The Jews, well, I don't know any of them on a personal basis. Ma's boss is a Jew. The man who owns the Reno movie house in Newclare is a Jew. Jews own clothing stores in town. All they ever say to you is: 'I'm telling you, you won't get this cheaper anywhere else.' They're white. They live far away, in places called suburbs that I don't even know how to get to. But Muslims, now that's a different story. Riverlea is chock-a-block with Muslims. In every street of thirty families, four or five are Muslim. We go to the same schools, play football together in the streets ...

'Who do they follow?' I ask Ma.

She smiles at my choice of words. 'Who do they follow? They follow the prophet Mohammed.'

Mr and Mrs Lang are Muslims – we have a nickname for Muslims: 'slamsies', from 'Islam'. The Langs live at the bottom end of our street. They're an old couple, in their late sixties or early seventies. If you're not even near your tenth birthday then being over sixty is ancient.

Mr Lang is a perfect oval, an egg in braces ... Moegamat Dumpty, I suppose, a strictly halaal egg. He has a bald spot surrounded by sparse grey hairs. Braces keep up his pants and thick glasses show him the way to town – where he goes once a week to buy spices for the *koeksisters* he and his wife sell on Sunday mornings. They also sell sweets (I especially like their nutty, brittle beetle nuts, which look like legless beetles), and popcorn in cones that they make out of quarter sheets of newspaper. A fair percentage of my pocket money ends up in a glass jar on the Langs' kitchen cupboard.

But the *koeksisters* are not for every day. Those are special and come, plaited and dipped in syrup and sprinkled with a confetti of coconut, on Sunday mornings.

Christian and Muslim kids all trudge, half-asleep, down to the Langs, dish in hand, for our half dozen or dozen. We sit on a little bench in their kitchen, yawning and staring at the Arabic holy script on the walls – always in green.

The Slamsies are our friends.

But there are kinds of inner circles that inevitably develop between the Muslims. They pray together and in the holy month of Ramadan you see children, *kufias* on their heads, taking little dishes of curry or pudding to Auntie Rashida or the Ali family. Ramadan is the fasting month and, to break their fast every evening, Muslim mothers cook special dishes, which they share with friends and family.

Every household has a 'Boeta'. Boeta Ibrahim or Boeta Gamat, usually the father or older brother. The Muslims greet each other with a *Salaam aleikum* (Peace be upon you), but when they greet us Christians it's a mere hullo. We're not part of the circle.

I find the Muslims a little weird. They seem to have only one song that they sing to God – and which wakes up the entire township around 4.30 am on Friday mornings, when it blares out from a loudspeaker on the roof of the mosque. They like the colour green. From their hearse, which collects dead bodies, to clothes to the biscuits they bake on their holy days – all green, green, green. Many Muslim men quite like the green weed too.

The Christians too have their own religious customs and rituals that bind them. We almost all eat fish on Fridays, we could be pointed out on the football fields on Sundays by our white shirts (worn to church that morning) with their talismans of tomato sauce and brooches of beetroot from our almost identical Sunday lunches of chicken curry, with jelly and custard for dessert.

Then, within the Christian community there are the Catholics, the Anglicans, the Ebenezers, the Methodists, New Apostolic Church, Dutch Reformed Church, Lutherans, Congregational Church ... These are called denominations. The first time I hear that word I take great pleasure in asking a friend:

'Which denomination do you belong to?'

'Huh?'

The Catholics are by far the strongest denomination in Riverlea. This is thanks to one Father Patrick McCullagh or Father Mac. Everybody knows him; he stands out like a sunburnt white Irish thumb on account of being the only white person in a sea of darker-skinned people. But it's not his skin colour that has made him famous in these parts. When I first hear about Father Mac I am both in awe of him and happy that I am not a Catholic.

Every day of the week, I straggle home from school with all the boys: Kurt, Ivan, Neil, Allan, Toolbag, Keith. We peer down mine-shafts, pop in at the shops to buy sherbet and bubblegum, play 'Ollie' along the way. But on Wednesdays half the *chommies* are missing, running home past all of us.

'Aw, gents. Why yous in a hurry? Here's some sherbert.'

'No thanks. Can't stop now. I'm late for catties. Father Mac's gonna *moer* me if I'm late again.' Catties? Catechism.

Ask Ivan Johnson about Father Mac. One day he's in the confessional and he's going: 'Forgive *chew-chew* me Father *chew-chew* for I have *chew-chew* sinned *chew-chew* ...' Father Mac yanks him out of the confessional and delivers two hot smacks to his cheeks.

'Chewing gum while asking God for forgiveness, you feckin stupid boy!'

It's not only the boys and girls who are scared of Father Mac. He scares the holy shit out of their parents too.

Mr Peffer beats up his poor wife from time to time... until Father Mac comes to hear about it. One Friday Father Mac storms into the Peffer home in Potomac Street just as Mr Peffer, steamed up by a few brandies, is piling into Mrs Peffer. The priest takes off his dog collar and his cassock and tosses them over a dining-room chair.

'Father, what are you doing?'

'That,' Father Mac says, pointing at the things he has taken off, 'is

Father MacCullagh.' Then, pointing a thumb at himself. 'And this is *Mr* MacCullagh. I see that you hit women, so I want to see how you'll fare with Mr Mac.'

'No, Father, please.'

'Mr. And by the way, Ralph, I was Dublin Middleweight Boxing Champion, 1939.'

There's a wham and a bam and a boom and a doof and, the next thing, Ralph Peffer is out for the count. When he gets up he's cured of woman abuse for ever. No prayers, no mass, no lighting a candle – just a good whack from Father Mac.

Riverlea still has a severe drinking problem. But Father Mac single-handedly reduces it by two or three per cent. Almost all the Catholic men go about with little green badges proclaiming that they are Pioneers. Shame, they look a little like babies deprived of their milk bottles. But their wives are so happy because now Ralphie or Eric or James comes straight home from work on Friday evenings and puts that pay envelope, sealed and stapled as it should be, into wifey's ever-loving hands. So instead of filling the coffers of the shebeens, the pay now buys bread and milk and tea and mealie meal and pays the rent. Will all this abstinence last? Nobody knows, but for the moment it's Father Mac's miracle. There are exceptions though. But these are exceptions at their own peril. One of them is Boy Brown.

Boy Brown scoffs at this 'pioneer shit'.

'Sissies,' he calls these men. He takes centre stage in the backyard of Foxy's shebeen, where he debates the issue with the other regulars – who all seem to be on his side. 'All week long, I have to put up with a white man telling me what to do. Then on Saturdays and Sundays when I wanna sit around with some friends, there's another white man trying to tell me what to do.'

'Tell them, ou Boy Brown!'

'You got a point there.'

Someone puts a double brandy and water into his hands and asks him to act out his version of the mass, just one last time.

Boy Brown leaps into action and the circle of drinkers goes quiet. This is a sketch they've all seen before but it's worth seeing a hundred times more.

Boy Brown takes a hat off somebody's head and presses it down on his own head. He does a wide-brim charade with his hands: he's wearing a sombrero. He slaps his pockets: he's packing two colts. He strides a few paces into the sunlight: he's gonna fetch his horse.

Then suddenly Boy Brown swings around, faces his audience, makes the sign of the cross and announces:

'Mea culpa, mea culpa, me a Mexican cowboy.'

Foxy's backyard explodes into laughter and somebody passes Boy Brown another drink.

The story doesn't end there.

Boy Brown's wife is a devout Catholic. Meisie is one of a group of women who spend almost all their free time in the house of the Lord. They make tea for Father Mac, clean the church and make sure there are always fresh flowers in the many vases in the church.

One day Boy Brown is very short of cash for a drink and so badly in debt at the shebeen that there is no hope of getting even a nip on the book. As he swallows the last of his brandy, he suddenly remembers where he's seen a stash.

'I'll be here now-now, gents,' he says. 'With cash.'

'No problem, Boy Brown. But you seem very sure.'

'I am. Rinse those glasses so long.'

He goes home, and heads straight for his bedroom and his wife's wardrobe. There's an old black handbag from the 1940s. It used to be for going out into town but now it's used for hiding money from hubby. And, it seems, that use has now also had its day. Boy Brown snaps it open and there's the money!

'Boy!'

He gets a bit of a *skrik*; he didn't hear Meisie come in.

'What are you doing with my money?'

'Oh fuck off, this is our money ...'

'It's the church's money. For flowers.'

'Fuck the church.'

'Boy! How can you say that?'

He brushes past her and arrives back at the shebeen, waving the five-rand note for all to see.

Things are going well at the shebeen, but not so well down the road at the Catholic Church.

Meisie stumbles into the church sobbing. Father Mac is sipping tea in his room, humming one of those many Irish songs. He hears the sobbing and comes out to see.

'Meisie, what's the matter?'

She tells him.

'The money for the flowers?'

'Y-yes, F-father.'

Boy Brown is doing his skit for the boys when he sees the black cassock sweep into the dusty backyard of the shebeen. The Mexican cowboy has nowhere to run.

Father Mac flings off his cassock with his familiar fighting words:

'That's Father MacCullagh, this is Mr MacCullagh.'

Mea culpa, mea culpa, mea maxima culpa.

We belong to the Ebenezer Church. The services are mostly in Afrikaans, very rarely in English. We call the preacher *Meneer* (Sir). Mr Conley, our *Meneer*, unsettles me one Easter Sunday morning. Whilst telling us about how Christ had died for us on the cross, he bursts into uncontrollable sobs, dragging out the service an hour longer than scheduled. He is putting on such a performance, as if Jesus was his very own brother and had died that very morning.

We Ebenezers are like one family. Not as close as the Catholics – and not half as big. But a family nevertheless.

A few months, maybe a year, after Ma's religious revelations to me, she's sick in bed, groaning and moaning in pain. She has a headache, backache, a fever.

She calls me to her bedroom and tries to sit up to talk to me.

'Go to Mr Fortune,' she says, leaving long painful pauses between each word. 'Ask him if I can please have a jar of menthol camphor. Tell him I don't have the money now but I'll pay him ... next week Friday.'

'Yes, Ma.' I nod. This is one chore I'm eager to do. If menthol camphor is going to take away Ma's pain, then I would go and fetch it in Cape Town let alone three streets down from where we live.

'And don't forget to say ...'

'Please and thank you – I know, Ma.'

I run out the front door into a Saturday afternoon that is turning into evening. The sun is going down behind the mine dumps and clouds of smoke are billowing out of chimneys as coal stoves are lit all over Riverlea to prepare the evening supper.

The Fortunes are Ebenezers like us. Cyril and Cecil, handsome twins, are my classmates and among my best friends. I spend a lot of time at their home. Every Friday afternoon they buy *True Africa*, a photo comic about the adventures of a muscular African hero called Samson, who goes about rural villages and urban towns fighting crime with his ever-present monkey, Jacko, on his shoulder. What the twins have in looks they sort of lack in reading skills so they call on me to do the honours. Every Friday afternoon after school about four or five boys make their way to the Fortunes'. We sit down in the sand on the shady side of their house. Somebody hands me the latest *True Africa* and I become the centre of our informal reading club.

I begin to read: 'The Leopard Men had been harassing these peace-loving villagers for far too long now and Samson decided to do something about it. Jacko hopped on to his master's shoulder and they set off for the distant village of Taung.'

There are also the speech bubbles, which go like this: 'Take that, you thug!' (in a serrated bubble to show us just how angry Samson is).

Mr Fortune has a regular job like most fathers. But in order to earn extra money he is also an agent for Watkins Products, the cosmetics company that manufactures salves, deodorants, facial creams and that kind of stuff. During the week Mr Fortune goes from door to door taking orders for this cream and that spray. Then on Friday evening and Saturday morning he comes delivering his products and collecting his money.

The Watkins Menthol Camphor is a heady, pungent ointment that comes in a flat green tin. Once, when I had a cold, Ma rubbed it on my chest so that I could have a good night's sleep. I stayed awake half the night trying to avert my nostrils – until I called Ma to wipe it off my chest.

In about eight minutes flat I'm knocking at the Fortunes' door, a little out of breath. A voice inside says, 'Come in.' I open the door and, sitting at the dining-room table, is the man himself. He has a ballpoint pen in his hand and is surrounded by receipt books and invoice books with carbon sheets sticking out of them.

Actually I know it's Mr Fortune even before I open the door because it's the same voice I hear on Sunday mornings in church singing, 'What a friend we have in Jeee-zus ...'

I say good evening, Mr Fortune. He says yes.

'Mr Fortune,' I begin – I had done a quick rehearsal on my way here – 'my mother asks if she can please have a tin of menthol camphor. She says she will definitely pay you next week Friday.'

He looks me up and down once or twice, with disapproval. He sits back in his chair and enlarges his eyes. 'Tell your mother that I don't give Watkins products on credit to people who have changed their agents, who don't ... who can't make up their minds who they want to buy from. Tell her to go to the new agent when she's in trouble, not the one she refuses to buy anything from any more.'

Now here is a man who's been waiting to get something off his own chest too. I'm stunned.

'Off you go,' he says.

'Good night, Mr Fortune.'

He doesn't bother to respond to that. I leave, making sure to close the door softly; I don't want to be called back and told to *close* the door and not *slam* it.

At home I report to Ma. Through her pain she frowns, trying hard to make sense of what I'm telling her. It's all a misunderstanding. She had once bought something from another agent, not believing this would be taken as a slight by Mr Fortune. And another time she had been in such financial difficulties that Mr Fortune's wonderful products, stuff like Body Mist deodorant and hand cream, just had to wait.

Ma's still in pain and I'm standing by her bed not knowing what to do. She twitches and makes little gasping noises and I'm at a loss.

'Listen,' Ma says, 'be a good boy and go to Mrs Lang for me. Tell her I've got backache and ask her for some *kruie*.'

'Krayer? What's that, Ma?'

This was the Afrikaans word for herbs. But, even if I spoke to Mrs Lang in English, which I planned to do, I was to use the word *kruie*.

'And tell Mrs Lang it's for my back.'

The trip to the Langs takes half the time it takes to get to Mr Fortune. I knock on the door and Mr Lang opens, in his usual braces and slippers. I greet him. He says, 'Hullo, little van Wyk,' smiles at me and waits for my order: popcorn, beetle nuts, Ice Kwenchies. But tonight I'm not here for sweets. I'm on a serious mission.

'My mother sent me to Mrs Lang, please Mr Lang.'

'Oh,' he says, 'Oh.' This has never happened before and he's thrown for a few seconds. He calls his wife and she comes waddling to the kitchen door, wearing long white socks, slippers, a long dress, a jersey and a scarf – even though it's a summer evening. I greet her.

'Hullo, my child.' She smiles.

'Mrs Lang, my mother sent me to ask you if you please don't have some *kruie* for her, for her sore back.'

'Oh shame, oh shame,' they chant a duet. Then they both bustle about in the kitchen. From the dresser drawer they haul out a bunch of what looks to me like dried out twigs. They wrap it in a sheet of newspaper; both pairs of old wrinkled hands trying to do the same work.

They hand it to me, shuffling in the doorway.

'Thank you ...'

'Don't say thank you!' they both chorus, almost aggressively.

I step back, a little alarmed.

'Do you understand me?' Mr Lang says.

'Yes, Mr Lang.' I take the parcel of brittle herbs from him, and almost say thank you again – it's such habit.

I run up the road wondering what's happening to me this evening. Everywhere I go adults are trying to bite my head off, no matter how polite I am.

At home I present Ma with the bouquet of *kruie* and tell her about my strange encounter.

'They sounded almost angry just because I said thank you.'

Ma nods. 'You're not supposed to say thank you for medicine. They feel it's their duty to give medicine.' She sits up in bed, and, for the first time, that evening, I see her smile.

Chris van Wyk was born in Baragwanath Hospital, Soweto in 1957, and went on to become an acclaimed poet, novelist, editor, and children's writer. He was educated at Riverlea High School in Riverlea, Johannesburg, where he still lives and works today. In 1979, van Wyk was awarded the Olive Schreiner Award for his collection of poems entitled *It is time to go home*, and, in 1998, was awarded the Sanlam Prize for the year's best South African short story for *Magic*.
Book Extracted: *Shirley, Goodness & Mercy* (Picador Africa, 2004)

Farmboy and Industrialist
Albert Wessels

… I was born in 1908, six years after the end of the Anglo-Boer War. The time in which I grew up and gradually developed an awareness was thus inevitably strongly influenced by the War and the conditions that followed it.

The first circumstance of which I became aware was the terrible poverty of the farmers. During the three years of the War, with the men on commando and some later prisoners of war, and the women either in flight or in concentration camps, the farms lay unworked. In the last years of the War the British military authorities, in their attempt to subdue the troublesome resistance of the Boer guerillas, undertook a programme of burning down farm houses and destroying the livestock. After the War the farmers, like my father and mother and also my grandparents, returned to farms that had been totally destroyed. They had to move into the shells of burnt out houses and, without livestock or seed, start up anew. It took years before they could again get on their feet.

What I remember of my first years is that everything was scarce and that nothing could be wasted. You had to eat what was put before you on the table. You had to look after your clothes. Every one had his own tasks in the house. For my brother and me it was a touchy matter that we had to make our own beds and sweep out our bedroom ourselves. We felt that this, after all, was women's work. Mother was hardly concerned with such complaints and we simply continued tidying our room. We all worked together in the garden, milked the cows, separated the milk and made butter. Our enthusiasm wasn't always great, but we knew we would quickly land in trouble if our daily tasks weren't properly performed.

New clothes were a rarity. That is probably why I still remember what my first suit looked like – a blue Mao-type jacket with a wide, embroidered white collar. All of course made by Mother.

Yet I cannot remember that we were ever conscious of poverty. That word simply never existed in our home. True, everything was scarce, and we realised that we had to save to get something together again. Things shall come right once more, Mother consoled us. Things will one day be as they were before the war when Oupa slaughtered a fat ox every year and made a lot of biltong, when they drove to church in the nearby village in a spider with four smart horses and a Griqua driver, when there were four orchards in the old garden. Work, save, and everything will come right again, she encouraged us.

This urge to save for a better future was so deeply impressed upon my young mind that it has become an obsession that I cannot get rid of. I am not unaware that my children and good friends sometimes mock me for cheese-paring, but it doesn't worry me. Unlike me, they didn't see how a people had to save and work themselves up, literally from the ashes of destroyed farms, so that their children would be assured of a normal life.

A second consequence of the War was that the young folk of that time grew up with a strong awareness of the events of the struggle. Khakies and Boere, Tommies and Redcoats played a big role in their imaginations. And there was need of a rationale for the defeat the Boers had suffered. On the one hand, there had been the superior power of the English army, its unlimited ammunition and war supplies, and its great stocks of food. On the other hand, there'd been our fathers and grandfathers who lived off mieliepap and braaivleis (often without salt) while on commando, who during the last part of the War could only fight with ammunition they had taken from the English troops, who had to get by with horses that were only skin and bone in the winter months.

When I think back to that time, I find it remarkable how that search for a rationale for the defeat took place without inordinate bitterness. In our imaginations and our games we of course beat up the English. But on a personal level people did not seek revenge. The children of English soldiers who were settled on crown lands they had received for war service soon became our playmates. Still, we remained aware that our parents had been defeated, and deep down a yearning for rehabilitation arose. It developed into an urge to prove that you were at least the equal of the conquerors and their children; and this urge was encouraged by the community in which we lived, and particularly by our teachers.

That urge has never left me. Early in life, especially under the influence of my parents, I learnt to accept English-speaking South Africans as fellow citizens. But a spirit of competition, a need to compete with them, worked strongly within me. In the business world I entered, all the people in the same field are of course your competitors, and you have to battle against them. The knowledge that I, as a child of a defeated nation, have striven to achieve equality in various fields hence always gives me pleasure.

Of the school on our farm, I don't have clear memories, but I do of the children who were there with me, like the Krauses, the Naudés and the Van Wyks. Most clearly I remember the black children who played with us. They joined us in light work on the farm, like bringing in sheep to the kraal or fetching calves in the veld. We usually swam together in pools or the big dam and played at clay stick shooting. At play there was complete equality, but one remained the *kleinbasie* to the black children.

My hero among our black servants was Outa Hendrik Kora. He was a proper Korana and a bachelor who had worked on and off for my parents and grandparents for more than thirty years. He was a great smoker of dagga but did it with dignity and style. He always knelt when he smoked, and before each pull on his long-stemmed pipe he recited a little verse in Korana, then took a mouthful of water, and blew out the smoke along with the water through a hollowed-out reed.

I always wondered what that doggerel meant, but he would never tell. Nor would he allow us a suck on his pipe.

It was many years later that I discovered that Eugène Marais, the well-known Afrikaans poet, who spent long periods in Boshof recovering from the effects of excessive morphine addiction, had written down that Korana, or Griqua, verse and translated it.

We learnt the 'facts of life' from old Kora. And of the great power of the Spanish fly: if you put one in your shirt pocket all the girls would run after you, he told us. Unfortunately we didn't like girls in those days, and still less the idea that they should run after us.

In the evenings after supper all the servants on the farm would come into our living room and sit in a row against the wall while Father conducted family prayers. After they had gone home, old Kora would remain behind and help with washing up the dishes. Then he would tell my sisters of a magic wand: you knocked on the table with it, and all the crockery would be in the washing-up basin in the kitchen; you knocked again and everything stood dried off in the pantry; and when you knocked once more, all would be neatly packed away on the shelves.

At the end of Std 1 I was sent to school in Dealesville. Dealesville is a small town between Bloemfontein and Boshof and is the religious and commercial centre of that community.

My school years there were very happy. Although the school was fairly small, it had excellent and inspiring teachers.

The first one I wish to mention is Mr Jan Viljoen who later became Minister of Education. When he was appointed principal of Dealesville in 1920 it was only a primary school up to Std 6. Within four years under his leadership it could offer tuition up to matric. I still remember how often he and my father, who was then chairman of the school commission, had to go to Bloemfontein to obtain further support from the Education Department and the Provincial Council. The Viljoen family were always great friends of my parents. Jan Viljoen's father and my father were comrades-in-arms and were together as prisoners of war in India; and they remained life-long, intimate friends. Our families also agreed on politics, and when the National Party split in the Thirties, Mr Viljoen, like my family, remained a supporter of General Hertzog.

The second teacher I remember with great respect was Dr SJ du Toit who succeeded Mr Viljoen as principal. He was a different kind of personality – very learned, a philosopher and an educationist, but perhaps not so good an organiser. In different ways he encouraged us to read. He for instance acquired various children's magazines and newspapers for us, as well as the publications of Arthur Mee.

Then there was Gawie Nienaber who arrived in Dealesville fresh from university. He was our German teacher, but his educational interests extended far wider. He encouraged us to work on our own and arrange our own outings. In various ways he was the real founder of the Voortrekker youth movement. And it was no surprise that besides all his academic work at the University College in Pietermaritzburg, where he soon obtained an academic appointment, he moreover became leader of the Voortrekkers in Natal.

In a book of school stories *Moffie en sy Maats* I later wrote, the two main characters among the teachers are based on Dr du Toit and Gawie Nienaber.

Boshof, where I later matriculated, was already a famous school in the Free State. Mr IW Malan, the principal, had brought together an excellent teaching staff and organised the school with military precision. From each of my teachers I received more than mere class instruction: they were professionals, true educationists, and shared my parents' belief that the Afrikaners would only raise themselves from their post-war poverty and backwardness by proper school education and higher training.

Although I matriculated at Boshof, I was more the product of the Dealesville school.

While I was at school, I, for the first time, earned something with my pen. Our local dominee, a Rev. du Toit, collapsed on the tennis court one hot summer's afternoon and died of a heart attack. He was an honoured minister and a number of dominees from the surrounding towns came to Dealesville for his funeral. The great occasion made me think of sending an article about it to the *Volksblad*. That same evening I wrote a report of the funeral and posted it immediately. Two days later it appeared prominently in the newspaper, and at the end of the month I received a cheque for seven shillings and sixpence.

That was my first cash income, but not my first business transaction. When I was about seven or eight years old, I heard one morning from Outa Jim, one of the black farmworkers, that one of his cows had died during the night and that he wanted to sell her calf for five shillings. I went to Mother and asked if she would lend me the money. Probably more from surprise than anything else she lent me the sum which I then took to Jim to strike my deal.

Later in the morning I heard that my father had wanted to buy the calf. Quite cheekily I could say: 'If you want to buy the calf, Pa, you'll have to buy it from me. But I don't want to sell.'

Years later that calf was sold as an ox for ten pounds, and until today I still feel rather aggrieved that I only got back my five shillings in cash. For the rest had to be put away in my savings box.

Albert Wessels was born on a farm in the Orange Free State in 1908. He went on to become a highly successful businessman and industrialist, including being the founder of Toyota South Africa. Even with all his business ventures, Wessels still managed to maintain interest in cultural matters, and was particularly concerned in the public affairs of the country and its people.
Book Extracted: *Albert Wessels – Farmboy and Industrialist* (Perskor, 1988)

Asking for Trouble – the autobiography of a banned journalist
Donald Woods

Far from the big cities of South Africa are the tribal reservations, and it was in one of these, the Transkei Territory, that I grew up among the Bomvana tribesmen of the Wild Coast. The Bomvanas wore red-ochred loincloths and blankets, lived in round mud huts with thatched roofs and believed in sorcery and witchcraft. Their young men settled arguments by fighting to the finish with battle axes, and as a child I grew accustomed to the fact, if not the spectacle, of human beings literally being chopped to death. The axe-fights took place every Sunday in our district, and it was safe to watch them from fairly close because the fighters never turned on anyone with whom they had no quarrel. The clashes were usually between rival groups of up to twenty, and bystanders were attacked only if they gave an impression of favouring one side or the other.

Although for years I was the only white child among tens of thousands of Bomvanas, I never felt in any danger among them; I could walk anywhere in the area and go into any of their huts. Apart from the axe-fights, violence was not among their chief characteristics. They had a disciplined society with rigid social rules. Tall, well-built people, they spoke with elaborate courtesy, and their code was based on generosity and communal sharing.

Their language was Xhosa, which has a variety of distinctive clicksounds, and as a white child living on a trading-post in Bomvanaland I spoke it as naturally as I spoke English. In fact, up to the age of five I expressed myself better in Xhosa than in English because it was spoken by all my Bomvana playmates and my nursemaid, Maggie Mzondo. My parents and my brother and sister also spoke it fluently.

Maggie was a *gqirakazi*, a witchdoctress, and we kids used to get her to *vumisa* for us, to go into a trance and wail her incantations to the spirits as she sagged to the floor with her eyes rolling back in her head. We loved it, although it was often scary. Maggie could 'smell out' evil-doers and cast spells on them – a valuable aid in imposing discipline on kids, especially at bedtime. My brother Harland and I would show her our Superman comics, explaining the stories to her in Xhosa, but her own bedtime stories were far more vivid.

One in particular used to send chills down our spines. It was about the *sigebenga* – the monstrous Xhosa spook who was all things terrible

– who entered a hut where children were sleeping and decided aloud in which order he would eat them up. '*Ndizaku qala nga le...*' he would begin. ('I'll start with *this* one ...') '*Ndi ze nga le ...*' ('Then I'll come to *this* one ...') '*Ndi ze nga le...ndi ze nga le... ndi ze nga le...*' ('Then *this* one ... then *this* one ... then *this* one.')

Maggie's impassive face was ominous in the dim nightlight as she intoned the singsong litany of ghastly inevitability. She told many frightening stories of the loathsome *sigebenga*, but that was the scariest. And though her stories were hardly conducive to lulling us into calm slumber we always pestered her for more – especially *'leya'* ('*that* one') in anticipation of which we would shudder and burrow deeper into the blankets while she composed her features to begin the tale.

Bomvana lore was full of bogeymen and sprites. The best known was Tikoloshe, the water-sprite who was only two feet tall and whose whole body was covered in grey hair. He had a long grey beard down to his knees and lived in the eroded banks of rivers. Tikoloshe would get you if you didn't behave. He could walk through walls, run like a horse and even fly. He could destroy entire herds of cattle, inflicting mysterious diseases on man and beast or causing people to act peculiarly against their better inclinations. He could also be blamed for anything that went wrong, so he was a scapegoat as well as a bogeyman. Another sprite was Ichanti, the watersnake, one of Tikoloshe's submarine minions, and a third was Impundulu, the lightning-bird. Knowledge of the ways and powers of these sprites was part of the qualification of the witchdoctors. It was believed that the most powerful witchdoctors rode about on baboons at night, dragging one leg and leaving a swathe through the underbrush and tall dobo grass. I was once shown such a swathe by my playmates, who gave a superior laugh when I said it was only the mark of a lightning strike. They were condescending – what could a *mlungwana*, a little white boy, know of such things?

Apart from her sorcery Maggie was a woman of substance. She and her husband cultivated several fields and had herds of cattle, sheep and goats. In view of this and her 'practice', it was never clear why she worked all her life as a domestic servant, unless it was because of the close bond between her and my mother. She worked for my mother for forty years, and it was often a stormy arrangement. My mother sacked her at least a dozen times, usually after they had traded insults and imprecations in Xhosa, Mom at the top of her voice and Maggie in a barely audible undertone. But Maggie would ignore these dismissals and turn up the next morning for work, busying herself about the kitchen as if nothing had happened. Mom would heave a sigh of relief and uphold the truce.

When my sister Joan was a baby Maggie saved her life. Workmen were moving a heavy wardrobe in a bedroom and it toppled over and was falling on the child when Maggie flung herself over her on all fours and took the weight of it on her back. Sometimes when Mom was feeling sheepish about allowing 'that cheeky devil Maggie' to resume work after a sacking she would mutter: 'After all, she *did* save Joanie's life ...'

Mom and Maggie were the same age, although from the time they were in their fifties Mom would often call her 'the old devil' as if there were a vast age-gap. At other times they were the closest confidants and would murmur away for hours in Xhosa, Mom in a kind of monologue punctuated by Maggie's regularly spaced moans of assent and grunts of comprehension. Then the roles would be reversed and the monologue would be Maggie's, with the moans of assent and grunts of comprehension coming from my mother.

These sounds were necessary in any protracted conversation in Xhosa. It was considered inattentive to hear a speaker out in silence for any length of time, so the listener had to come in regularly with 'awwww' or 'ehhhh' or simply a noise in the throat.

Much of Dad's social life was with local elders of the Bomvanas. At sundown he would often have a drink with five or six of his favourite acquaintances among them, but never inside the house or in any of their huts – usually out in the yard. A servant would bring out a chair for him, and the elders would sit on the ground around him, smoking long-stemmed pipes as they chatted about crops or local events. The servant would bring a bottle of Cape brandy, a water jug and two glasses, one glass for Dad and the other for the tribesmen. Dad would pour out his measure, exactly up to a pattern on the glass, then add water. Then the bottle and the other glass would be handed round the circle and each would pour his own measure, again up to the pattern on the glass, constituting about a triple-shot of neat brandy. The Bomvanas never added water, always gulping the neat brandy down in one draught, followed by a loud 'Aaahh!' to cool their burning throats, smacking their lips in exaggerated appreciation. Sometimes I would lean against my father's chair, being four or five years old, or sit on the ground to listen to the talk. Then the old tribesmen would engage me in some conversation, always solemnly, as if I were an adult, never like the old tribeswomen who clucked and made baby-talk noises like '*Mah-na-seh!*' ('Isn't he cute?').

Joan, Harland and I were all given Xhosa names at birth by the tribesmen, as a mark of friendship. Mine was 'Zweliyanyikima', 'the world shakes'. Such names were quite arbitrarily given and were not connected to any event, there having been no earthquakes or tremors anywhere in Bomvanaland in living memory. Given at birth, Xhosa names were always complimentary. Given to adults, they would be more specific in reference to a characteristic or physical feature of the person named. As I grew older I was given additional names and could be hailed by any of them by members of different black communities, but in Bomvanaland I was always known as Zweliyanyikima. My father, who as a trader loaned money at interest, was called 'Masumpa', 'He who makes a gift then takes back a part of it'. His assistant, Glenn Turner, was called 'Ginyizembe', 'He swallowed an axe', because of his quick temper.

Adults, and especially elders, conversed with strict formality when children were around, and never joked about sex or other natural functions in their presence. When I leant against my father's chair as he drank brandy in the yard with the elders, one of them would address me formally: 'Greetings, Zweliyanyikima. Are you well?' I would reply: '*Molo, Mekene. Hayi, ndisahleli.*' 'Greetings, Mekene: No, I am well.' Mekene might then inquire after a sheep which the headman had given me for my birthday. Was the sheep well? No, the sheep was well. Then I would ask if he was well and he would reply that no, he was well, and thus the niceties of etiquette would be observed.

The Bomvanas loved practical jokes or straight-faced leg-pulling, and when a tribesman noted in the district for his big feet was persuaded by my father that there was going to be a new tax according to the area of ground a man's feet covered, they laughed about it for months and never let the big-footed one forget his gullibility.

The only Bomvana whose hut my father ever visited socially was a venerable elder for whom he had enormous respect. He was Belwana, and he was in his nineties. When Belwana saw Dad's black Buick pull up by the roadside near his kraal he would walk all the way down to the road to accompany him to the hut. The vigorous old man, bareheaded, barefoot and wearing only a loincloth, would utter a formal welcome and he and Dad would walk together as they talked. They sent each other gifts from time to time – a bag of tobacco, a goat, a blanket or a carved stick.

In South Africa the Bomvanas were regarded as the most primitive of all the tribes people and Bomvanaland as the most remote area of the country. It was part of the Transkei Territory, set aside by the white government a hundred years before as a reservation for Xhosa tribes such as the Pondos, the Tembus and the Bomvanas. The Bomvanas were so called because in Xhosa the word Bomvu means red, and the reference was to the red ochre they used to stain their blankets and loincloths. It wasn't simply that they liked the colour – it kept away lice and ticks.

A Bomvana in full dress looked magnificent, especially the young men and the old women. In addition to the loincloth and the blanket worn as a cloak over one shoulder, the young men wore intricately patterned bead necklaces, amulets, anklets and waist-bands in the brightest colours, made by their girlfriends to traditional designs. The old women dressed even more splendidly. Their basic garment was the *mbaco*, an ankle length skirt with the hem ornately patterned in rows of braid, and a braided bodice – both a light orange colour – over which the blanket was worn like a cloak. Scarves and bead necklaces of many colours adorned the neck, and surmounting all this was the magnificent head-dress. This was like a flared turban of coloured cloths extending outward and upward, contributing to the regal appearance of the old women. They looked stately as they walked along the road in all this gear, often with a long-stemmed beaded pipe clenched in their teeth and sometimes with a bucket of water or shopping bundle balanced on top of their turbaned heads.

The Bomvanas went barefoot at all times, and from early youth developed a thick sole as hard as horn which trod thorns and pebbles without any pain. Quite often while talking to you they'd stand on one foot and lift the other sole to pick out thorns and burrs as impersonally as if out of a strip of leather.

Bomvanaland stretches along the south-eastern coast of South Africa between the Kei and Umtata rivers, extending inland from thirty to fifty miles. Where we lived, near the mouth of the Bashee River, was the heartland of it. Every five miles there was a trading-post in which a white trader was licensed to trade with the tribespeople; the trading concession of each station extended in a circle for a five-mile radius. If blacks wanted to establish trading-stations they could trade within a two-mile radius, but there were few black traders. Throughout the Transkei Territory, about the size of Wales, there were about seven hundred white traders. Whites from outside the territory looked on our white trading community in the Transkei as strangely different because we spoke the complex Xhosa language which they couldn't understand and because, as they saw it, we lived 'among the savages'.

Traders sold basic commodities to the tribespeople – blankets, axes, buckets, hoes, sickles, spades, medicines, mirrors, beads and so forth. They sold grain on credit during times of famine, after a drought for instance and when harvests were good they bought produce from the tribesmen – hides, skins and wool for bigger markets. Traders were also recruiting agents for the gold mines and functioned as postal agents, money-lenders, pension officers and scribes for illiterates.

The first white settlers in South Africa had been Dutch, who colonized the Cape of Good Hope in 1652 and whose descendants, later known as the Boers and later still as the Afrikaners, had trekked inland and evolved their own culture and language – Afrikaans, an offshoot of Dutch. Later the British Empire had annexed South Africa, and after the Napoleonic Wars the British government encouraged young Britons to settle in the country. The 1820 Settlers, as the first wave of these immigrants were called, were given land grants as farmers in the Eastern Cape area between the places now known as Port Elizabeth and Grahamstown.

One of these settlers was twenty-one-year-old Frederick Woods, my great-great-grandfather. Little is known of the first two generations of Dad's family in South Africa, apart from the fact that Frederick was said to have come from Cornwall, but his grandson, James Woods, my grandfather, became a wealthy ostrich-farmer in the days when ostrich-feathers were the fashion in Paris and London. When the designers dropped the ostrich-feather as a means of adornment, grandfather James was ruined. He became a transport-rider, leading ox-wagon supply teams inland to the diamond fields of Kimberley. He later settled in Peddie, a small town between Grahamstown and the port of East London, and became a cattle-dealer and butcher.

It was in Peddie that Dad was born, one of sixteen children, and he had little schooling. His first job, at the age of twelve, was as a butcher-boy, and at fourteen he became a postal clerk. His family were strict Wesleyan Methodists, and while still in his teens Dad became a lay preacher of some local renown. At the age of nineteen he walked two hundred miles to the Transkei coast with the ambition of becoming a trader and owning his own trading-station. He worked for several traders as an assistant, then began to look around for his own trading-site. He found it near the banks of the Bashee River, within a few miles of where the river runs into the ocean. It was called Hobeni, place of doves, and consisted of a couple of run-down mud huts – one for living in and one functioning as the trading-shop. It was owned by a man of Irish descent named Frank Lawlor, from whom Dad at first leased it. After a few months he felt he could convert Hobeni into a profitable station and bought it. Frank Lawlor lived ten miles away on a large station called Madwaleni. He took a liking to my father, who thereafter often saddled his horse and rode to Madwaleni to visit the family. Then in his mid-twenties, Dad was regarded as one of the leading sportsmen in the white community.

Christened Walter John Woods, he was always called Jack, and during his visits to the Lawlor place four of Frank Lawlor's daughters used to scramble to the window to 'get a look at Jack Woods'. He was tall and good-looking, and the Lawlor girls were impressed with his elegant riding-coat and boots. He, in turn, was impressed with one of the youngest, Edna, and after several years of formal courtship they were married when she was twenty. Dad was twenty-six and by now fairly wealthy, having paid Frank Lawlor the last instalment for Hobeni.

Mom's ancestors had come from Ireland after one of the potato famines of the middle 1800s. Originally from County Cork and parts of Wicklow, they were tenant farmers and at least some of them had been involved in rebellion against British rule; my uncle Fintan Lawlor was almost certainly called after the Irish revolutionary, Fintan Lalor.

Grandmother Alice Lawlor, a second-generation South African, had as a child been taught phrases like 'Erin Go Bragh!' and 'Up the rebels', which she uttered with feeling from time to time throughout her life. Her mother had been one of the 'Kennaway girls', a shipload of Irish girls brought to South Africa on the sailing ship *Kennaway* to provide wives for the German Legionaries hired by the British government to police the frontier between the settler farmers and the Xhosa warriors – the colonial authorities fearing the mercenaries might take black wives and dilute the white race. The *Kennaway* missed its anchorage point at the port of East London and was wrecked on a beach, but all the girls were rescued. However, after her arrival great-grandmother Warren rejected the Germans and fell in love with an Irishman named Kelly. She was fifteen, he was forty-two, and for some years after they married he was still buying dolls for her. She would sit on his lap, fascinated by his pocket watch, and he would chuckle to friends: 'She's only a child!'

They had several children and one of their daughters was my grandmother, Alice Kelly, who met, married and bore thirteen children to Frank Lawlor. Edna Lawlor, my mother, was the sixth of them, born at Madwaleni. A governess was engaged for the primary education of the children, then they were sent to boarding-school at the convent in Umtata, sixty miles away, by ox-wagon. It used to take them three days to get to school, crossing river drifts and going up and down hills with no roads of any kind, through forests, and across wide maize-fields.

Granny Lawlor was a formidable woman. She was sturdily built and wore her waist-length grey hair in a plaited bun. She had handsome Irish features, and many years later when I paid my first visit to Ireland I saw counterparts of her and my mother in the features of the women in a Tipperary market place. One of my earliest memories of her was seeing her swing a shotgun up to her shoulder to blast a treesnake which then slithered down headless in a grove of trees at Madwaleni. Wild Coast treesnakes are bright green, but they blend so well into foliage that it takes a keen eye to spot them if they keep still. They are called boomslangs – in Afrikaans 'boom' means 'tree' and 'slang' means 'snake' – and are one of the most poisonous snakes in the world. Their venom dissolves the walls of blood-vessels, and a badly bitten victim oozes blood from the eyes, the nose, the mouth and the ears. The venom also attacks the nervous system and death results from this and from rapid destruction of the blood cells. Unlike most snakes, which withdraw their fangs after striking, the boomslang keeps chewing at the wound to inject more venom because its biggest fangs are at the back of the upper jaw, deeply grooved to carry the poison as far into the wound as possible.

The boomslang Granny Lawlor shot was about four feet long, but often they grow to six feet. They are fast-moving, especially in trees, and because of this and their brilliant green colour they are often mistaken for another deadly snake, the green mamba. But the mamba has a flat head and is usually found further up the coast in Natal. The boomslang has a round head and big round eyes, and when angry it inflates a hood behind its head like a cobra. It also rears up off the ground to strike, like a cobra, but herpetologists have established that its venom, drop for drop, is more poisonous than that of any cobra or viper. Boomslangs usually avoid human beings and only attack if they feel cornered or threatened. They eat chameleons, birds, mice and frogs, and especially like birds' eggs. The speed of their strike against a bird on a branch is like a blur.

Things went well for my parents in the first few years of their marriage. They added on to the house and shop at Hobeni, and trade was good. As a trader's daughter Mom was a help in the business, and at weekends they went to dances and gymkhanas all over the district. The dances held at the trading-stations were formal affairs, with dance-cards to be filled in by the ladies. They danced reels, schottisches, mazurkas, waltzes and barn-dances, and bands of musicians were hired from Umtata by whichever trader was the host for the occasion. Between dances there would be musical events by talented amateurs, and officers of the Cape Mounted Riflemen and the Transkei Mounted Rifles would often attend.

Returning from one of these dances my parents saw their home in flames. Hobeni and everything they had was destroyed. What started the fire was never known. There was no insurance, and they had to start from the beginning again. They were living in a tent, still clearing away the rubble, when a representative of the wholesale suppliers arrived to take an order for goods. Dad explained that they had no money, apart from some pieces of gold coin that had fused together in the blaze, and couldn't place an order. The representative, a Mr Neuper, said he had instructions from his managing director to extend credit for a complete re-stocking of all the goods lost in the fire, to help Hobeni back on to its feet. Dad placed the order, and when he was finished Neuper said: 'Now I have instructions that when you have completed your order I am to double it, and to tell you the company will defer payment for whatever length of time you require.' Dad asked why. 'I asked that myself,' said Mr Neuper. 'All the boss would reply was that he liked young Woods's face.'

Then came help from another quarter. Dad's ledgers and account books had all been destroyed in the fire and there were no records of amounts owed by the local tribesmen, but one after another they came forward to acknowledge or pay off their debts in grain or goats or cattle or money. Those who couldn't pay anything at that time brought relatives who took their debts over, because Bomvanas believe that settlement of debt involves the honour of a whole family. With all this support, and working at first out of tents, then mud huts, Mom and Dad earned good profits, and by the time their first child was born Hobeni was rebuilt on a larger scale than before. The new buildings were solid brick and mortar and the homestead, shop and outbuildings were spaciously laid out ...

Donald Woods was born in 1933, and raised in the Transkei. In 1950, after hearing a parliamentary debate, his conservative views changed because of what he called 'the great obscene lie of apartheid'. He started out as a law student, later turning to journalism, and, in 1965, became the editor of the *Daily Dispatch*. While there, he formed a friendship with black consciousness activist Steve Biko, and tried to persuade government officials to speak to Biko. When Biko was killed, Woods' reaction led to him being banned by the government, and he eventually fled, with his family, to London. After the fall of apartheid, Woods returned to South Africa as an honoured man. He died in London in 2001, after a long fight with cancer.
Book Extracted: *Asking for trouble: The autobiography of a banned journalist* (Penguin, 1987)

References

www.infoplease.com
www.worldbank.org
www.nb.co.za
www.worldwriters.english.sbc.edu
www.people.africadatabase.org
www.southafrica.info
www.clarkesbooks.co.za
www.motlc.wiesenthal.com
www.polity.org.za
wi.essortment.com
www.aaregistry.com
www.southafrica.info
www.collectorspost.com
www.literature.kzn.org.za
http://eu.wiley.com
www.chico.mweb.co.za
www.litnet.co.za
www.sahistory.org.za
www.cca.ukzn.ac.za
www.adebooks.com
www.legacy-project.org
www.newafricabooks.co.za
www.librairie-compagnie.fr/afrique-sud/auteurs/hirson.htm
www.contemporarywriters.com
http://literature.kzn.org.za/lit/23.xml
http://psychcentral.com/psypsych/William_Plomer
http://en.wikipedia.org, http://breyten-breytenbach.biography.ms/

Copyright Acknowledgments

The author and publisher gratefully acknowledge the following persons and instances for permission to quote copyright material:

An extract from *Long Walk to Freedom: The autobiography of Nelson Mandela* by Nelson Mandela (Macdonald Purnell, 1994) reprinted with permission of the Nelson Mandela Foundation; an extract from *Asking for Trouble: the autobiography of a banned journalist* by Donald Woods (Penguin,

1987) reprinted with permission of the publisher, Victor Gollancz, a division of The Orion Publishing Group; an extract from *Beside Myself - An Autobiography* by Antony Sher, (Hutchinson, 2001) reprinted with permission of the Random House Group Ltd; an extract from *Never been at home* by Zazah Khuzwayo (David Philip, 2004) with permission of New Africa Books; an extract from *The Calling of Katie Makanya* by Margaret McCord (David Philip 1997) reprinted with permission of New Africa Books; an extract from *The South African Autobiography* by William Plomer (David Philip, 1980) reprinted with permission of New Africa Books; an extract from *To my Children's Children* by Sindiwe Magona, (David Philip, 1990) reprinted with permission of New Africa Books; an extract from *Memoirs* by Ahmed Kathrada (Zebra Press, 2004) (ISBN 1868729184), in the first edition; an extract from *Part of my soul* by Winnie Mandela (Penguin, 1985) reprinted with kind permission of Rowohlt Verlage; an extract from *Hearing Grasshoppers Jump* by Raymond Ackerman, (David Philip, 2001) reprinted with permission of New Africa Books; an extract from *Every Secret Thing* by Gillian Slovo (Little, Brown and Company, 1997) reprinted with permission from Time Warner; an extract reprinted from *The Coyaba Chronicles: Reflections on the Black Experience in the 20th Century* by Peter Abrahams, pages 1-7: 'The Loved Ones' by permission of Ian Randle Publishers; an extract from *Boyhood: scenes from provincial life* by JM Coetzee (Vintage, 1998) reprinted with permission from David Higham Associates; extract from *Boy from Bethulie* by Patrick Mynhardt (Wits University Press, 2003) reprinted with the permission of the author and the publisher; an extract from *Towards the Mountain* by Alan Paton (David Philip, 1980) reprinted with kind permission of Alan Paton Will Trust; an extract from *Shirley, Goodness & Mercy* by Chris Van Wyk (Picador Africa, 2004) reprinted with the permission of Pan Macmillan and the author; an extract from *Down Second Avenue* by Es'kia Mphahlele (Picador Africa, 2004) reprinted with the permission of Pan Macmillan and the author; an extract from *Call me Woman* by Ellen Kuzwayo (Picador Africa, 2004) reprinted with permission of Pan Macmillan; an extract from *My Traitor's Heart* by Rian Malan (The Bodley Head, 1990) reprinted with permission of The Random House Group Ltd; an extract from *Armed and Dangerous* by Ronnie Kasrils (Jonathan Ball, 1993) reprinted with permission of Jonathan Ball; an extract from *Final Postponement – reminiscences of a crowded life* by Cecil Margo (Jonathan Ball, 1998) reprinted with permission of Jonathan Ball; an extract from *Blame me on History* by William Bloke Modisane (AD Donker, 1963) reprinted with permission of Jonathan Ball; an extract from *Across Boundaries: The Journey of a South African Woman Leader* by Mamphela Ramphele (The Feminist Press, 1996) reprinted with permission of New

Africa Books; an extract from *I Remember King...* ...Denis Hirson (Jacana, 2004) reprinted with kind per... ...and Blake Friedmann Literary Agency, London; an... ...*in Paradise* by Breyten Breytenbach (Jonathan Cap... permission of the author; an extract from *Memory*... Mattera (Ravan Press, 1987) reprinted with perm... Publishers; an extract from *My Story* by Miriam Make... (1988) reprinted with permission of Siyandisa Music (... of the Z M Makeba Trust. Copyright Miriam Makeba and... all rights reserved; an extract from *Who's laetie are you?* ...*...wetan boyhood* by Rrekgetsi Chimeloane (Kwela Books, 2001) reprinted with permission of NB Publishers.

Every effort has been made to trace copyright holders or their assigns. The author and publisher apologise for any inadvertent infringement of copyright and, if this is drawn to their attention, will be pleased to make the necessary correction in any subsequent edition.